Y SWIM LESSONS ®

YMCA Character Development

CARING
HONESTY
RESPECT
RESPONSIBILITY

the youth and adult

AQUATIC PROGRAM MANUAL

Produced Under A Grant From The Aquatic
Resources (Wallop-Breaux) Trust Fund
Administered By The U.S. Coast Guard

YMCA

We bu...
strong familie...

148489

YMCA of the USA.
    The youth and adult aquatic program manual/YMCA of the USA.
        p. cm. — (YMCA swim lessons)
    Includes index.
    ISBN: 0-7360-0048-8
    1. Swimming—Study and teaching. 2. Swimming for children—Study
    and teaching. 3. Aquatic sports—Study and teaching. I. Title.
    II. Series.
GV836.35.Y65 1999
797.2'1'083—dc21   98-37672
                                                       CIP

ISBN: 0-7360-0048-8
Published for the YMCA of the USA by Human Kinetics Publishers, Inc.
Item no.: Y5419
Copyright © 1999 National Council of Young Men's Christian Associations of the United States of America

Permission notices for material reprinted or adapted in this book from other sources can be found on page vi.

Project Coordinator: Laura J. Slane
Writers: Pat Sammann and Laura J. Slane
Acquisitions Editor: Pat Sammann
Developmental Editor: Elaine Mustain
Assistant Editor: Melissa Feld
Copyeditor: Sarah Wiseman
Proofreader: Debra Aglaia
Indexer: Craig Brown
Book Design and Composition: Studio Montage
Photographer (cover and interior): Tracy Frankel
Photo Editor: Laura J. Slane
Illustrator: Cindy Wrobel
Printer: Quest Graphics

Printed in the United States of America
10 9 8 7 6 5 4 3 2

Copies of this book may be purchased from the Y Program Store,
P.O. Box 5076, Champaign, IL 61825-5076, 1-800-747-0089.

The YMCA of the USA does not operate or manage any YMCA Swim Lessons Programs.

Contents

Acknowledgments iv
Credits vi

Chapter 1 *Overview of the Youth and Adult Aquatic Program* **2**
Changes in the Youth and Adult Aquatic Program 3
Common Elements of YMCA Aquatics Programs 3
The Five Components of Each Level 4
Program Level Structure 6
Objectives Summary Chart 7

Chapter 2 *Polliwog Level* **10**
Component 1: Personal Safety 11
Component 2: Personal Growth 20
Component 3: Stroke Development 22
Component 4: Water Games and Sports 25
Component 5: Rescue 29
Summary 33

Chapter 3 *Guppy Level* **34**
Component 1: Personal Safety 35
Component 2: Personal Growth 42
Component 3: Stroke Development 44
Component 4: Water Games and Sports 49
Component 5: Rescue 60
Summary 63

Chapter 4 *Minnow Level* **64**
Component 1: Personal Safety 65
Component 2: Personal Growth 70
Component 3: Stroke Development 72
Component 4: Water Games and Sports 76
Component 5: Rescue 89
Summary 91

Chapter 5 *Fish Level* **92**
Component 1: Personal Safety 93
Component 2: Personal Growth 99
Component 3: Stroke Development 101
Component 4: Water Games and Sports 104
Component 5: Rescue 114
Summary 117

Chapter 6 *Flying Fish Level* **118**
Component 1: Personal Safety 119
Component 2: Personal Growth 123
Component 3: Stroke Development 124
Component 4: Water Games and Sports 126
Component 5: Rescue 139
Summary 141

Chapter 7 *Shark Level* **142**
Component 1: Personal Safety 143
Component 2: Personal Growth 144
Component 3: Stroke Development 145
Component 4: Water Games and Sports 151
Component 5: Rescue 156
Summary 161

Chapter 8 *Porpoise Level* **162**
Class Format 162
Component 1: Personal Safety 162
Component 2: Personal Growth 166
Component 3: Stroke Development 167
Component 4: Water Games and Sports 169
Component 5: Rescue 170
Club Format 173
Summary 177

Appendix A: Drills for Improving Strokes and Building Fitness 178

Appendix B: YMCA Wetball Rules of Play 190

YMCA Swim Lessons Level Logos 194

Resource Organizations 196

Additional Resources for Your Aquatics Program 197

Index 198

Acknowledgments

The YMCA of the USA would like to acknowledge the contributions of the following people to the *Youth and Adult Aquatic Program Manual.* Staff leadership for this project was coordinated by Laura J. Slane.

Thomas Clark
YMCA Scuba
Norcross, GA

Kathi Cook
West Park, NY

Dr. Jerry DeMers
California Polytechnic
State University
San Luis Obispo, CA

Diane Erb
South Side/Carondelet YMCA
St. Louis, MO

Janet Gabrielson
United States Diving
Indianapolis, IN

Linda Garcia
Wheeler Regional Branch YMCA
Plainville, CT

Theresa Hill
Buehler YMCA
Palatine, IL

Marcia Humphrey
Gwinnett Family YMCA
Northbrook, IL

Dr. Ralph Johnson
North Greenville College
Tigerville, SC

Dr. Stephen Langendorfer
Bowling Green State University
Bowling Green, OH

Marianne Mackey-Smith
Bob Sierra Family YMCA
Tampa, FL

Jan McGah
YMCA of Greater St. Louis
St. Louis, MO

Karen Martorano
YMCA of Metropolitan Detroit
Detroit, MI

Terri Pagano
University of North Carolina
Chapel Hill, NC

Cami Ramo
YMCA of Greater New Bedford
New Bedford, MA

Pat Sammann
YMCA Program Store
Champaign, IL

Stephen Smith
Schroeder YMCA
Brown Deer, WI

Debby Speck
Lake County Central YMCA
Painesville, OH

Barb Straube
Rich Port YMCA
La Grange, IL

Al Wagner
University of Pittsburgh
Pittsburgh, PA

John Wingfield
United States Diving
Indianapolis, IN

Pat Wolfe
Southwest Branch YMCA
Saratoga, CA

Laura J. Slane
Lynne Vaughan
Mary Zoller
YMCA of the USA

We would like to thank the staff and members of:
Chino Valley YMCA
Chino, CA

Crescenta Canada YMCA
La Canada, CA

Deb Anderson
Chino Valley YMCA, Chino CA

Georgia Harrison
Crescenta Canada YMCA
La Canada, CA

for their help and assistance with our photo shoot.

The YMCA of the USA is grateful to the United States Coast Guard for its support of the YMCA Swim Lessons Program.

We would like to thank the following companies for their donation of equipment and supplies for the photo shoot for this book.

Adolph Kiefer and Associates (Phone: 847/872-8866)
Polywog Tube (#600510), Mesh Water Polo Cap (#600028), Kiefer Synchro Nose Clip (#690200), Kiefer Kona Silicone Snorkel (#810485), Kiefer Lahaina Silicone Mask (#810815), CPR Basic Learning System (#HLS100), Visor with Lifeguard (#909500), Kiefer Fin (#810002, #810003, #810004), Workout Dumbell Waveeater (#650610), Kiefer Barbell (#650603), Vest Type II Toddler (#621307), Underwater Slalom Game Set (#643027), 3/pk Connector Water Log 9" (#650590), YMCA Rescue Tube (#620042Y), Diving Brick (#600044), Type II Child Lifevest (#621107), Vest Type II Child (#621207), Vest Type II Univ Adult (#621007), #3 Water Polo Wetball Jr. Ball (#606603), Dive Toys Pool Pals Set of 5 (#651002)

Printworks, Inc. (Phone: 414/421-5400)
YMCA Staff Tee (#43071), YMCA Staff Polo (#43082), J-Collar Theme Polo (#43112), Character Development Hot Top (#43505), Character Development Tee (#43123), Y Times 4 Tee (#43125)

Recreonics, Inc. (Phone: 502/456-5706 or 800/428-3254)
Water Woogles (#94071), Catalina Boat Kit (#94059), "Freddy Fish" Funny Float 29" (94124), Rubber Duckie, Yellow (#94150), Dive F/The Tropical Fish Game (#94150), Dive Brick (#92260), Recreonics "Superboard" (Yellow #92212.Y, Red #92212.R, Blue #92212.B), Deluxe Junior Floating Fins (#92442, #92440), Advanced Tempered Glass Dive Mask and Snorkel Set (#92450), Infant's Head Ups Vest, Orange (#12284.O), Foam Type II Life Vest (#12279, #12280, #12281)

Credits

Front flip turn and back crawl flip turn skill descriptions (chapter 6), reprinted, by permission, from ASEP, *Rookie Coaches Swimming Guide,* (Champaign, IL: Human Kinetics), 59-60.

Ball passing skill description and discussion guidelines (chapter 3); rotary kick skill description and discussion guidelines (chapter 5); how to block the ball and overhand shot skill descriptions and discussion guidelines (chapter 6); and wetball offensive and defensive strategies discussion guidelines (chapter 8); adapted, by permission, from B. Barnett, and B. Wigo, 1996, *United States Water Polo Wetball Coaching Manual: Junior Water Polo for Beginning Swimmers,* (Colorado Springs, CO: U.S. Water Polo), 25, 90, 209-210, 224-225.

Canoe righting instructions (chapter 6), adapted, by permission, from Boy Scouts of America, 1989, *Canoeing* (Boy Scouts of America Merit Badge Series), (Irving, TX: Boy Scouts of America), 62-63.

Rowboat righting instructions (chapter 6), adapted, by permission, from Boy Scouts of America, 1993, *Rowing* (Boy Scouts of America Merit Badge Series), (Irving, TX: Boy Scouts of America), 66-67.

Canoe scull skill description (chapter 3); dolphin, oyster, and waterwheel skill descriptions (chapter 4); ballet leg, kip, and corkscrew skill descriptions (chapter 6); and front walkover skill description (chapter 7); adapted, by permission, from Forbes, M., 1989, *Coaching Synchronized Swimming Effectively,* (Champaign, IL: Human Kinetics), 29-31, 40-41, 47, 69-70, 83-86, 110-111.

Stroke variations skill descriptions (chapter 6); and accordion and star patterns skill descriptions (chapter 7), adapted, by permission, from Gundling, B., and J. White, 1988, *Creative Synchronized Swimming,* (Champaign, IL: Human Kinetics), 18-19, 114-116.

First aid for an unconscious victim with an obstructed airway discussion guidelines (chapter 7), adapted, by permission, from National Safety Council, 1997, *First Aid and CPR Standard*, (Sudbury, MA: Jones and Bartlett Publishers, Inc.), 30. Copyright © 1997 by Jones and Bartlett Publishers.

Shock treatment discussion guidelines (chapter 7), adapted, by permission, from National Safety Council, 1995, *First Aid Handbook*, (Sudbury, MA: Jones and Bartlett Publishers, Inc.), 36, 38. Copyright © 1995 by Jones and Bartlett Publishers.

Ice rescue discussion guidelines points 1 and 2 (chapter 7), adapted, by permission, from The Royal Life Saving Society Canada, Alberta and Northwest Territories Branch, "Watersmart tips, ice safety, how thick is thick enough?" Royal Life Saving Society Canada web site.

Push pass skill description (chapter 2); dribbling a ball skill description (chapter 2); how to shoot the ball discussion guidelines numbers one and two (chapter 6); and "Introduction to Water Polo" (appendix B), adapted, by permission, from D. Sharadin, 1993, *United States Water Polo Level One Coaching Manual,* (Carmel, IN: Cooper Publishing Group).

Various drills in appendix A, adapted, by permission, from *The Complete Book of Swimming* by Dr. Phillip Whitten, copyright © 1994 by Dr. Phillip Whitten. Reprinted by permission of Random House, Inc.

the **youth** and adult

CHAPTER one

Overview of the Youth and Adult Aquatic Program

The purpose of the YMCA Youth and Adult Aquatic Program is to help participants lay a good foundation of basic aquatic skills.

We hope this leads them to develop a lifelong appreciation for aquatic activities, which include not only swimming but also lifesaving, lifeguarding, and aquatic sports.

This revision of the Youth and Adult Aquatic Program is oriented toward student-centered learning. It is designed to ensure the student's safety, provide the student with regular, progressive success, and make the learning process more enjoyable.

The YMCA Youth and Adult Aquatic Program is divided into seven levels:

1. Polliwog
2. Guppy
3. Minnow
4. Fish
5. Flying Fish
6. Shark
7. Porpoise
   (sometimes offered in a club format)

At each level of the Youth and Adult Aquatic Program, participants are involved in activities relating to five components:

1. Personal safety
2. Personal growth
3. Stroke development
4. Water games and sports
5. Rescue

We also encourage you to find opportunities to teach your students more about the physics of swimming throughout the program. When students understand the principles underlying swimming instruction, they can apply those principles to improve the efficiency and comfort of their strokes.

This manual provides you with objectives for each level and a sample teaching strategy for each objective. However, in order to use this material properly, you will need to participate in the YMCA aquatic training and certification programs, and you will have to get to know your participants and tailor classes to meet their unique needs. The goal of the Youth and Adult Aquatic Program is to develop the total person. Sensitivity to each person's individual needs is the key to a successful aquatic experience.

The rest of this introductory chapter describes the changes made in this version of the Youth and Adult Aquatic Program and the rationale behind them, plus the common elements of all YMCA aquatics programs. It also lays out the five components found at each level (with a Skill Summary Chart summarizing all class objectives) and the structure of each level.

Changes in the Youth and Adult Aquatic Program

The Youth and Adult Aquatic Program had not been revised since 1986. This revision, done in 1998, provided a good opportunity to take a thorough look at the program. The new version offered here expands on YMCA philosophy and aquatic program concepts and incorporates recent research relating to learning how to swim. The program is now more student-centered, with developmentally appropriate activities. This change was made in order to

→ ensure the student's *safety;*

→ enhance the student's *enjoyment* of the learning process; and

→ provide consistent, progressive *success* for the student.

The underlying assumptions in this program are the following:

→ Student learning is the central focus of the program.

→ Learning should be an active process, ultimately controlled by the student.

→ Learning is a holistic process.

→ Learning is a process of lifelong change.

→ Learning movement changes, such as learning to swim, is best understood as resulting from a linked system involving the learner, the tasks, and the environment.

→ Changes in movements, such as swimming, occur when the relationships, or linkages, between the learner and task, learner and environment, or task and environment are altered.

→ An instructor's role in the learning process is best envisioned as being a guide, facilitator, and agent of change.

→ Effective teaching most often occurs *indirectly* when an instructor engages students to explore, guides their discovery process, and systematically sets task goals and demands that match the students' developmental readiness to achieve the goals and meet the demands.

In addition, the new program should do the following:

→ Build a foundation for lifelong appreciation of aquatic sports and activities

→ Incorporate character development

→ Provide education for parents

→ Increase understanding of how and why we can swim

→ Increase safety awareness for participants and their parents

→ Provide family activities that reinforce learning from class

→ Increase boating safety awareness

Common Elements of YMCA Aquatics Programs

The Youth and Adult Aquatic Program has some elements in common with other instructional YMCA aquatics programs:

→ *Series swimming.* Series swimming, or sustained swimming, is one of the most effective methods of developing skills, strength, and endurance. Depending on the swimmers' level of ability, series swimming might be kicking or swimming lengths or widths. This is an important fitness component of the class.

→ *Peer grouping.* Children learn better when they are grouped by age as well as ability. The fact that those grouped children are likely to have school or hobbies in common enhances group rapport.

→ *Closed-end classes.* YMCAs maintain classes at a fixed ratio of participants to instructors. The number of class periods is set at the beginning, and each class session has a distinct beginning and end.

→ *Use of whole pool.* During the class, the entire pool is available to participants. This availability enables you to use different parts of the pool as appropriate for different activities, and it makes students more aware of the entire pool area.

→ *Use of instructional flotation devices.* Instructional flotation devices, when used properly, aid skill development. Such devices free swimmers from worrying about staying afloat so they can concentrate on learning new skills and build strength and endurance. These devices should be used only for teaching purposes and should not be worn throughout an entire class period.

→ *Use of games.* Games can be important tools for enhancing learning. At each level, skills should be reinforced with games that focus on those skills. Appendix A of *Teaching Swimming Fundamentals* offers some games, and both instructor and students can make up their own.

The Five Components of Each Level

As stated earlier, each level contains five components: personal safety, personal growth, stroke development, water games and sports, and rescue. Here is a brief description of each.

Component 1: Personal Safety

Every student participating in the YMCA Youth and Adult Aquatic Program should become safety conscious around water. The information learned in these classes often forms the basis for accident prevention. Role playing also can be used to teach personal safety; if students imagine themselves in particular danger situations, the importance of the skills they are learning becomes more immediate.

Objectives for survival skills are included in all levels. Students learn the floating, swimming, and relaxation techniques necessary for support in deep water when swimming to shallow water is not possible. By teaching floating, the resting stroke, and proper treading techniques, as well as important safety and self-rescue principles, you emphasize the desired outcomes of safety and survival.

Boating safety is an important part of Youth and Adult Aquatic Program classes. Many people now boat, but they may not be aware of the dangers of boating and open water or know what to do in case of a water emergency. Students need to learn how to move around in a boat safely, the importance of wearing lifejackets and what types should be worn, and some basics about boat handling and safety. These students also share handouts and ideas from class with their families, making family members more aware as well. Beyond the basic information presented in this program, additional boating safety information is available from the YMCA of the USA, the U.S. Coast Guard Auxiliary, the U.S. Power Squadrons, the U.S. Sailing Association, the U.S. Canoe Association, or your local American Red Cross Chapter. Throughout the book, look for this icon— ⛵. It identifies material on boating safety.

You may notice in the manual that we are using rafts to demonstrate boating safety skills. Because we are teaching mainly in swimming pools, it can be more practical to use rafts than boats. While these types of rafts may be appropriate for teaching basic boating safety skills, be sure to point out the difference between the actions of the rafts used in class (which are flexible and pliable) and actual boats (which have rigid boat hulls).

Component 2: Personal Growth (Character Development)

The first commitment of all YMCA programs is to the personal development of each participant. YMCA programs need to be structured and conducted so that each person improves his or her own self-esteem.

One way to improve self-esteem is to develop capabilities. Those who learn new skills also learn to believe in themselves and have a healthy self-image.

Another way to build healthy self-esteem is to behave in line with our own values. Through Youth and Adult Aquatic Program lessons, students can learn more about the core values of caring, honesty, respect, and responsibility and how those values play a significant role in all their activities. In the Youth and Adult Aquatic Program, participants spend time making values decisions. They are asked to think about the consequences of choices and to work to close the gap between stated values and actual behavior. They interact with others in planned activities that test their personal values and help build family and community values. This is called character development.

You, as an instructor, will be responsible both for being a role model, exemplifying the core values in your behavior, and for making character development an integral part of your swimming program. Through preplanned activities and spur-of-the-moment opportunities, you can teach, practice, and celebrate good values.

Component 3: Stroke Development

When students are building endurance and striving to perfect strokes, encouragement and goal setting are important. Discourage competing with others or trying to move on quickly to the next level. Becoming a good swimmer takes time and practice.

You may use flotation belts and other instructional flotation devices (IFDs) to help beginners learn stroke movements. IFDs encourage swimmers to move hundreds of yards, promoting strength and endurance, and permit swimmers to try new skills or accept new challenges with confidence. Although IFDs may accelerate learning, endurance, and adjustment to the water, they are not a substitute for an instructor's vigilant eye. Providing competent supervision is always necessary when children and beginners are in or near the water.

An important part of learning new strokes is understanding how and why they work. Throughout the program, take opportunities to explain why a principle of physics applies to a new stroke or why a certain concept of exercise physiology works the way it does. This enhances students' cognitive understanding of the skills and experiences involved. The section in chapter 7 of *Teaching Swimming Fundamentals* entitled "The Physics of Swimming Instruction" provides a list of basic physics concepts and sample lessons for teaching them.

Component 4: Water Games and Sports

Students will be introduced to a variety of strokes and swimming safety skills in the Youth and Adult Aquatic Program; however, the program does not stop there. To give participants a well-rounded and fun aquatic background, the program includes opportunities to take part in recreational and competitive aquatic activities. It also includes time for playing games and introduces aquatic sports.

Playing sports and games is a major shift from programs that focus only on stroke mechanics and water safety. Well-organized water games and sports, integrated with the other elements of the Youth and Adult Aquatic Program, become an important program feature. This concept distinguishes the YMCA program from others and helps hold the interest of many more participants.

The following sports are highlighted at different levels of the program (other sports such as windsurfing, kayaking, and surfing can be part of the Porpoise Club):

→ *Synchronized swimming skills* are presented to allow students to experiment with different body positions in the water, achieve higher levels of physical fitness, and make future decisions about participating in the instructional, art, or competitive synchronized programs. Also, the sculling experience enhances swimming skills.

→ *Springboard diving skills* are included to encourage students to try movement exploration and to provide them with a maximum of fun and success with a minimum of embarrassment and failure.

→ *Underwater swimming* adds an element of excitement and exploration to the program. The proper and safe use of masks and fins helps the student discover the underwater environment.

→ *Introduction to small craft and boating* opens new possibilities for recreational and competitive water activities.

→ *Wetball* is a three-level progressive program that leads to playing water polo. Students learn the basic water polo skills and correct positioning through drills and games.

→ *Competitive swimming* prepares students to compete in YMCA league programs and possibly in cluster, field, and national championships. Some teams also compete in U.S. Swimming–sponsored competitions. Competition is organized by age groups.

Teaching for each of these water sports is done based on the skill ability of students at each level. If students progress through all the levels, they should attain a basic knowledge of each of these sports. At the final level, Porpoise, students can refine their skills and add new activities.

Aquatic games are included at all levels; not only are these games fun, they can also help students develop skills to reach specific learning goals. Games can provide motivating opportunities to use skills in new and different ways and in varied situations. In addition, games can create "teachable moments" in which real-life situations can be used to illustrate values in action. Look at appendix A in *Teaching Swimming Fundamentals* for game ideas to work into your classes.

Component 5: Rescue

With proper training, even young children can perform basic, nonswimming rescues and provide simple aquatic emergency care. At each level of the Youth and Adult Aquatic Program, skills are introduced to prepare the student to respond to emergencies.

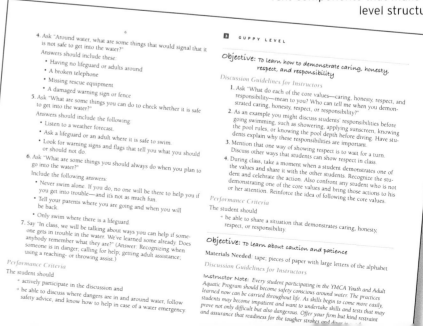

Objectives Summary Chart

The chart shown in table 1.1 summarizes the objectives at each level for each of the five components.

Program Level Structure

The rest of this manual describes each of the objectives for the components of each of the seven levels and sample methods of teaching them. Each chapter contains the information required to teach the objectives for one level and is made up of the following parts:

→ *Overview.* The first part of each chapter briefly describes the topics covered in this level and lists the objectives and prerequisite for the level.

→ *Component.* This next part identifies which of the five components is being discussed.

→ *Objectives.* Several objectives are given for each component. Each objective is followed by discussion guidelines and performance criteria sections.

→ *Skill description.* Often a skill description precedes the discussion guidelines. When one or more new skills are to be introduced, a description of each of those skills can be found here. This information is here to help you in guiding students to discover the best way to perform each skill.

→ *Discussion guidelines for instructors.* Discussion questions and orienting methods to use in teaching are presented. However, each skill can be led in many different ways, and you need to develop alterna-

tive methods as part of your growth as an instructor. If specific equipment or materials are needed to carry out the teaching instructions, those materials are listed under *Materials Needed.*

→ *Performance criteria.* This section tells you the minimum that students should be able to perform in order to successfully reach the objective.

→ *Summary of performance criteria.* At the end of each chapter is a list of the criteria to be met for each objective described in the chapter.

Also, scattered throughout the chapters are *Instructor Notes.* These are cautions and recommendations for instructors to follow regarding specific activities.

Two appendixes at the end of the manual provide additional helpful information for teaching. Appendix A contains stroke drills for you to choose from to aid students in improving their strokes; appendix B gives the rules for wetball.

For handouts that can be sent home with children, look in the *YMCA Swim Lessons Administrator's Manual.* It includes parent handouts and Family Huddle handouts. The parent handouts are parent education pieces on safety and parenting issues. The Family Huddle handouts offer fun activities children can do at home, on their own, and with their parents, that reinforce what is taught in class. The handouts also include tips to parents on developing their child's values and on water safety. Handouts are provided for each class level except the Porpoise level.

Text components that make up level structure

Table 1.1 Objectives Summary Chart

Level	Personal safety	Personal growth	Stroke development	Water games and sports	Rescue
Polliwog	• Pool rules • Class expectations • Walk away from wall, turn and grab wall; take feet off floor • Front and back float • Wear PFD • Jump into pool with PFD, paddle front, kick on back • Get into and out of boat • Jump away from side, turn, and return to side • Sun safety	• Self-confidence • Interpretation of core values • Enjoy game	• Paddle on front, side, back wearing float belt	• Flat/stationary sculling and finning • Tub • Climb down/climb up pole • Dribble ball • Pass and catch ball	• Danger recognition • Yell for help • Ask adult for assistance • Dial emergency number • Reaching assist
Guppy	• Diving safety rules • Front and back float • Tread water • Select, wear PFD • Jump into deep water, paddle back float • HELP Position • Bobbing • Getting into/out of boat safely • Sitting and moving in boat	• Danger recognition, safety, and emergency procedures • Share situation showing core value • Safety precautions	• Front alternating paddle • Front symmetrical paddle • Side alternating paddle • Back alternating paddle • Back symmetrical paddle	• Front/back somersault • Canoe sculling • Jump into deep water • Jump off 1-m diving board • Kneeling dive • Throw/catch ball; dribble ball; pass and catch ball; shoot goals	• Reaching/throwing assists • Rescue breathing
Minnow	• Diving safety rules • Boating safety tips • Resting stroke • Treading water • Swimming front/back wearing PFD • Capsized boat • Swimming with clothes on • Shallow-water blackout	• Goal setting • Demonstrate core values in class • Heart rate	• Front alternating paddle • Front rudimentary breaststroke • Rudimentary sidestroke • Back alternating over-arm stroke • Back symmetrical rudimentary elementary backstroke	• Circle kick • Dolphin/oyster • Water wheel • Combining synchronized swimming skills • Stride dive (low and high positions) • Standing dive off deck • Jump off 1-m diving board feet first with arm swing • Dribble and pass while swimming, shoot ball • Play wetball	• Throwing/reaching assists • Conscious obstructed airway maneuver • Rescue breathing

Table 1.1 Objectives Summary Chart (continued)

Level	Personal safety	Personal growth	Stroke development	Water games and sports	Rescue
Fish	• Skin diving safety • Currents • Floating • Treading water • Swimming with clothes on • Huddle position • Safe-boating tips • Getting back into a boat after falling overboard/getting into and out of a swamped boat • Sun safety • Leg cramps	• Teamwork • Reinforce core values • Safety/cooperation through games	• Crawl stroke • Breaststroke • Elementary backstroke • Back crawl • Sidestroke • Butterfly stroke	• Headfirst/feetfirst sculling • Plank • Stroke variations • Standing dive off 1-m diving board • Juggle, pass, catch, dribble ball while swimming, shoot ball • Change from crawl to backstroke quickly • Tread water with rotary kick • Play wetball • Headfirst/feetfirst surface dives • Using mask and fins	• Throwing assist • Accident prevention • Rescue breathing • First aid
Flying Fish	• Backyard pool safety • Waterpark safety • Floating with clothes on • Treading water • What to do if a boat capsizes • Healthy lifestyle • Health-related fitness components	• Personal ground rules for risk • Understanding *adventure, risk taking* • Goal setting for core values	• Crawl stroke • Breaststroke • Elementary backstroke • Back crawl • Sidestroke • Butterfly stroke	• Swim underwater • Sailboat • Ballet leg • Kip • Stroke variations • Create synchronized swimming routine • Three-step approach front dive off a 1-m diving board • Shoot, block ball into goal • Ball-handling • Rotary kick in all directions • Play wetball • Use of snorkel • Starts and turns	• Reaching assist • Throwing assist • Rescue breathing

Table 1.1 **Objectives Summary Chart** (continued)

Level	Personal safety	Personal growth	Stroke development	Water games and sports	Rescue
Shark	• Rafting, tubing safety • Open-water safety • Swimming in rough water • Target heart-rate range	• Service to others • Discussion of core values	• Crawl stroke • Breaststroke • Inverted breaststroke • Back crawl • Overarm sidestroke • Butterfly stroke • Trudgen crawl • Individual medley	• Front walkover • Combine synchronized swimming skills with partner and team • Water polo medley • Pass the ball • Play wetball • Wear skin diving gear and dive for an object	• Ice safety and rescue • Excessive heat/cold conditions • Shock • Rescue breathing • Opening obstructed airway
Porpoise*	• Tread water • Get into/out of boat from deep water • Disrobing, inflating clothing in water	• Leadership • Setting goals • Observing and reinforcing core value behavior • Components of fitness	• Increasing stroke speed • 200-yd individual medley • Double-trudgen crawl	• Create synchronized swimming routine with group • Offensive/defensive strategies in wetball • Play Wetball	• Hyperventilation • Swim carrying a heavy object • Approach crawl stroke • Side entry/approach crawl to retrieve object • Rescue breathing

* The Porpoise level also can be a club experience in which participants apply their skills to an ever-widening circle of aquatic activities. These activities are an introduction to what may become lifelong pursuits.

CHAPTER two

Polliwog Level

Developing the total person in a YMCA swim class starts at the Polliwog, or beginning, level.

Some people first learning to swim may be afraid of the water; others may be uneasy about the class itself; others still have had little or no experience with the water. Some students will have been through preschool swimming programs and will be familiar with the environment and eager to learn.

Helping people learn to swim, however, is only one of your responsibilities as an instructor. Developing students' mental and spiritual capabilities is as crucial as developing swimming skills. Sensitively guide new swimmers toward problem solving through questions and discussions of safety and the basic physics of swimming and toward character development through values activities. Remember that students learn based on success.

While enrolled in the Polliwog level, the student is

→ introduced to pool rules;

→ acquainted with class expectations;

→ oriented to the pool surroundings and water and to the use of instructional flotation devices;

→ helped to learn the front float and how to take a breath and to recover to a stand from a glide;

→ helped to learn the back float and the resting float;

→ given an explanation of the correct use of U.S. Coast Guard–approved personal flotation devices (PFDs) and allowed to practice wearing them;

→ helped to learn how to get into and out of a boat safely;

→ helped to learn to step or jump away from the pool wall, turn around, and reach for the wall without assistance;

→ involved in a discussion of sun safety;

→ gaining self-confidence;

→ involved in a discussion of the core values at the YMCA;

→ helped to learn relaxation and fun in the water through a game;

→ helped to learn the front paddle stroke;

→ helped to learn the side and back paddle;

- → introduced to finning and sculling;
- → introduced to the tub, a synchronized swimming skill;
- → allowed to experience going underwater;
- → helped to learn to pass and catch a ball and to dribble a ball across the pool;
- → introduced to victim and danger recognition and reaching assists; and
- → given practice in calling for help or going for or phoning for adult assistance.

Prerequisite: None

Component 1: Personal Safety

Objective: To learn the pool rules and the importance of pool safety

YMCA Cool Pool Rules

It Takes Two to Enjoy the Pool!

Always swim with a friend or where a lifeguard or parent is present.

Enjoy the Pool Safely!

No running in or near the pool area.

Swimmers Use Their Mouths for Breathing!

No food, drink, or gum is permitted in the pool area.

Help Keep the Water Clear!

Always use the restroom and take a soap shower before entering the pool.

Be Prepared!

Learn safety, rescue, and first aid.

Discussion Guidelines for Instructors

1. Talk about why we need rules.
2. Ask students what rules they think would be important.
3. Let the students decide why these rules will help keep them safe.
4. Have the students put the rules into their own words.
5. Let students create their own additional rules.
6. Ask the students if they can think of any other good ways to be safe in the pool, at the beach, at home, and at the YMCA.
7. Talk about how rules relate to values.

Here is a sample of the questions you might use to discuss pool rules: "How can we help keep the water clean (or respect the water)?" Look for answers such as *Always shower before entering the pool* or *Use the restroom before coming to class.*

"Why don't swimmers chew gum in the pool?" Look for answers such as *Swimmers need to breathe through their mouths.*

"Why is it your responsibility to throw away your gum before getting into the pool?" Look for answers such as *So I won't choke* or *So another swimmer doesn't step on it.*

"Why should you wait for your instructor before you get into the pool?" Look for answers such as *It's safer to wait until the instructor is there, so he or she can help you.*

"How do we move when in the pool area?" Look for answers such as *We always walk.*

"Do we splash other swimmers? Why or why not?" Look for answers such as *We don't splash because we respect others' likes or dislikes* or *We don't because we care about how others feel.*

"What can we do to help ourselves get ready for swimming lessons?" Look for answers such as *We bring our towels* or *We put on our flotation belts.*

"How do we care for the swim equipment?" Look for answers such as *We pick it up and put it away, We don't break it,* or *We use it the way it should be used.*

The rules become an important part of the pool environment when the students tell each other about infractions and become self-disciplined.

Instructor Note: *Also be aware of the following important safe teaching guidelines for yourself:*

- *Keep students in view at all times. Never turn your back.*
- *Never ever leave your class unattended, even for a few seconds*
- *Comply with your local YMCA lifeguard policy.*
- *Be aware of students' limitations.*
- *Clear the pool at the end of class.*
- *Have a quick method of communication for control and pool evacuation.*
- *Know your emergency procedures so well that they are almost automatic.*
- *Be sure rules are posted in a visible place.*
- *Take and record attendance.*

Performance Criteria

The student should

→ participate actively in the discussion,

→ be able to repeat the rules, and

→ be able to discuss the rules.

Objective: To learn class expectations that help make class fun and enjoyable for all

Discussion Guidelines for Instructors

Instructor Note: *Introduce some basic class expectations for conduct so students immediately learn what is acceptable and unacceptable behavior in class. The following expectations can help you get started. You can use these as is, adapt them, or add to them. Remember to keep them simple.*

- *Speak for yourself…not for anybody else.*
- *Listen to others…then they'll listen to you.*
- *Avoid put-downs…who needs 'em?*
- *Take charge of yourself…you are responsible for you.*
- *Show respect…every person is important.*

1. Discuss the importance of each expectation with your group.
2. Let the students decide why these expectations will help make class more pleasant.

3. Have the students put the expectations in their own words.
4. Let students create their own additional reasonable expectations if they like.

Performance Criteria

The student should

→ participate in the discussion,

→ be able to repeat the expectations, and

→ be able to discuss the class expectations.

Objective: To learn to walk away from the pool wall, turn around, and reach and grab onto the wall without assistance; to be comfortable being in the water; and to take the feet off the floor while wearing an IFD

Materials Needed: instructional flotation devices (IFDs)

Discussion Guidelines for Instructors

1. Have students as a group walk around and explore the pool area.

2. Ask, "Do you know where the shallow water is? Where are the steps or ladder? Where is the deep water? Are you ready to get in?"

3. Have the students sit on the pool edge as you stand in the water facing them. Ask the following series of exploratory and problem-solving questions to help guide the children to enter the water safely: "Can you put a body part in the water while staying on the deck?" Repeat, asking, "Can you put another body part in the water?" as children try their feet, legs, hands, arms, and so on.

4. "Safely, can you put two body parts in at once?" Repeat, looking for unique combinations.

5. "Safely, can you get all the way into the water feet first? Safely, can you do it another way?"

6. "While you are in the water, what body parts can you get or keep out of the water?" Repeat the question, looking for other options.

7. "Can you get two body parts out of the water and only touch bottom with one body part?" Repeat, asking for different solutions. (This is working toward floating and buoyancy.)

8. "Can you make air bubbles in the water?" Possible solutions may be splashing with the hands or feet or blowing bubbles through the mouth or nose.

9. "Can you make bubbles with your ears? No, I guess not. How about with your elbow? What body part works best in making bubbles?"

10. "Can you make bubbles with just your nose? How about with just your mouth? How about both?"

11. "Has anyone seen a fish underwater? What do they do? What would it be like if you tried to talk to a fish? Show me."

12. "Can anyone hum? What songs can you hum? How about 'Pop Goes the Weasel'? Does anyone know 'Row, Row, Row Your Boat'?" Say "Try humming one of those songs underwater. What happens?" or "Can anyone hum 'Row, Row, Row Your Boat' underwater?"

13. Ask students who can step out to you (you are about two feet away from the wall) to give you a celebration signal after they step. It could be a high five, or clapping, or cheers to celebrate success. Students may suggest alternative celebration techniques. After they step out, help them turn around and reach for the wall. Continue practicing until they can step out, turn around, and reach for the wall by themselves. (Being able to step out and turn around to reach for the wall is an important safety skill.)

Instructor Note: If your pool is too deep for students to stand in, encourage them to give you a high five while holding on to the side with one hand.

These steps may be done with or without students' wearing flotation (or float) belts, depending upon the students' comfort in the water. Flotation belts are used to help students participate with more confidence and to allow the entire class to spend more time in the water, rather than just taking turns one-on-one with you.

You can alter the body position of a student by moving the flotation belt from the child's hips to the chest. For each individual child, put it in the most helpful place that still allows him or her to balance safely.

Students who are reluctant to put their faces in the water can paddle in the water with float belts or kickboards. This allows them time to get used to the water without the fear of putting their faces underwater until they are ready.

To encourage students to get their faces wet, ask them to pretend they are washing their faces at home in the bathtub. Alternatively, you can ask them a progressive series of questions such as the following. First ask them "What can you use to wash your face? Show me how." They may use washcloths, sponges, or just their hands. Then continue by asking, "Can you wash your nose with one hand? With two hands? Can you wash your chin with one hand? With two hands?" Finally, follow with "Can you wash behind your ears? Can you wash your cheeks? Can you wash your whole face? Can you wash your hair?"

Additionally, while holding on to the side in the water, students can go through a movement exploration series using "Who can?" questions to help them get used to being in the pool. Examples are "Who can see the bottom?" and "Who can hold their breath and put their face in the water?" At this level, do not force students to do anything that frightens them. You can achieve more using a sense of humor, exploration, and fun than by pushing, urging, or coercing.

polliwog

Performance Criteria

The student should

→ be able to walk away from the wall, turn around, and reach and grab onto the wall without assistance,

→ be comfortable being in the water, and

→ take his or her feet off the floor while wearing an IFD.

Objective: To learn how to back or front float, with or without support, and to be able to take a breath and to recover to a stand

Materials Needed:
various flotation devices; kickboards, one for each student

Skill Description

The student does the front (prone) float with the front of the body down in the water, usually with the face in the water. The position may vary in the angle of the body in the water, the position of the arms, the degree of symmetry, and the amount of bend at the elbows, shoulders, hips, and knees. To do a front float, the student should be able to hold his or her breath, should not be afraid to put the face into the water or to float, and should be able to right himself or herself from the prone position to standing.

The student does the back (supine) float with the back of the body down in the water. The position may vary in the same ways as the front float; however, the student does not have to be able to hold his or her breath or put his or her face into the water as in the front float. He or she still should not be afraid to float and should be able to right himself or herself from the supine position to standing.

Keep in mind that because all body types are different (depending on the amount of muscle mass and bone density versus fat), students will float at different levels and positions in the water. Some might not float at all without using their arms or legs for stability and support. Also consider this factor when evaluating students' floating skill.

Discussion Guidelines for Instructors

Have students sit in a circle on the deck or stand in the shallow end of the pool. Say "Let's play a game. We're at the beach. It's warm, and the water is

beautiful. Show me or tell me some safe things we might be doing at the beach." (Answers: Sunbathing, building sand castles, swimming.) "OK, if we were in the water swimming, we might get tired. What could we do if we were tired?" (Answers: Get out of the water; rest; stand up.) "What if we got tired and were too deep to stand up? How could we rest?" Have them show you their ideas, then have them try to stand up, float on the back, and roll over.

Instructor Note: *Give students the opportunity to experiment, first verbally, then physically, with different methods of staying afloat. Make a game of this by having students time each other, by letting them vote on the most fun way to stay afloat, or by having a friendly contest of showing how many different variations of floating they can do. Talk about various types of flotation devices, such as inner tubes, water logs, float belts, barbells, kickboards, and beach balls. Have several such devices around the pool so students can have fun choosing the best ones.*

Buoyancy

Ask the following series of questions:

1. "With your shoulders underwater, who can balance on the big toe? Can you do this on land? It would hurt, wouldn't it?"

2. "Why is it easier to balance in the water than on land?" (Answer: The water holds you up.)

3. "What does this mean?" (Answer: That we can float in the water.)

4. "Why does the water hold us up?" (Answer: The pressure of the water does it.) For a more detailed answer, use the flotation lesson from "The Physics of Swimming" section of chapter 7 in *Teaching Swimming Fundamentals.*

Front float

Ask the following progressive series of questions:

1. "Can you get your feet off the bottom? Show me."

2. "How many different ways can you get your feet off the bottom?" (Examples: Jump up, feet off momentarily; lift one foot; hold on to the side; hold on to someone else; hold on to the instructor; use a flotation belt.)

3. "Who can keep both feet off the bottom for one second? Two seconds? Three seconds?"

4. "How many ways can you do it?"

Front float

5. "What position is best?"

6. "What happens when I pull you? This is like going for a ride."

7. "What is your body like?"

8. "Where did your feet go?"

Instructor Note: *As you move through this process, students should become more familiar with being in the water. As students relax while going for a ride, see if they can try to put their faces in the water while on their ride. Then try to see if they will let you release their hands for a few seconds. Ask them what it feels like when they are floating by themselves. Then ask them how else they could float if you didn't just hold them. What else could they use to help them? (Answers: Flotation belts, water logs, kickboards, holding on to the side.) Then have students try the rides with the belt on and a kickboard under each arm.*

Recovery to a stand

1. Say "Now that we can float, how can you stop?" Have them try their ideas while they are on their ride. (Examples: Putting feet down, pushing back against the water, grabbing the wall.)

2. After a few attempts, ask them which way was easier or better for them. Point out those who drew their knees to their chest, pressed down with their hands, and lifted their heads. This helps position the feet and legs under the hips and makes it easier to stand.

Getting a breath

Ask "If you had your face in the water and you wanted to be able to float longer on your stomach without standing up again, what could you do? Show me." (Examples: Roll over, lift head.) Continue with guiding questions until they try to press their arms down and lift their heads.

Back float

Ask the following series of questions:

1. "Who can get both feet off the bottom and still keep your face dry? How would you do this?" (Examples: side or back positions, hanging on to the side, using an IFD, using another person.) If they need a hint, say "Use a different body position."

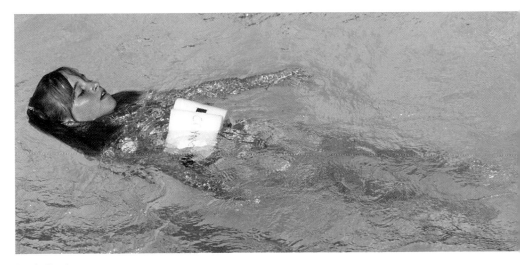

Back float

2. "What seems to work best for your body—being straight or bent?"

3. "Where can you put your arms when you are on your side? When you are on your back? Does it make a difference where you put them?"

4. Distribute one kickboard to each student. Then ask "Can we pretend this kickboard is a pillow? (Wait for responses.) What could you do with it if it were a pillow? Cuddle it? Put it under your head? Sit on it?"

5. "What if it were a piece of bread—a big piece of bread? Pretend your body is another piece of bread. Let's spread peanut butter and jelly all over your body and make a sandwich using the kickboard!"

6. "Can you be a peanut butter and jelly sandwich with the bread facing some other direction?"

7. "How can you float on your back using a kickboard? On your side?"

Instructor Note: *Start by supporting the students' heads while taking them for a ride. As the students become comfortable, tell them that you are going to release their heads, but will stay right by them if they need anything. You also can try using a water log.*

8. "Now that you can float, how can you stand back up? Let's see." (Examples: drop hips and sit; push with arms; roll over; sink down and stand; thrash around a lot.)

9. "Which methods of trying to stand up kept your face dry?"

10. "Which methods of trying to stand up do you like best?"

Instructor Note: *To stand up from the back float, students should look toward their feet and drop their hips down (like sitting in a chair) as they circle their arms forward.*

Performance Criteria

The student should

→ be able to support himself or herself in the water for 30 seconds with or without a float belt,

→ be able to demonstrate the front and back float,

→ be able to take a breath on the front float, and

→ be able to recover to standing from both the front and back float.

⚓ **Objective:** To learn about United States Coast Guard-approved (USCG) personal flotation devices (PFDs) and to be able to select one, put it on, secure it, and take it off; to understand the difference between a PFD and an IFD

Materials Needed:

PFDs, one for each student, and various types of IFDs

Discussion Guidelines for Instructors

Instructor Note: *PFDs are personal flotation devices that have been determined to be in compliance with U.S. Coast Guard specifications and regulations related to performance, construction, or materials. Look for the U.S. Coast Guard stamp of approval on the device to confirm that it is certified. IFDs are used for specific teaching purposes during swimming. They may help students float, but they are not designed for use in emergency situations and are not certified. These are important and critical differences that both students and parents need to know and follow.*

Various types of PFDs and IFDs

1. Show students a PFD and ask them "What is this called?" (Answers: A lifejacket or a PFD.)

2. Ask "What is it used for?" (Answer: To help you float.)

3. Ask "When should you wear it?" (Answer: Whenever you are in a boat or in other water-related activities.)

4. Show students examples of instructional flotation devices (IFDs), such as a kickboard, belt, and water log. Ask "What are these used for?" (Answer: To help you swim better.)

5. Ask "How is one of these different from a PFD?" (Answer: PFDs are designed to be worn for safety in the water; IFDs are for play or instructional use only.)

6. Discuss the available types of PFDs and why we wear them, explaining at a level suitable for the cognitive level of your students. Make the following points:

   • PFDs are made in high-visibility colors. Ask students why this is important. (Answer: So you can be seen more easily in the water.)

   • A PFD has proven and tested buoyancy. Show where this is stamped on the PFD and let everyone see it. Ask students why this would be important. (Answer: To know it's a real PFD.)

   • PFDs may have different kinds of fasteners. Have students practice fastening all the various types.

   • PFDs keep you warmer in cold water, which can help prevent hypothermia. Explain to students that, if they should fall into cold water and have to stay there for a while, their body temperature could be cooled down to where it is dangerous. A PFD could help hold their heat in.

   • PFDs come in many sizes and styles so people can select the one that fits most comfortably and for the right purpose. Ask students questions such as the following: "How can you tell if a PFD fits properly?" "Could you wear an adult PFD? Why or why not?" "Could you wear one that your little brother or sister would wear? Why or why not?" and "Who should wear PFDs?" (Answer: Everyone who is boating or engaged in whitewater activities.)

7. While on the deck, have students practice putting lifejackets on and securing them. Allow students to check each other to see if the lifejackets are on correctly.

8. Have students get in the water and test their lifejackets to see if they fit properly.

9. Have students take off their lifejackets and store the lifejackets in their proper place.

Instructor Note: According to the National Safe Boating Council and the U.S. Coast Guard (1997), to test for proper fit, lifejackets should fit properly with all zippers, straps, ties, and snaps correctly secured. Have students enter the water and walk into water up to their necks. Have them lift their legs and tilt their heads back, in a relaxed floating position. Their mouths should be out of the water, and they should be floating without any physical effort. If a student's lifejacket "rides up," try securing it more tightly to the body. If it still rides up, the student may need a smaller lifejacket or a different style. Students should be comfortable and able to float with very little effort.

Performance Criteria

The student should

   → be able to secure and take off a PFD and

   → be able to discriminate between a PFD and an IFD.

⚓ Objective: To learn how to jump into a pool wearing a PFD (giving the PFD a hug), paddle stroke 10 yards on the front, then turn on the back and kick 10 yards

Materials Needed:

PFDs, one for each student. Place a mark on the pool indicating where students should swim to.

Discussion Guidelines for Instructors

1. Distribute a PFD to each student, and have the students put the PFDs on. Tell them that you will check each one to see if it was fastened properly and if it fits right.

2. Now have students try paddling while wearing a PFD. Ask if it's easier or harder to do while wearing a PFD.

polliwog

Paddling while wearing a PFD

3. Say "Let's see how many ways you can paddle with your lifejacket on." (Examples: front, back, side)

4. Ask "Who can turn around in circles?"

5. Ask "Can you roll onto your back? Roll back on your stomach? On your side? Change front to back without rolling? Back to front?"

6. Ask "Which of you can paddle out to me?" Gradually increase the distance between you and the students until you are on the other side of the pool. "Can you come back without touching the other wall? Can you paddle on the front? On the side? On the back?"

7. Say "Let's try to jump into the pool. Do you need to do anything different with your PFD?" (Answer: Cross the arms over the jacket.)

8. Have all the students line up on deck as you stand in the water 5-10 feet away indicating the spot where they should jump. Have the students, one at a time, call out the name of someone they respect and why, then jump to the correct spot and paddle out to you.

9. Say, "Let's see if you can jump in and paddle out to me. Give yourself a big hug and say 'Oh, I'm so good.' Say that when you jump in."

10. Ask, "Can you jump in, paddle to the mark (place a mark on the side of the pool at the distance you want them to swim), roll onto your back, and then paddle back while on your back?" Gradually increase the distance until students can perform this for 10 yards.

Performance Criteria

The student should

→ be able to jump into a pool wearing a PFD (giving the PFD a hug), paddle stroke 10 yards on the front, then turn over onto the back and kick 10 yards.

⚓ Objective: To learn how to get into and out of a boat safely with assistance

Materials Needed:

PFDs, one for each student; a boat (canoe, rowboat, dinghy, inflatable raft)

Discussion Guidelines for Instructors

1. Have a boat on the deck, such as a canoe, rowboat, dinghy, or small inflatable raft.

2. Have the students select and put on PFDs (you should wear one, too).

3. Ask students what safety rules should be followed in and around boats. Discuss some of the basic boating safety rules such as the following:

- Never enter a boat without an adult with you.
- Always wear a PFD whenever you are in a boat.
- Always stay seated when in a small boat.
- Maintain three points of contact when getting in and out.
- Step in the center to keep the boat balanced.

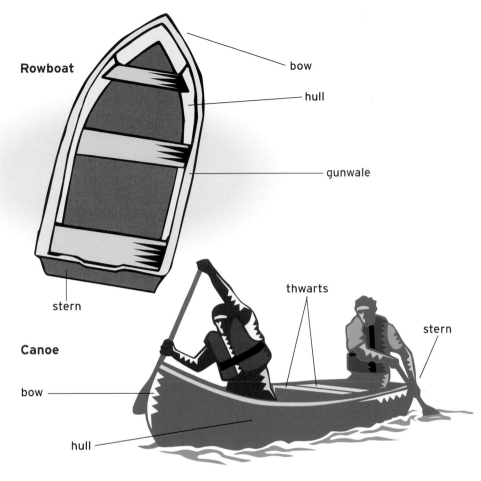

Rowboat

bow

hull

gunwale

stern

Canoe

thwarts

stern

bow

hull

4. Explain the names of the different parts of the boat.
5. Explain how to get safely into and out of a boat:
   - Climb into the boat by stepping into the middle, keeping your weight low (which keeps your center of gravity low). Stabilize yourself by placing your hands on the edges. You should maintain three points of contact.
   - Exit by doing the reverse.
6. Practice with the boat on the deck and provide assistance.

Performance Criteria

The student should

→ be able to get into and out of a boat with assistance while wearing a PFD.

Objective: To learn how to jump in away from the pool side, paddle to the surface, turn, and return to the side without assistance in deep water

Materials Needed: IFDs

Discussion Guidelines for Instructors

1. In shallow water, have students step out away from the side of the pool and get back to it without assistance and without wearing an IFD.
2. In deep water, have the students try to jump out away from the side, paddle and kick up to the surface, and turn around and return to the side.

Instructor Note: *Be there in the water to make sure they jump out into the pool and to assist if necessary. Have a kickboard, rescue tube, or water log with you and keep it between you and the students. It will provide additional support. Students may or may not wear IFDs at first, depending on their comfort level.*

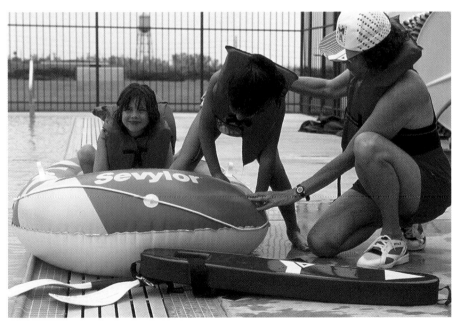

Getting into a raft while on the deck

polliwog

Performance Criteria

The student should

→ be able to jump out away from the side, paddle to the surface, turn, and return to the side without assistance.

Objective: To learn about sun safety

Discussion Guidelines for Instructors

1. Ask "What do you put on to protect yourself from the sun? What is something else you can put on? Anything else?" Continue asking until you get the following items:

   • Sunscreen (minimum 15 SPF)

   • Hat

   • Sunglasses

   • T-shirt or other clothing

2. Ask "What else can we do to protect ourselves from the sun?" Continue asking until you get the following:

   • Drink lots of water.

   • Stay in the shade and limit time in the sun, especially when the sun is hottest (usually between 11 A.M. and 3 P.M. during Daylight Savings Time).

   • Reapply sunscreen regularly, especially after being in the water.

Performance Criteria

The student should

→ participate in the discussion and

→ know at least one way to protect himself or herself from the sun.

Component 2: Personal Growth

Objective: To gain self-confidence

Discussion Guidelines for Instructors

Using the following discussion activities, orient students to the YMCA and weave these themes throughout the Polliwog level. Begin each class with these ideas:

→ Welcome students and encourage them to get to know each other.

→ Introduce yourself to students in new ways each time the class meets by sharing something new about you and asking them to share something about themselves.

→ Reassure students that they will never be asked to do anything that they cannot do or is dangerous. Ask them "If you were really scared to do something I asked you to do in the water, what would you do?" (Answer: Tell you I am scared.)

→ Have students share their favorite pastimes and other things that are going on in their lives. Do this in different ways each session.

→ Discuss the YMCA Pool Rules—why we need them and whose responsibility they are. (See earlier pool rules objective under the Personal Safety component).

→ Try relaxation exercises. Have students back float and ask "What would a rock do in the water? What would a feather do? What would Jell-O look like or feel like in the water?" (If your muscles are tense and tight, it's harder to float than when you feel light as a feather and your muscles are loose.)

→ Talk about goal setting. Discuss completion guidelines for Polliwogs and how each student will learn at an individual pace. As the program progresses, encourage individuals to identify their own progress. Celebrate successes at each class meeting. Teach students that you want them to do their best.

Performance Criteria

The student should

→ participate in the discussion and activities.

Objective: To describe what the terms caring, honesty, respect, and responsibility mean

Discussion Guidelines for Instructors

1. Say "In swimming, as in everything else we do, we must learn to get along with others."

2. Ask "Does anyone know what *caring* is?" (Answer: To love others, to be sensitive to the well-being of others, to help others.) "Have you seen anyone being caring? Tell me about it."

Instructor Note: *You may want to try the following activity. If a student is having trouble completing a skill, ask the other students for ideas to help him or her. Share those ideas with the student and have the class encourage that student to keep trying. Explain to the class that it's a good idea to help others who are having trouble if you already know how to perform a skill. Tell them that this is a way to demonstrate caring for others.*

3. Ask "Does anyone know what *honesty* is?" (Answer: To tell the truth; to act in such a way that you are worthy of trust; to have integrity, making sure your actions match your values.) "Have you seen anyone being honest?"

4. Ask "Does anyone know what *respect* is?" (Answer: To treat others as you would have them treat you; to value the worth of every person, including yourself.) "Have you seen anyone being respectful?"

5. Ask "Does anyone know what *responsibility* is?" (Answer: To do what you ought to do, to be accountable for your behavior and obligations.) "Have you seen anyone being responsible?"

6. Say "These are very important ideas because they help us get along with others. We see and watch other people all the time. We need to learn to do what is right so we do it all the time, even if no one is watching."

Instructor Note: *Refer to chapter 2 of* **Teaching Swimming Fundamentals** *if you need to know more about the social and emotional development of the age group in your class. This will help you to modify your discussion of values appropriately for your class. Pay attention to "teachable moments" as opportunities to talk about values. During class, take a moment when a student demonstrates one of the values and share it with the other students. Recognize the student and cele-brate the action. Also confront any student who is not demonstrating one of the core values and bring those actions to his or her attention. Reinforce the idea of following the core values.*

Performance Criteria

The student should

→ participate in the discussion and

→ give an interpretation of what caring, honesty, respect, and responsibility mean to him or her.

Objective: To have fun in the water through a game

Materials Needed: flotation belts

Discussion Guidelines for Instructors

Here is one example of a game to play. Let students wear flotation belts if they wish.

Heads, Shoulders, Knees, and Toes: The leader faces a line of swimmers standing in the shallow end. When he or she calls out the word *head,* the swimmers should touch their heads with both hands. The leader then calls out the words *shoulders, knees,* and *toes,* and the swimmers touch the corresponding part. Make the game splashy so that everyone gets wet. To make it exciting, move from one body part to another as quickly as possible.

Many other games are appropriate. See appendix A in *Teaching Swimming Fundamentals* for more games, or make up your own.

Performance Criteria

The student should

→ actively participate and

→ show enjoyment by smiles, laughter, or other signs.

Component 3: Stroke Development

Objective: To learn and improve the front paddle stroke

Materials Needed:

flotation belts, one for each student; kickboards, one for each student

Discussion Guidelines for Instructors

Instructor Note: *Have students wear flotation belts while working on these skills. Allow some time in class for them to attempt the same skills while not wearing a belt. Discuss with the students what the belt is doing when they wear it and why they should take it off to try the same skills.*

Front paddle stroke

Ask the following series of questions:

1. "When you are on your front in the water, what do you do to make yourself move? Can you move forward? Can you move backward? What can you do with your arms that helps make you move forward? What about your legs?"

2. "When you are paddling on your front, what are your legs doing? How many ways can you make your legs move? Which ways make you move forward best? Which ways seem easier to you?"

Instructor Note: *After asking each question, have the students try their ideas. Point out those students who are performing appropriate or creative movements. Emphasize that there is more than one good way to move the arms and legs in the water. At this point students can move their arms and legs either symmetrically or in alternation; both are acceptable. Refer to chapter 7 of* **Teaching Swimming Fundamentals** *to remind yourself of the standard progression of the stroke. Move the flotation blocks on the flotation belt to the back to make it easier for students to swim on the front (paddle stroke), and adjust the location of the blocks on the trunk to help with body positioning. Work with students until they are able to move a few feet without your assistance.*

3. "Is there a way to make paddling easier or better for you?" Give each student a kickboard. Ask "Can you walk the kickboard to me? Is there another way to hold the kickboard and walk to me? Any other ways? When was it easier? Was it lying on top of the water, flat, or was it vertical, up and down? It goes pretty easily when it is flat, right?" Then ask "When you are swimming, which way do you think you swim—flat or up and down? Maybe a little bit of both right now. But what can you do to make yourself flatter on the water?" (Answers: Put the face in the water, kick the feet harder, keep the toes near the surface.) "Let's try that."

4. "If you wanted to swim longer than you can in one breath, what could you do? (Answer: Get a breath of air.) "How many different ways can you try to get a breath? Let's try a few. Can you lift your face up? Can you roll over onto your back? Can you turn your head or face to the side? Which was easier?" Have students try to get a breath. Once they can swim and get two or three breaths, move on to the next activity.

5. "How can we get across the pool more quickly? Is there something different we could do with our arms or legs to help make that happen? Let's try some of your ideas."

Instructor Note: *Work on getting students to reach out as far as they can with their arms. Also see if you can get them to kick their legs over a smaller range and slightly faster, maybe with less knee bend. Gradually lengthen the distance so students move from paddling a few feet to going across the pool.*

6. "How many ways can you get across the pool to the other side now? Show me!" (Examples: walk on deck, walk in shallow water, hold on to the gutter and move hand over hand.)

7. "How many ways can you get across the pool without touching the bottom or side of the pool? Let's see."

8. "Can you go across with your head up and feet down? How about with your head up and your feet up? How about with your head in the water and your feet up? Which way was easiest and fastest?"

Performance Criteria

The student should

→ be able to paddle on the front for 25 yards while wearing a flotation belt and 20 feet without an IFD. He or she can move the arms and legs in whatever way is effective for him or her.

Objective: To learn the back paddle

Materials Needed: flotation belts, one for each student

Discussion Guidelines for Instructors

1. Say "Show me another way to get across the pool with your face out of the water, but not on the side."

2. Ask "Can you float in the pool looking up at the ceiling? Let's see. What can you look at to guide you? How should your body be—straight or bent at the hips?"

3. Ask "When you are on your back in the water, how can you make yourself move? Can you move forward? Can you move backward? What can you do with your arms that helps make you move to the other side of the pool?

4. Ask "When you are paddling on your back, what can you do with your legs? How many ways can you make your legs move? Which ways make you move best? Which ways are easier?"

Back paddle stroke

Instructor Note: *After asking each of these questions, have the students try their ideas. Point out students who perform creative movements. At this point students can move their arms and legs either symmetrically or alternately; both are acceptable. Arm recovery can be in or out of the water, although in-water recovery may be best for most Polliwog-level swimmers. Make it easier for the students by moving the flotation blocks on their belts so the blocks are on their stomachs instead of their backs. This will help students float with their heads back and stomachs up. Work with students until they are able to move a few feet without your assistance.*

Performance Criteria

The student should

→ be able to paddle on the back for 25 yards while wearing a flotation belt and 20 feet without an IFD. He or she can move the arms and legs in whatever way is effective.

Objective: To learn the side paddle

Materials Needed: flotation belts, one for each student

Side paddle stroke

Discussion Guidelines for Instructors

Ask the following series of questions:

1. "Show me three positions you use to move in the water. How about holding on to the side? Holding on to a partner or me? Using a float belt? Without support?"

2. "Can you try it on your side? Show me how many ways you can move on your side."

3. "Can you get across the pool with one shoulder out of the water and your feet off the bottom? Let's see."

Instructor Note: *At this stage, students may have difficulty with the side paddle. The exploration of trying to find an efficient way to move on the side is what is important right now. A specific arm and leg movement is not necessary at this time, and they can use arms and legs either symmetrically or alternating.*

When they are wearing flotation belts, twist the flotation blocks so that the blocks are on the side of the trunk nearest to the surface to assist with students' movement and position.

Performance Criteria

The student should

→ be able to paddle on the side for 25 yards while wearing a flotation belt and 20 feet without an IFD. He or she can move the arms and legs in whatever way is effective.

Polliwog Series Swim Information

The YMCA recommends that students at this level wear flotation belts (regardless of whether other IFDs are used) and swim along the pool wall. They begin by walking across the width of the pool. Then they paddle across the width. Begin teaching this skill by having students go only as far as an endpoint marked by a safety cone before they exit and walk back to the starting point. As they build strength, increase the swimming distance until they can begin doing full lengths. When students paddle lengths, they should begin in the deep end and move toward the shallow end.

During early series swims, you should be in the water with the class for safety reasons as well as to give students the security of having you face-to-face with them. If more than one class is swimming together, some instructors should be in the water and some on deck. Instructors in the water should have an IFD or rescue tube with them. A lifeguard should be stationed on deck, at waterside, or in a chair, at all times. If possible, he or she should be located near the series swimming.

Component 4: Water Games and Sports

Objective: To learn how to fin and scull

Materials Needed: kickboards, one for each student; flotation belts

Skill Description: Finning

To fin, the student starts by doing a back float with the arms at the side and hands relaxed. He or she then bends the elbows and draws the hands up, scooping the water. The student then flexes the wrists and pushes the water with the palms toward the feet. The scooping movement is a short stroke, with the hands about a foot away from the sides of the body.

Finning

Discussion Guidelines for Instructors

Ask the following series of questions:

1. "Can you move through the water without using your legs? How? How many ways? Which way is better? Can you try it on your back?"

2. "What happens when you move your hands up? Down? Flat? Side to side? Back and forth?"

3. "What do your hands look like?" (Answer: Fish fins.)

4. "Have you ever watched a fish swim? Can you use your 'fins' and swim while watching the sky? Can you move your fins while on your side?"

5. "Can you fin real fast? Real slow? What's the difference? Which one is easier to help you float and move?"

6. "What happens if you move your hands down by your hips? By your waist? Where else can you move your hands? Which way are your thumbs pointing? Are they up, then down?"

7. "Which way is easier?"

8. "Let's see how far you can go."

Skill Description: Sculling

Sculling is a method for supporting the body and, if desired, moving it through the water using only the hands. The angle of the palm determines movement and direction. Sculling is a rapid "figure-eight" action.

The student holds the hands flat, fingers together, and wrists loose and flexible to allow sideward action. The wrist should not bend up or down but should rotate around the forearm unless directed otherwise. Pressure is constant, down and/or against the water. The student swings the arms away from the shoulders. The arms are straight or bent slightly and rotated in a figure eight pattern.

Flat or stationary sculling, in which the body does not move, is done in the back float position. The student stretches the body, toes at the surface and ears in the water. He or she performs the sculling action near the hips, with hands flat. The arms swing away from the body about 10 inches. The student applies downward pressure as the hands scull away from each other, thumbs angled. Hands are downswept out about 10 inches, turned so that the little finger is angled down, and then returned to the starting point. The pressure should be constant and even, not stopping as the palms are angled.

Sculling relates to all stroke mechanics. The "**S**" pattern or "heart" pattern used in strokes is the same as sculling: When hands move out, hands are pitched out; when hands move in, they are pitched in.

Discussion Guidelines for Instructors

Ask the following series of questions:

1. Say "With finning you moved, right? With sculling, we want to stay in one place. How do you think we might do this?"
2. Say, "Let's see you try your ideas."

Kickboard drill

1. Have students stand in shallow water and give each student a kickboard. Say "Place your arm and hand on the kickboard. Move the board back and forth on the surface of the water. Pitch your hand out when you move the board outward. Pitch your hand in when you move the board inward. See how fast you can move the board back and forth without losing the kickboard."
2. Ask "Why does the board stay in place? Can you feel the pressure of the board against your hand?"

Instructor Note: *Hand pitch is an important concept to learn. It is essential in creating lift force for an efficient stroke (Bernoulli Theorem). You should begin teaching the concept at this level because it will take students some time to learn it.*

Pitch practice

1. Have students stand in the water with their hands on the deck. Say "Pretend you are smoothing sand on the deck."
2. Then have students stand in the water with their hands on the surface of the water and try the same motion.
3. Now have students drop their hands below the surface of the water and perform the motion.

Performance Criteria

The student should
→ perform a "finning" action by pushing or straightening the hands and arms from the elbows and
→ be able to do flat or stationary sculling for one minute wearing or not wearing an IFD.

Objective: To learn how to do the tub

Materials Needed: kickboards, one for each student; IFDs

Skill Description

To do the tub, the student begins with a stationary scull, drawing the knees toward the chest as the hips sink. The shins remain at (not above) the surface of the water. The sculling is performed at the hips to support the position. To turn, the student sculls by cupping the hand on the side he or she wants to turn toward and pulling in short pulls.

The tub

Discussion Guidelines for Instructors

Ask the following series of questions:

1. "Can you float on your back? Now, can you make yourself real small without coming out of your float?"
2. Distribute one kickboard to each student. Then ask "Do you think you could balance a kickboard on your shins? Let's see you try."
3. "Is there any other way you can hold the kickboard on your shins?"

4. "How many different ways can you move in this position? Are there any other ways?" (Answers: Forward, backward, circle left, circle right.)

5. "Who can move the kickboard in this position toward the other side of the pool? Can you come back without turning around? See how far you can go."

Instructor Note: *When first starting this skill, the use of IFDs may help students achieve success more quickly. As they grow more confident, they should perform the skill without an IFD.*

Performance Criteria

The student should

→ be able to do the tub with the hands only,

→ be able to move forward and backward, and

→ be able to circle left and right.

Objective: To learn about going underwater

Materials Needed:

toys or objects heavy enough to sink; a pole long enough to extend from the water's surface to the bottom of the pool. Mark the pole with plastic, colored tape in one-foot increments so students can see the water depth.

Discussion Guidelines for Instructors

1. Start in shallow water. Drop toys or other objects into the pool. Say "There's treasure on the bottom of the pool. All we have is this pole. How can we bring the treasure up?"

Instructor Note: *Hold the pole steady vertically and let the students try to get down to the treasure. To reach the bottom of the pool, the students pull themselves under the water by going hand over hand down the pole. They return to the surface by climbing up the pole. If any child appears to have discomfort with their ears, they may need to be equalized (see page 53).*

2. Ask "Would it be easier to get down if the treasure were on land or in the swimming pool?" (Answer: On land.) "Why do you think so? (Answer: The water supports you, making you buoyant.)

Going down the pole

3. Say "Now we are going to try something else. Can you hold on to the pole going down, pick up the treasure, and climb back up?"

4. Ask "Can you climb down, pick up the treasure, let go, and swim up? How many ways can you swim up?"

Performance Criteria

The student should

→ be able to climb down and up a pole in shallow water.

Objective: To learn how to dribble a ball across the pool

Materials Needed:

8″ foam balls, beach balls, or small playground balls, one for each student

Skill Description

Dribbling the ball is what is done to move the ball across the pool without passing. The student can do this by walking, running, or swimming to move the ball forward without holding it, using crawl or breaststroke arm movements. The ball should move on the wave created by the body moving forward. Controlling the ball takes a lot of practice.

Instructor Note: *If students can't stand comfortably in the shallow end, this may be difficult for them. Modifications may be needed such as the use of a tot dock or IFDs.*

Discussion Guidelines for Instructors

Ask the following series of questions:

1. "How many ways can you get the ball across the pool?"

2. "How can you get the ball across the pool without touching the ball with your hands? Let's see you try." Start with going only 10 to 15 feet, and gradually increase the distance.

3. "What are things you can do to keep the ball from getting away from you?"

4. "Is it easier if you go faster or slower?"

5. "Is it easier moving your arms underwater or above the water?"

Walking and dribbling a ball

Performance Criteria

The student should

→ be able to dribble the ball across the pool.

Objective: To learn how to do the push pass

Materials Needed:
8″ foam balls, beach balls, or small playground balls, one for each pair of students

Skill Description

The push pass is an easy way to shoot or pass the ball. The student picks the ball up with one hand and holds it at shoulder height. He or she then throws the ball in a shotput motion.

Instructor Note: *The ball size is important for success. The ball should be small enough for students to throw with one hand, but large enough to make catching easier. However, at this level, the students will be using two hands; the younger students are not usually able to use one hand yet.*

Discussion Guidelines for Instructors

1. Have students stand in a circle. Show the ball and ask "How can you get the ball to someone in the circle? How many different ways can we get the ball to others?" (Examples: One hand, two hands, over the head, walk it to them, bunny hop it to them.)

2. After they have exhausted all their ideas, have them move one step back, making

Passing the ball

a bigger circle. Now ask "How can we get the ball to someone across the circle without moving away from our own spot?"

3. Say "Let's try again. Let's see if we can get the ball to someone else faster."

4. Say "This time, name the person you want the ball to go to before you throw it."

5. Have the students get into two lines, facing each other. Now each student has a partner. Give a ball to each pair and say "Now see how many times you can get the ball back and forth from your partner." Once they have done it successfully 10 times, have them take a step farther apart and try it again.

Performance Criteria

The student should

→ be able to pass and catch the ball with one or two hands.

Component 5: Rescue

Objective: To learn how to recognize a victim in danger

Discussion Guidelines for Instructors

1. Tell the following trigger story to your students:

   "You and a friend are playing on a hot summer day. Your friend tells you she wants to play in a backyard swimming pool in your neighbor's yard. The family is not home, but your friend says she is going anyway. You follow and watch her jump into the pool. You see she jumped into the deep end but is not swimming. She can't seem to reach the side of the pool, either."

2. Ask the following questions for discussion:

   Question 1: Now, let's deal with the problem of your friend. How can you tell your friend is in trouble?

   Discussion

   • Look of fear and panic

   • Inability to yell or speak

- Upright position in the water
- Hands waving or thrashing
- Bobbing motion of head and body

Question 2: Can people in trouble in the water yell for help? Why or why not?

Discussion: Usually not. They are simply concerned with trying to breathe.

Question 3: What are some situations that might be dangerous?

Discussion: Ask students to describe some potentially dangerous situations. Their replies might include playing with matches, crossing the street, riding a bike without a helmet, or running on a slippery hill; try to include water-related situations, such as a nonswimmer floating into deep water or being pushed into the water from the deck.

Question 4: When you recognize danger, how do you call for help?

Discussion:

- Stay calm.
- "Yell, 'Help!'"
- If no one is available to help, look for something to throw that floats or something to reach to the person in trouble. Stay on deck and do not enter the water to help.
- If you have to call for help,
  a. dial the emergency number (such as 911, if your city has it) or dial 0;
  b. give your name, location, and the nature of the emergency; and
  c. wait for instructions.

Question 5: What are the dangers to you in trying to help someone?

Discussion: Issues students should consider include these:

- What might happen if I get in the water to help?
- What is in or under the water?

- How big is the victim? Am I strong enough to bring the victim in without getting in trouble myself?
- Can I do what it takes to help the victim?

Reinforce that these dangers are why the students should not enter the water to help the person in trouble.

Question 6: What is not good about this story? What did you or your friend do right? Do wrong?

Discussion: It was wrong to not respect other people's property. It was right to be caring and help a friend.

Performance Criteria

The student should
  → be present for the trigger story and discussion and
  → be able to describe two examples of a dangerous situation.

Objective: To learn how to get help when needed

Discussion Guidelines for Instructors

1. Ask "If a problem came up, how could you get an adult's attention? Show me."
2. Ask "When should you yell for help? Is it OK to yell for help as a joke?"

Instructor Note: *Always teach students to yell "Help!" instead of "Lifeguard," so they are more likely to be helped right away.*

3. Say "Let's see how you can yell for help."

Performance Criteria

The student should
  → know when to yell for help.

Objective: To learn how to go for adult assistance

Discussion Guidelines for Instructors

1. Say "Sometimes if someone needs help, yelling may not be enough. You may have to go get an adult to help."

2. Ask, "What can you do? What would you need to tell the adult?" (Answers: Stay calm; look for an adult or lifeguard; tell him or her what you saw and say "Help! Call 911.")

Performance Criteria

The student should

→ be able to go to an adult for assistance.

Objective: To learn how to call on the telephone for help

Materials Needed: a toy telephone

Discussion Guidelines for Instructors

1. During the class prior to this activity, ask students to make sure they know their home phone number and address for the next class.

2. Ask "What number do you call to get help?" (Answer: 911 or the local emergency number.) "What would you need to tell them?" (Answer: Your name, the phone number and address of where you are, and what happened. You should not hang up until the person on the phone tells you to do so.)

3. Using the toy phone, have the students practice calling the emergency number. One student pretends to be the one calling the emergency number, and the other pretends to be the dispatcher on the other end of the line.

Performance Criteria

The student should

→ participate in the activity and

→ know his or her own phone number and address, the emergency number to call, and not to hang up until told to.

Objective: To learn about and practice reaching assists

Materials Needed:
child-sized items that could be used in a reaching assist

Skill Description

Reaching assists are used to help distressed swimmers without endangering the rescuer. Many items can be used to perform a reaching assist: a pole, a towel, a piece of clothing, or a piece of lumber (watch for splinters). A rescuer also can extend an arm or leg. At this level, because of the size and age of the students, we will concentrate on extending objects rather than an arm or leg.

To perform an assist, the student first establishes a firm base of support by lying down or crouching, spreading the legs, and keeping the weight low and away from the victim. He or she extends the object within reach of the victim and either slides it under the victim's armpit or presses it against the victim's side. Once the victim has grasped the object, the student maintains position and, with weight shifted away from the victim, pulls him or her in slowly, hand over hand. The student should communicate with the victim, reassuring the victim as he or she is brought to safety.

At this level, emphasize that students should not get into the water to rescue. Teach students how to grab and hold onto an item extended by a rescuer.

Instructor Note: *The reaching assist is introduced before the throwing assist because throwing requires more cognitive and motor skills than reaching.*

Discussion Guidelines for Instructors

1. Share the following trigger story with your students:

   "Two boys, Bob and Jamie, were fishing at the end of a dock. Bob reached out with a fishing net to scoop up the fish he had just caught. But he leaned over too far and fell off the dock into the water. Jamie called, 'Are you OK?' Bob didn't answer and just kept thrashing around in the water. He was trying to reach the dock, but he wasn't close enough to hang on."

2. Ask the following questions for discussion:

   Question 1: What would Jamie see Bob doing in the water that would tell him Bob needs help?

   Discussion: The look of panic, thrashing upright in the water, an inability to speak clearly, and bobbing under the water.

   Question 2: What are some of the things Jamie could do to help Bob?

   Discussion: Call for help, look for something to reach to him or something to throw to him that floats. He should not go into the water.

   Question 3: What should Jamie not do?

   Discussion: He should not go into the water. He also should not simply do nothing or run away.

   Question 4: What if Jamie had nothing to throw to Bob?

   Discussion: Look for something to reach. Something is always available, even if it's just clothing.

   Question 5: Because the boys were fishing, what kinds of things could Jamie use to help?

   Discussion: An oar, pole, stick, towel, shirt, and so on.

   Question 6: If Jamie used the fishing pole to help Bob, where should he place the end so that Bob could reach it most easily?

   Discussion: He should extend the pole to Bob's side under the armpit to avoid injuring Bob's face or chest.

   Question 7: What should Jamie say to Bob to get him to hold onto the pole?

   Discussion: "Stay calm, grab the pole, and let me pull you to the side."

   Question 8: If Bob were really scared when he grabbed the pole and pulled hard, what might happen to Jamie?

   Discussion: Jamie could be pulled into the water.

   Question 9: What could Jamie do so he would not fall in so easily?

   Discussion: He could lie or stand crouched on the deck with his legs spread apart so his center of gravity would be low. He then could slowly pull Bob to the side.

3. Have students take turns pretending to rescue you, using extension items. Have them tell you, as you role play the victim, what to do: Look at me; keep your head up; kick your feet; grab and hold on to the item extended.

Performance Criteria

The student should

→ be able to perform a reaching assist.

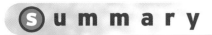

Summary

Polliwog

Summary of Performance Criteria

Component 1: Personal Safety

- Participate in the discussion and be able to repeat and discuss the pool rules.
- Participate in the discussion and be able to repeat and discuss the class expectations.
- Walk or swim away from the pool wall, turn around, and reach and grab onto the wall without assistance; be comfortable being in the water; and raise feet off the bottom while wearing an IFD.
- Be self-supporting in the water for 30 seconds with or without a float belt, demonstrate the front and back float, take a breath on the front float, and recover to standing from both the front and back float.
- Secure and take off a PFD and discriminate between a PFD and an IFD. ⚠
- Jump into a pool wearing a PFD (giving the PFD a hug), paddle stroke 10 yards on the front, and then turn on the back and kick 10 yards. ⚠
- Get into and out of a boat with assistance while wearing a PFD. ⚠
- Jump out away from the side, paddle to the surface, turn, and return to the side without assistance.
- Participate in the discussion and know at least one mode of protection from the sun.

Component 2: Personal Growth

- Participate in the discussion and activities related to self-confidence.
- Participate in the discussion of core values and give an interpretation of what the core values mean.
- Actively participate in a game and show enjoyment by smiles, laughter, or other signs.

Component 3: Stroke Development

- Paddle on the front for 25 yards while wearing a flotation belt and 20 feet without an IFD.
- Paddle on the back for 25 yards while wearing a flotation belt and 20 feet without an IFD.
- Paddle on the side for 25 yards while wearing a flotation belt and 20 feet without an IFD.

Component 4: Water Games and Sports

- Perform a "finning" action by pushing or straightening the hands and arms from the elbows and do flat or stationary sculling for one minute with or without an IFD.
- Do the tub with the hands only, move forward and backward, and circle left and right.
- Climb down and up a pole in shallow water.
- Dribble the ball across the pool.
- Pass and catch the ball with one or two hands.

Component 5: Rescue

- Be present for the trigger story and discussion and be able to describe two examples of a dangerous situation.
- Know when to yell for help.
- Be able to go to an adult for assistance.
- Participate in the practice for dialing the emergency number and know own phone number and address, the correct emergency number, and when to hang up.
- Perform a reaching assist.

polliwog

CHAPTER *three*

Guppy Level

At the Guppy level students are building on the confidence and abilities they developed in the Polliwog level.

Some students may become too confident and overestimate their skills and abilities; therefore, lessons in caution and patience are important. Others' confidence still needs considerable bolstering, for water activities can be frightening.

Students begin to refine their personal safety skills and strokes to become more efficient as they increase their endurance and overall fitness. The students are slowly being introduced to deeper water and are gradually increasing their ability to rescue others.

While enrolled in the Guppy level, the student is

→ helped to learn the safety swim;

→ helped to learn diving safety;

→ helped to learn the front and back float performed without an IFD;

→ developing treading skills without an IFD;

→ helped to learn the correct use of PFDs and allowed to try performing a safety swim while wearing a PFD;

→ given an explanation of the heat escape lessening posture (HELP);

→ helped to learn bobbing;

→ helped to learn how to get into and out of a boat and how to sit and move around in a boat properly;

→ involved in a discussion of safety precautions around water;

→ involved in a discussion of the meaning of the core values in everyday life;

→ developing caution and patience around water environments;

→ helped to learn the following strokes: front alternating paddle (with rudimentary rhythmic breathing), front symmetrical paddle, side alternating paddle, back alternating paddle, and back symmetrical paddle;

→ helped to learn synchronized swimming skills, including the front- and back somersault and canoe sculling;

→ helped to learn diving skills, including swimming up to the surface, jumping off a one-meter board, and performing a kneeling dive;

→ helped to learn skills needed in wetball, including throwing and catching a ball, passing the ball to a partner, and shooting toward large targets (goals); and

→ helped to learn more about rescue skills such as reaching and throwing assists and rescue breathing.

Prerequisite:

→ Successful completion of the Polliwog requirements

Component 1: Personal Safety

Objective: To learn about diving safety

Discussion Guidelines for Instructors

1. Ask "Who knows what *diving* into the pool means? How is it different from climbing in or jumping in?" (Answer: Diving is going in headfirst.)

2. Ask "What are some things we should know before we ever dive into the pool?" Discuss the following general diving safety rules:

   • Follow posted diving rules.

   • Dive only into water that is **at least 9 feet deep** when diving off the side and **at least 11½ feet** when diving off of a one-meter board.

   • Dive with arms extended and hands grabbed.

   • Dive only when you know the water and the bottom are clear of obstructions and other swimmers.

   • Swim directly to the nearest side of the pool after going off the diving board. (Follow local pool rules.)

   • Use the diving board one person at a time.

   • Don't dive off the board until the person in front of you has swum to the side or has cleared the area.

Instructor Note: *It's dangerous to use starting blocks as diving boards, especially if they are not in nine-foot, or deeper, water. They are intended for competitive swimming purposes only and are to be used only under the supervision of a swim coach.* Check the document "Risk Management Involving Starting Blocks or Platforms, Water Depth, Deep Diving Starts, and Supervision" in Principles of YMCA Aquatics *and the* Design Safety Checklist *in* YMCA Pool Operations Manual *for more specific guidelines.*

Do not allow children to slide off a mat on the side of the pool or slide down a water slide headfirst. Sliding like this runs the risk of causing head and neck injury.

Lead the discussion by asking a series of linked questions. Here's an example for the rule "Dive only in water that is **at least 9 feet deep** when diving off the side and **at least 11½ feet** when diving off of a one-meter board."

"How can we find out how deep the water is?" (Answers: Look at the pool depth markers; try to touch the bottom with your feet and see how far the water is above your head; do a feetfirst surface dive; ask the lifeguard; place a pole in the water that is a known height or is marked by feet.)

"How deep should the water be before you dive in?" (Answer: At least 9 feet deep for diving off the side and at least 11½ feet when diving off of a one-meter board.)

"Why should it be nine feet deep?" (Answer: That provides a diving envelope or cushion to slow the body down, like high jump or pole vault cushions.)

"How much of the pool should be that depth?" (Answer: Wherever a diver might dive in and start coming up, the diving envelope.)

3. Ask if they can think of any other rules.

Performance Criteria

The student should

→ participate in the discussion and

→ be able to name the four most important diving safety rules:

Follow posted diving rules.

Dive only in water that is **at least 9 feet deep** when diving off the side **and at least 11½ feet** when diving off the one-meter board.

Dive with arms extended and hands grabbed.

Dive only when you know the water and the bottom are clear of obstructions and other swimmers.

guppy

Objective: To learn to do a front and back float without wearing an IFD

Instructor Note: This is the first of a series of activities in this section that interrelate and build upon one another. They offer multiple opportunities to practice and reinforce skills.

Materials Needed: flotation belts, one for each student

Instructor Note: Allow them to try while wearing a flotation belt the first couple times. Then have them try floating without a belt. The first time you use IFDs in class, explain to the children how and why IFDs are used.

2. Ask "How many different ways can you float?"

3. Ask "Is it easier to float if you take a big breath of air or not? Try it."

Front float without an IFD

Back float without an IFD

Discussion Guidelines for Instructors

1. Relate the following trigger story to your students:

"While swimming with friends, you accidentally walk past the shallow water into water slightly over your head. It will take one minute for the group leader to get you out of the deep water. You have no float belt. How could you stay afloat for that minute? Show me some ways you could stay afloat."

Possible solutions include doing a front, back, or side float; treading water; or performing a safety swim.

Performance Criteria

The student should

→ be able to float for one minute on the front and one minute on the back without wearing an IFD.

Objective: To learn how to tread water

Materials Needed:

IFDs, one for each student (flotation belt, kickboard, water log, etc.)

Skill Description

Treading water is a survival skill that helps keep the head out of the water in deep water. The student essentially swims upright with the mouth or face out of the water for breathing. Arm actions that can be used while treading include downward finning, wide sculling symmetrically or alternately, and downward short pushing (not effective). Leg actions that can be used during treading include a scissors kick, double scissors kick, a circle (whip or breaststroke) kick, a rotary (eggbeater) kick, or a flutter kick (not effective). The body position may be vertical to slightly inclined forward or back.

Treading water with a water log

To tread water, the student should have no fear of deep water, have relatively effective arm and leg actions, have some buoyancy (either internal or from an IFD or PFD), have the ability to turn around and change positions, and be able to perform all movements smoothly and comfortably.

Discussion Guidelines for Instructors

1. Have all students put on IFDs. Then ask "Who can do a 'dog paddle' or 'human stroke' (whatever you have called it) without moving anywhere?"

2. Ask "How are your arms moving? Can you move them in a different way and still stay in place? Another way?" Continue having students try different ways.

3. Ask "How are your feet moving? Can you move them another way and still stay in place? Another way?" Continue having students try different ways.

4. Ask "Is it easier to be up and down in the water to stay in place? Why? What happens if you lean forward? Backward? What position is easier?"

5. Ask "Which arm movements seem to go best with which leg movements? Show me."

Continue having students try different ways.

Instructor Note: *At this level the most effective stroke to use is an exaggerated scull in the upright position. Emphasize that the arm action helps to stabilize the body and that the leg action is basically a big, slow kick. The more space the body takes up (with bigger motions), the easier it will be to keep the head out of the water.*

At this level it doesn't matter what kick the students use; it's more important that they feel comfortable in the water. Students may choose to use a scissors, whip, eggbeater, or bicycle kick, or even a flutter kick. (The flutter kick will not work very well, so you might encourage the students who used it to kick wider, thus changing their flutter kick to a scissors kick.) They may wear flotation belts or other IFDs to build their confidence and to enable them to spend more time practicing in the pool.

6. Explain the purpose of treading water.

7. Ask "Why is it important to know how to tread water?" (Answers: For rescue; to rest from swimming; for sports and games.)

Performance Criteria

The student should

→ be able to tread water for 20 to 30 seconds with or without an IFD.

guppy

⚓ **Objective:** To learn more about PFDs and their correct use

Materials Needed: PFDs, one for each student

Discussion Guidelines for Instructors

1. Help students select the type and size of PFD most appropriate for them.

2. Have students put on and secure the PFD properly. Watch to be sure they perform this correctly. Then, test the fit of the PFD they selected (see page 17).

3. Have students practice entering and exiting the pool from a sitting and standing position, wearing a secured PFD.

4. Have students practice balance and swimming skills in the water wearing secured PFDs. Ask them "Can you lean forward? Backward? To the side? Can you go from forward to backward quickly?"

5. Ask "Can you roll over or turn around? How do you do it? With your arms? With your legs? What leg kicks work well? What arm actions work well?"

6. Remind students that new swimmers or children on or near water must have competent adult supervision from someone trained in water safety.

7. Discuss when and where PFDs are necessary; for instance, they should always be worn while boating or while engaging in whitewater activities.

8. Say "We are on a camping trip and go canoeing. The canoe tips over and goes downriver. You are in the river and start to paddle, then get tired. What can you do to keep going and rest some?" (Answer: Keep your PFD on and float feetfirst so you can protect yourself from oncoming rocks or other hazards.)

Performance Criteria

The student should
→ be able to select, put on, secure, and take off a PFD.

Objective: To learn how to do a safety swim

Back float with a PFD

Skill Description

The safety swim consists of jumping into deep water, doing a paddle stroke for 15 feet, rolling to a back float for 10 seconds, then returning to the side using a paddle stroke. This is done without wearing an IFD, however students may wear an IFD when they first attempt this skill. As they progress, they should perform the safety swim without an IFD.

Discussion Guidelines for Instructors

Say "To do a safety swim, we need to be able to swim in deep water and paddle on our front and back, showing how we can change directions. Who thinks he or she can do that?"

Performance Criteria

The student should
→ be able to jump into deep water, paddle stroke 15 feet, roll to a back float for 10 seconds, then return to the side using a paddle stroke without wearing an IFD.

Objective: To learn about the heat escape lessening posture (HELP)

Materials Needed:
PFDs, one for each student; students should wear clean shirts and pants to class over their swim suits and bring large plastic bags with their names on them to hold wet clothing.

Skill Description
The HELP (Heat Escape Lessening Posture) was developed to help people preserve body heat when they are immersed in cold water. To get into this position, the student floats in a tuck position with legs squeezed together and crossed at the ankles. He or she presses the arms against the sides and holds the PFD across the chest, keeping the head above water.

Discussion Guidelines for Instructors
1. At the previous class meeting, tell students to wear a clean shirt and pants over their swimming suits and to bring plastic bags with their names on them to hold the wet clothing after the activity. Send home a note with students explaining what the students need to bring to class and why.
2. Ask "If you are cold, what can you do? If you go outside in the winter time, what do you usually put on? Is there anything on your head? What type of clothing do you have on? Why do you think you wear these things?"
3. Ask "Now, if you were in cold water, what could you do to stay warmer? Anybody have any ideas?"
4. Have students select a PFD and put it on. Tell them to jump into the water and try a few of their ideas.
5. Say "Let's think for a second. Should your head be in the water or out if the water is cold?"
6. Ask "Would you be warmer if you spread yourself out or pulled yourself together?" Continue until students are doing the HELP position.
7. Then ask "Would you want to keep your clothes on or take them off in the water? Why?"

8. Have students get out of the pool and take off their PFDs and outer clothing, wring out the excess water from the clothing, then put the wet clothing into plastic bags.

Performance Criteria
The student should
→ be able to maintain the HELP position continuously for two minutes and
→ have an understanding of its purpose.

Objective: To learn how to bob

Materials Needed: IFDs

Skill Description
Bobbing consists of repeated bubble blowing in series, with the body mostly submerged. It helps students learn how to inhale with the face above water, then exhale under the water. The student inhales through the mouth and exhales through the nose and mouth with the lips pursed in order to force more air out through the nose. Doing this helps keep water out of the nose. With arms at the sides, the student inhales and brings the arms up with palms up over the head and submerges. He or she then surfaces by exhaling and returning the arms to the sides.

Bobbing

Discussion Guidelines for Instructors

1. Ask "Who can blow bubbles underwater? Show me. Who can do this without holding on to the side? How far down can you go?"

2. Ask "What can you do to make it easier to go under the water? Show me."

3. Then ask "What can you do to come to the surface?"

4. Ask "Can you do this faster? Slower? Can you do this while moving across the pool? With partners?" Make it a see-saw game.

5. Say "This is what we call bobbing. Let's talk about what we've been doing."

6. Ask "What happens when we breathe air in? What happens to the air? Where does it go?" (Answer: The air goes into our lungs, bringing oxygen for our brain and body.)

7. Ask "When we swim, how can we breathe and swim if our faces are in the water?" (Answer: We have to lift or turn our heads to breathe air in, then let the air out into the water.) "What does the air coming out underwater cause?" (Answer: Bubbles.) "We already know how to blow bubbles. Tell me again where the air comes out?" (Answer: The nose and mouth.)

8. Say "Bobbing like we've been doing helps us get better at breathing while we are swimming. It is also good to know how to bob if we get tired while swimming in medium depth water. We can rest a bit by bobbing."

Instructor Note: *When you begin to work on bobbing, first have students try it in shallow water; then you can move them into deeper water. Some students may be more comfortable wearing an IFD, especially while initially practicing in the deep water, even though the IFD will make it difficult for them to go underwater very far. If you have smaller IFDs, you might use them, as they provide some support but allow students to go under more easily. As these students progress, have them try the skill in deep water without IFDs.*

Give students a specific number of bobs to do. Caution students not to do too many bobs because it could cause them to hyperventilate.

Performance Criteria

The student should

→ be able to perform 10 bobs in deep water without an IFD, getting a breath each time.

⛵ **Objective:** To learn how to get into and out of a boat safely and independently while wearing a PFD

Materials Needed:

PFDs, one for each student; one or more boats (canoe, rowboat, dinghy, inflatable raft)

Discussion Guidelines for Instructors

1. Say "We are going to learn more about boating today. What should we always do first before we get near or into a boat?" (Answer: Select, put on, and secure an appropriately sized PFD.)

2. Say "We're going to talk about how to get into and out of a boat, then try it. To get into a boat, where do you think you should step in—at the front, the back, or the center of the boat? Near the side or in the middle? Can you just step in, or do you think you should do something else?" (Answers: You should enter in the center and middle of the boat. You also should reach over and hold on to the side of the boat, stay low, and try to maintain at least three points of contact with the boat at all times.)

3. Say "When you get out of the boat, you do the same things—stay low, hold on to the side of the boat, and get out from the center of the boat. Remember, maintain three points of contact to help you keep your balance."

4. Put the boat into the water at the side of the pool; then have each student practice getting into and out of the boat properly.

Instructor Note: *Steady the boat and be sure to spot the students as they enter so that they do not fall or slip. If possible, have aides or parents assist as well, and have more than one boat available so students do not have a long wait in line. When practicing boating skills, instructors, parents, and aides should wear lifejackets as well as the students.*

Getting into a raft

Performance Criteria

The student should
- → be able to get into and out of a boat safely and independently from the side of the pool while wearing a PFD.

 Objective: To learn how to sit properly and move around in a boat

Materials Needed:
PFDs, one for each student; one or more boats (canoe, rowboat, dinghy, inflatable raft)

Discussion Guidelines for Instructors

1. Say "Now we know how to get into and out of a boat safely all by ourselves. What did you notice when you got into the boat? Were you steady like standing on the pool deck, or did you feel different? The way you balance in the boat is different from the way you balance on deck, isn't it?"

2. Ask "How do you think you can keep balanced in the boat?" (Answers: Stay low in the boat, use three points of contact, hold on to both sides of the boat, if possible, and stay seated near the center. Don't sit on the side of the boat. Keep the weight balanced between the front and back of the boat, and keep the knees bent.)

3. Ask "How can you move around safely in a boat without capsizing it?" (Answers: Stay low and near the center of the boat. Keep the weight balanced between the front and back of the boat and side to side. Maintain three points of contact. Only one person in the boat should move at a time. Secure the oars or paddles in the boat.)

4. Ask "How can you move around safely in a canoe without capsizing it?" (Answers: The person in the bow (front) moves slowly backward in a low crouching position to the center of the canoe, while holding onto the sides of the canoe. Next, the person in the stern (back) moves forward to the center in the same way, crosses over the other person, and continues forward to the bow. Once in position, the other person may move to the stern.)

5. Have students put on their PFDs and take turns sitting and moving around properly in the boat at the side of the pool.

Instructor Note: *Steady the boat and be sure to spot the students as they enter so that they do not fall or slip. If possible, have aides or parents assist as well, and have more than one boat available so students do not have a long wait in line.*

Performance Criteria

The student should
- → actively participate in the discussion and
- → be able to demonstrate the proper way to sit in and move around in a boat.

Component 2: Personal Growth

Objective: To become aware of safety precautions

Discussion Guidelines for Instructors

1. Ask "What do you think causes many accidents in water?" (Answer: They can be caused by the way my friends and I behave; they can be the result of not thinking before doing something.)

2. Ask "What are some things you should remember when playing with friends around the water?"

3. Say "Know where there are water dangers. What are some danger areas around the water?"

   Answers should include the following:

   • Stay away from water if no adult is present.

   • Avoid playing so close to water that, if you trip, you might fall in.

   • Stay away from hills, or banks above water; they may be slippery.

   • Keep away from canals, rivers, streams, and gravel pits; the water tends to be deep.

   • Don't play around locks, dams, and streams, where water can flow very fast.

   • Only swim in open water when a lifeguard is around.

   • Don't dive into water if you can't see the bottom or don't know how deep the water is.

4. Ask "Around water, what are some things that would signal that it is not safe to get into the water?"

   Answers should include these:

   • Having no lifeguard or adults around

   • A broken telephone

   • Missing rescue equipment

   • A damaged warning sign or fence

   • Big waves

   • Not being able to see the bottom

5. Ask "What are some things you can do to check whether it is safe to get into the water?"

   Answers should include the following:

   • Listen to a weather forecast.

   • Ask a lifeguard or an adult where it is safe to swim.

   • Look for warning signs and flags that tell you what you should or should not do.

6. Ask "What are some things you should always do when you plan to go into the water?"

   Include the following answers:

   • Never swim alone. If you do, no one will be there to help you if you get into trouble—and it's not as much fun.

   • Tell your parents where you are going and when you will be back.

   • Only swim where there is a lifeguard.

7. Say "In class, we will be talking about ways you can help if someone gets in trouble in the water. We've learned some already. Does anybody remember what they are?" (Answer: Recognizing when someone is in danger; calling for help; getting adult assistance; using a reaching or throwing assist.)

Performance Criteria

The student should

→ actively participate in the discussion and

→ be able to discuss where dangers are in and around water, follow safety advice, and know how to help in case of a water emergency.

Objective: To learn how to demonstrate caring, honesty, respect, and responsibility

Discussion Guidelines for Instructors

1. Ask "What do each of the core values—*caring, honesty, respect,* and *responsibility*—mean to you? Who can tell me when you demonstrated caring, honesty, respect, or responsibility?"

2. As an example you might discuss students' responsibilities before going swimming, such as showering, applying sunscreen, knowing the pool rules, or knowing the pool depth before diving. Have students explain why these responsibilities are important.

3. Mention that one way of showing respect is to wait for a turn. Discuss other ways that students can show respect in class.

4. During class, take a moment when a student demonstrates one of the values and share it with the other students. Recognize the student and celebrate the action. Also confront any student who is not demonstrating one of the core values, and bring those actions to his or her attention. Reinforce the idea of following the core values.

Performance Criteria

The student should

→ be able to share a situation that demonstrates caring, honesty, respect, or responsibility.

Objective: To learn about caution and patience

Materials Needed: tape, pieces of paper with large letters of the alphabet

Discussion Guidelines for Instructors

Instructor Note: *Every student participating in the YMCA Youth and Adult Aquatic Program should become safety conscious around water. The practices learned now can be carried throughout life. As skills begin to come more easily, students may become impatient and want to undertake skills and tests that may prove not only difficult but also dangerous. Offer your firm but kind restraint and assurance that readiness for the tougher strokes and dives is not far away.*

1. Before class begins, tape a different letter on each piece of safety equipment around the pool. When class starts, tell everyone in the class to go and find two letters and bring them back. When everyone returns, have each student explain where he or she found the letters and how to use the equipment on which the letters were found. Discuss why it's their responsibility to learn to help save lives and prevent accidents.

2. Discuss the following questions, encouraging students to respond. For each question, ask students whether their responses demonstrate caring, honesty, respect, or responsibility.

Question 1: You and your best friend have been taking swimming lessons. You are visiting a new swimming pool and your friend says, "Race you to the deep end." What should you do to be safe and still have fun?

Discussion: Discuss the pool rules and suggest games for the shallow end to get used to the water. (This relates to the values of respect and responsibility.)

Question 2: You and your sister are going to the beach with an older neighbor. The neighbor falls asleep or is not paying attention because he is absorbed in a book. Your sister wants to go off and explore because you've never been to this beach before. What should you do?

Discussion: Remember the rule that an adult trained in water safety, must be present when you are around water: Wake or interrupt your neighbor, and ask him to come along exploring. (This relates to the value of responsibility.)

Question 3: You and a new boy in class go to the swimming pool in his building. You both know how to float and do a few strokes. He wants to race you in the water from the shallow end to the deep end. There is a lifeguard on duty. What should you do?

Discussion: Encourage your friend to stay in the shallow end. If you race, use IFDs and ask the lifeguard where it would be safe for you to race. Maybe you can race across the pool width instead. (This relates to the values of honesty and caring.)

Question 4: You are at a motel with your parents and friends. Everyone decides to stay in the room and watch a movie, but you are restless. Your parents let you go to the game room. You're wearing your bathing suit and want very much to go to the motel pool. What should you do?

Discussion: Ask your parents if you can go to the pool, and have an adult come with you when you swim. (This relates to the values of honesty and respect.)

guppy

3. Then say "As your skills grow, remember that even the best swimmers need to be careful." Give them some safety tips for the pool:
   - Watch out for slippery decks. Be careful when walking, and never run near the pool.
   - Check the water depth of the pool. If it isn't deep enough, 9 feet or more for diving from the deck and 11½ feet for diving from a one-meter diving board, do not dive. (Caution students against diving into backyard in-ground or above-ground pools if the pools are not at least 9 feet deep.)

4. Tell students that, although swimming pools (especially backyard and motel pools) can be dangerous, waterways such as rivers, lakes, streams, farm ponds, and quarries are much more hazardous. Say that they need to ask themselves the following questions before using an inland waterway:
   - Are there currents, and are they too strong?
   - Is there pollution?
   - What kind of fish, or other aquatic animals, live in the water?
   - Is there junk lying on the bottom that is dangerous?
   - Do boats use this waterway?
   - Is there a lifeguard?
   - Do I feel very safe?

5. Talk to students about beach precautions. Discuss ocean currents, wave action, undertows, riptides, and changing water conditions during the day. Look for posted warnings of beach conditions or signs of danger. Provide students with the following rules that help the lifeguard keep the beach safe:
   - Never call for help just for fun.
   - Respect what the guard tells you. Do not talk to him or her unnecessarily.
   - Avoid unsafe areas.
   - Swim long distances along the shore, not away from it.
   - Dive only when you know the water is at least nine feet deep and the bottom is clear.
   - Stay away from boats and surfboards.

- Remember to always swim with a buddy who can help you if you need it.

Performance Criteria

The student should
   → participate in the discussion and
   → show awareness of safety precautions through discussion in class.

Component 3: Stroke Development

Objective: To learn and practice the front alternating paddle stroke with rudimentary rhythmic breathing

Instructor Note: *Previously learned skills for floating, treading, safety swimming, and bobbing all connect to stroke development in a variety of ways for practice and improvement. Help students build those connections.*

Materials Needed:

toy fish that sink or other heavy objects; water logs, one for each student; kickboards, one for each student; flotation belts, one for each student

Discussion Guidelines for Instructors

Instructor Note: *Key ideas for you to change progressively in your questions include the following:*
   - *Whether or not the legs or arms move*
   - *How the legs or arms move—at the same time or taking turns*
   - *Whether the legs and arms move fast or slow or with bigger or smaller motions*
   - *Whether the arms come out of the water*
   - *Whether the face is in the water or not*
   - *Whether the students are using an IFD (water log or kickboard) or not*
   - *How far the students can swim—from the side out, out and back to the side, or across the pool.*

   1. Ask "Can you push out toward me from the wall with your legs and paddle on your front without your feet touching bottom? How far can you go?"

Taking a breath while doing the front alternating paddle stroke

2. Ask "Can you do it without moving your arms and legs? How far can you go now? Can you do it now by moving your arms and legs?"

3. Say "Let's see if you can get here letting only one hand out of the water at a time."

4. Ask "How about moving faster? Moving slower?"

5. Ask "Can you make your movements bigger? Smaller?"

6. Say "Show me the way that you think works best."

7. Ask "Can you get here making long movements? Who can get here making the least number of arm movements?"

8. Say "Let's see who can make the arms touch the legs while they swim."

9. Drop a few toy fish or other heavy objects into the water near the sides and let them sink into the pool. Then say "Let's see who can look for fish (or the other objects) in the pool. Can you lift your head and tell me when you see one?"

10. Ask "Who can swim holding their hands in different ways?" Guide students to try swimming with a closed fist, then with the hand flat and open, and then with fingers spread wide. Ask "Which way was easiest? Which way do you think was fastest?"

11. Hand out kickboards, one to each student. Then say "This time we are going to use a kickboard. Let's see if you can move the kickboard to me with one hand on the board at a time."

12. Have students return the kickboards, then hand out water logs, one to each student. Say "This time we are going to try using the water log the same way. How did that work? Was it easier or harder?"

Instructor Note: *Students should wear flotation belts and a water log for additional support when they start this skill. As they become stronger and more secure and their stroke becomes more effective, use just the belts, then no IFDs at all.*

13. Have students return the water logs, then say "Let's try paddling out to me without the board or log." After they do it, ask "How did that work?"

Performance Criteria

The student should

→ be able to swim a front alternating paddle stroke for 25 yards with or without an IFD, using rudimentary rhythmic breathing. He or she should be able to swim with the face in the water and get a breath and return the face to the water. Arms alternate and can stay underwater or rudimentarily come out on recovery.

Objective: To learn and practice the front symmetrical paddle stroke (lead-up to breaststroke)

Materials Needed: IFDs, one for each student

Discussion Guidelines for Instructors

Have the students try the following steps first wearing IFDs and later without them.

1. Ask "Can you paddle moving both hands the same way at the same time? Show me."

guppy

Front symmetrical paddle stroke

2. Say "Let's try it again another way."

3. Ask "Can you go farther?"

4. Ask "Can you paddle moving both legs in a circle, instead of up and down?"

5. Say "Let's try it going faster. Then try going slower."

6. Say "Try using big movements, then small ones."

7. Ask "Who can go all the way across the pool using both arms at the same time?"

Performance Criteria

The student should

→ be able to swim a front symmetrical paddle stroke for 25 yards with or without an IFD. The arms and legs should move roughly symmetrically and simultaneously and should remain underwater.

Objective: To learn and practice the side alternating paddle stroke

Materials Needed: IFDs

Discussion Guidelines for Instructors

1. Ask "Who can swim with only one shoulder out of the water? Can you swim another way? Let's try swimming with the other shoulder out of the water. Are you on your side, sort of?"

2. Say "Try again, going slow. Try with long pulls."

3. Say "Try again, going fast. Try with short pulls."

4. Say "This time, try moving one leg and one arm at a time. What can you do?"

5. Ask "Can you make the movements real small? Now try with movements that are big and slow."

6. Ask "Which way works best?"

7. Ask "When you swim with your shoulder out (on your side), is your face in or out of the water? Can you try it with your face in? How about out?"

Side alternating paddle stroke

8. Ask "Which way is easier? Why? Which way makes it easier to get a breath?"

9. Say "We are going to play a new kind of hide-and-seek. In this game, the person who is 'It' cannot see your face, but you also cannot swim underwater. I'll be 'It' the first time. How can you swim past me without me being able to see your face? Let's try it."

10. Ask "Is it easier to move your arms faster or slower? Use bigger or smaller movements?"

11. Ask "Is it easier to move your legs faster or slower? Use big kicks or smaller ones?"

Instructor Note: *Be sure to provide students with opportunities to swim on both sides. For students who are wearing flotation belts, move the flotation blocks to one side under the arm, rather than the front or back.*

Performance Criteria

The student should

→ be able to swim a side alternating paddle stroke for 25 yards with or without an IFD. The arms and legs should make alternating motions and remain underwater.

Objective: To learn the back alternating paddle stroke

Materials Needed: IFDs

Discussion Guidelines for Instructors

1. Say "Remember the back float? Show me how you back float. Where should your head and face be? What about your feet and legs? What shape is your body in?"

2. Say "Great! What do you remember to do when you want to stand up? Show me how you do it."

3. Say "Suppose we want to move around—even go across the pool—on our backs. Show me what might make you move." Students may use arms, legs, or both.

Back alternating paddle stroke

4. Ask "I see some of you are moving your arms—can that help you swim on your back? Sure it can! Show me one way to move your arms without having them come out of the water. Show me another way." Continue having students show you different ways.

5. Ask "Can you try making your arms move bigger? What about move smaller? Which way makes you go farther more easily? Can you make your arms move any other ways? How high can you get an arm out of the water? How far can you reach over your head?"

6. Ask "Can you make your arms take turns? Can you make them work at the same time?"

7. Ask "Can you show me ways to move your arms and let them come out of the water? Can you show me ways to pull them, taking turns and coming out of the water?"

8. "What about your legs? How can you move your legs? Can you show me any other ways? Is it easier to do a big kick or a smaller one? Is it easier to go farther with soldier legs (stiff) or boiling spaghetti legs (loose)? With legs taking turns or going together at the same time?"

Instructor Note: *For students wearing flotation belts, move the flotation blocks to the stomach while they are working on this stroke. As students progress, have them practice without the belts.*

guppy

Performance Criteria

The student should

→ be able to swim a back alternating paddle stroke with or without an IFD. The student's arms and legs should make alternating motions that are effective enough to move him or her 25 yards.

Objective: To learn and practice the back symmetrical paddle stroke (lead-up to elementary backstroke)

Materials Needed: IFDs

Discussion Guidelines for Instructors

1. Say "Let's see if you can move on your back, moving your arms the same way at the same time."

2. Say "Let's see how many ways you can swim on your back without letting your arms get out of the water. Are there any other ways?"

3. Say "This time, let's see if you can move your arms the same way at the same time and swim on your back. What happens when you bring your arms back to push again? How can you make it easier?" (Answer: Keep the arms closer to the sides, streamlined.)

Back symmetrical paddle stroke

4. Ask "How about your legs? Can you make them move the same way at the same time, too? What ways can they move at the same time? How about up and down? Try it. How about going outward? How about in a circle?" Continue with other ways the legs can move. Students may need to take time to sit on the side and perform the circle kick to learn how to do it.

5. Say "Let's try doing this real slow. How did that work? How about trying it fast?"

6. Say "Now try to make your movements real small. Can you make them real big? Which one works best?"

7. Say "This is a good stroke to help you rest when you get tired. Why do you think it helps you rest?" (Answer: Because you can glide with your face out of the water.)

Instructor Note: *For students wearing flotation belts, move the flotation blocks to the stomach while they are working on this stroke. As students progress, have them practice without the belts.*

Performance Criteria

The student should

→ be able to swim a back symmetrical paddle stroke (lead-up for elementary backstroke) for 25 yards with or without an IFD. The arms and legs should move symmetrically and simultaneously and should remain underwater.

Guppy Series Swim Information

Students at this level should wear a flotation belt until they have gained the confidence and strength to be able to complete lengths easily. They should swim by the wall or in the first lane, **always starting at the deep end,** and they should exit the pool at the end of the length and walk back to the deep end. Walking back allows them to rest between lengths and to enjoy their accomplishment of completing an entire length. Have students stretch before beginning their series swim. Use static stretching only, no bouncing or ballistic movements. Lifeguards should be stationed on the deck, at the waterslide, or in a chair, at all times. If possible, they should be located near the series swimming.

Component 4: Water Games and Sports

Objective: To learn how to do a front and back somersault in the water

Materials Needed: gym mats (optional)

Skill Description: Front Somersault in Water

Instructor Note: *Before giving students directions for the front somersault, make sure they are comfortable with the face in the water and are able to hold their breath for at least 15 seconds. (Exhaling through the nose during the somersault helps keep water from going up the nose. Discourage students from holding the nose because it makes it difficult to perform the stunt evenly.) Because this is a new water experience, expect students to have some disorientation. Wearing a flotation belt will hamper this movement, so encourage only those who are comfortable without a flotation belt to try it. Have them try this in water in which they can stand up easily. You may want them to work together with buddies.*

To perform the front somersault, the student gets into a front float or glide, then pulls the knees into a tight tuck position. The student reaches down with the arms, tucks the chin, and circles the arms in a big motion

to finish the circle. He or she completes the figure by extending the legs backwards and returning to the front float.

Discussion Guidelines for Instructors

1. Ask "Want to try something fun? Who can do a forward roll?" If mats are available, have students try this on deck first. "Show me— I'll help!"

2. After they have tried doing a forward roll, say "Great! Can anyone do this in the water? Do you suppose it's harder or easier in the water? Right, a little of both. Why?" (Answer: It's easier because the water supports you; but it's harder because you have to hold your breath and keep water out of your nose.)

3. Say "Let's get into the water and try. What do we have to do first? Do we have to get upside down? Do we have to roll forward?" Continue asking questions and letting them try.

Skill Description: Back Somersault in Water

Instructor Note: *Again, before giving students directions for the back somersault, make sure they are comfortable with the face in the water and are able to hold their breath for at least 15 seconds.*

Front somersault

Back somersault

guppy

guppy

To perform the back somersault, the student gets into a back float and assumes the tub position. He or she then takes a breath and drops the head and shoulders back below the water. The student circles the arms backward and around in a circular motion (like swinging a jump rope) as the body finishes the rotation in the original tub position. He or she completes the figure by extending the legs and returning to the back float. The body should be tightly tucked throughout the somersault.

Discussion Guidelines for Instructors

1. Say "This time, see if you can make your circle starting from a back float. Let's see you try. Are there any other ways to do this?"

2. Ask "Would it be easier if you were smaller or bigger? Let's try it both ways."

3. Ask "What can you do with your hands to make it easier to turn over? Do you move them big or small?"

Somersault skill exercise

Once students can do both the front and back somersaults, have them attempt this exercise:

1. Say "Do a tub."

2. Say "Do a tub to a back somersault."

3. Say "Choose a partner. Now, side by side, do a back float, a tub, and then a back somersault."

4. Say "Again, with a partner, start with toes touching, repeat what you just did, and finish with your toes touching."

5. Say "Find another pair of partners to work with. Then repeat what you just did, starting and finishing with all your toes touching."

6. Say "Now, with your partner, side by side, do a front somersault."

7. Say "Get back together with the other pair of partners. Form a line, then do a front somersault."

8. Repeat the previous skills and combinations to music.

Performance Criteria

The student should

→ be able to do a front and back somersault in the water with assistance.

Objective: To learn about canoe sculling

Materials Needed: IFDs

Skill Description

The canoe scull keeps the body stationary or moving headfirst. In the canoe scull, the student extends the body in a front layout (front float) and places the arms beside the body in a comfortable position between the hips and shoulders. He or she arches the lower back slightly by pressing up with the heels and slightly down with the shoulders. The student hyperextends the wrists sharply and turns the palms out, away from the body. The elbows are bent and the hands almost touch underneath the body.

Canoe scull

The student leads with the wrists, sweeping the hands out about a foot from the body by extending the elbows. Without stopping, the student then rotates the hands so the palms face inward and sweeps the hands back toward each other by bending the elbows. The movement of the hands resembles a figure eight. The fingers and thumb should be held close together in order to exert maximum pressure on the water, but the wrists and elbows should be relaxed. To remain stationary, the student should keep the palms facing down; to travel, the student should have the fingertips facing down.

Discussion Guidelines for Instructors

1. Ask "If you wanted to move on your front without moving your legs and not showing me your arms or hands, how could you move?"

2. Ask "Where is the heaviest part of your body? (Answer: Your hips.)

3. Ask "Do you think if you tried placing your hands near your legs and hips it might help? Give it a try." After they have tried, ask "Where is it easier to put your hands? Right at your hips, or farther down toward your feet?"

Instructor Note: *The use of IFDs is recommended for learning this skill. As students become stronger and more comfortable have them try it without the use of IFDs.*

Performance Criteria

The student should

→ be able to demonstrate canoe sculling for 30 seconds with or without an IFD.

Objective: To learn how to swim up to the surface

Materials Needed:

a kickboard, rescue tube, or water log; a shepherd's crook; a pole long enough to extend from the water's surface to the bottom of the pool. Mark the pole in one-foot increments so students can see how deep the water is.

Discussion Guidelines for Instructors

1. In shallow water, review climbing down to the pool bottom and up using a pole.

2. Say "Now let's try climbing down and then letting go and swimming up to the surface." Hold the pole vertically in the water while students try climbing down it, then swimming up.

3. Ask "If you wanted to come up faster, what could you do?"

Swimming up to the surface after going down the pole

4. Ask "Did you notice anything when you went underwater? Did you feel any pressure or tightness in your ears? To make it feel better, we can equalize the pressure. First try either wiggling your jaw or swallowing with your mouth closed. If that doesn't work, try pinching your nose with your thumb and finger. Keep your mouth closed and try to blow air out your nose gently. You should feel a little 'pop' in your ears. Now, let's try it." Students practice equalizing the pressure. Then say "If your ears hurt when you go under or they won't pop, come back to the surface."

5. Move students to the deep water. Ask "Who can jump into the water and touch the bottom of the pool with their feet?"

6. Ask "What can you do to go deeper into the water? Try your ideas."

7. Ask "Does it work better if you spread out your arms and legs or if you keep them together? Try it both ways."

8. After the students surface, have them paddle to the ladder and climb out of the pool.

Instructor Note: *Have students jump out at least five feet. Mark five feet with a kickboard, rescue tube, or water log to provide students with a visual cue (you also can use these items for rescue purposes). Once students can perform this skill successfully, they can then try jumping off the diving board. Have a shepherd's crook available as a safety pole to grab on to.*

Performance Criteria

The student should

→ be able to jump into deep water and swim up from at least five to seven feet.

Objective: To learn how to perform a kneeling dive

Materials Needed: several sinkable objects

Skill Description: Surface Glide and Recover

This is the first of a series of skills that progresses to performing a kneeling dive.

Surface glide

Surface glide to the bottom

To perform a surface glide, the student pushes off the side with both feet, in shallow water. He or she slides on the surface with arms extended, hands grabbed, and with legs straight. The eyes should be open. When the student is ready to stop, he or she pulls the hands down and brings the knees forward, raises the head, and places the feet in standing position.

Discussion Guidelines for Instructors

Ask "Who can pretend to be an arrow or rocket (hold your hands over your head to make the point of the arrow or rocket) that has been shot from a bow and then hits the target?"

Skill Description: Surface Glide to Bottom

To do the surface glide to the bottom, the student glides to the bottom with arms extended and hands grabbed and touches it with the hands. He or she then brings the knees to the chest, puts the feet on the bottom, and pushes off to glide to the surface.

Discussion Guidelines for Instructors

1. Ask "How many different ways can you touch the bottom of the pool with your hands over your head?"

2. Say "This time, touch the bottom, but don't put your feet on the bottom until after you touch it with your hands."

guppy

Squatting on the bottom of the pool

Equalizing pressure

Ask "Did you notice anything when you went underwater? Did you feel any pressure or tightness in your ears? To make them feel better, we need to equalize the pressure. Do it this way: Pinch your nose with your thumb and finger. Close your mouth and try to blow air out your nose gently. You should feel a little 'pop' in your ears. Now, let's try it." Students practice equalizing the pressure. Then say "If your ears hurt when you go under or if they won't pop, come back to the surface."

Skill Description: Flying Porpoise

The flying porpoise is performed in four to six feet of water. The student starts by standing on the bottom, with arms extended and hands grabbed. He or she then bends the knees and jumps up, reaches out, and then glides to the bottom. After the student touches bottom, he or she places the feet on the bottom and stands up.

Instructor Note: *The water depth depends on the height of the students. Shorter students should perform this skill in shallower water.*

Discussion Guidelines for Instructors

1. Say "With your hands over your head, let's see if you can look like a porpoise swimming in the ocean."

2. Say "Now let's see if you can go all the way to the bottom and jump way out of the water. Imagine you are jumping through a hoop held above the surface of the water."

3. Ask "Can you do it faster? Can you make your jumps longer? How many times does it take to get across the pool? Let's see if you can do it with one less time."

guppy

Flying porpoise

guppy

Headfirst surface dive

Skill Description: Headfirst Surface Dive

The headfirst surface dive is done in deep water. The student starts with a surface glide with arms overhead. He or she then takes a breath, tucks the chin, and reaches toward the bottom, lifting the legs and gliding. The student exhales slowly and gently during the descent and ascent.

Discussion Guidelines for Instructors

1. Put some sinkable objects on the bottom of the pool. Then say "Let's see you try to get the objects on the bottom of the pool." After they try, ask "Are there any other ways you can get the objects?"

2. Say "Let's see if you can get near the items by going headfirst with arms overhead. Let's see how many different ways you can think of to get close to the objects."

3. Say "This time when you are swimming, don't stop, but try to go and get an object."

Skill Description: Kneeling Dive

Instructor Note: *Once diving is moved to the deck, tell students not to equalize pressure. The diving speed will be too great for students to dive without keeping their hands above the head at all times to prevent injury.*

The kneeling dive is performed in water at least nine feet deep. The student kneels (with one knee up and the other down) on the edge of the deck with arms extended and hands grabbed. The head is between the arms with the eyes focused on the entry point. The lead foot is positioned so the toes are over the edge of the pool. The student leans forward and touches the water before pushing with the feet. He or she glides toward the bottom, then swims up to return to the surface.

Instructor Note: *The kneeling dive should be taught in water at least nine feet deep. A large plastic loop may be held on the surface of the water to create a target for the diver.*

Discussion Guidelines for Instructors

1. Have students get into the kneeling position with one knee up and the other down with arms extended and hands grabbed and the head between the arms.

guppy

Kneeling dive

2. Say "Let's see if you can get into the water with your hands first. Look at where you want to dive in. When you surface, begin paddling across the pool."

3. Say "This time when you try it, after your arms and hands are underwater, stretch yourself as far as you can."

4. Say "Let's try again and see if you can get to the surface faster."

5. Ask "Would it help if, once your hands were underwater, you reached them up toward the surface? See if you can dive, surface, and paddle 15 feet."

Performance Criteria

The student should

→ be able to perform a kneeling dive with assistance, glide, then paddle 15 feet.

Objective: To learn how to jump into the water from a one-meter diving board

Instructor Note: *Try this activity only if your students can strongly grip the stair or pool ladder railing when they get out of the pool. If they cannot do this, they will not have the hand strength to hold the railing for the diving board stairs.*

Materials Needed:

a kickboard or water log, a one-meter diving board, flotation belts

Discussion Guidelines for Instructors

1. In the deep end of the pool, have students jump out to a kickboard or water log at least five feet away from the side. Then ask them to swim to the other side of the pool.

Instructor Note: *When you want students to practice **jumping** into water from the side, check the water depth. Because of differing body size and height, a rule of thumb is that the water should be at least five feet deep for children and nine feet deep for adults.*

2. Ask "When you jump in from the side or from a height, why do you want to jump out a few feet?"

3. Ask "Is it easier to jump in with your feet together or apart? How would you keep water from going up your nose?"

4. Say "We are going to try this off the diving board. What are a few things you need to remember when you use a diving board?" Review the diving safety rules covered in Component 1 of this level:

   • Follow posted diving rules.

   • Dive only in water that is **at least 9 feet deep** when diving off the side and **at least 11½ feet** when diving off of a one-meter board.

   • Dive with arms extended and hands grabbed.

   • Dive only when you know the water and the bottom are clear of obstructions and other swimmers.

   • Swim directly to the nearest side of the pool after going off the diving board. (Follow local pool rules.)

- Use the diving board one person at a time.
- Don't dive off the board until the person in front of you has swum to the side or has cleared the area.

5. Ask "When you climb up the ladder, what should you do?" Answers include the following:
   - Grab the hand rails tightly with both hands or, if the rails are too big for your hands, hold on to the rungs/steps.
   - Only release one hand at a time as you climb.
   - Step slowly up the ladder.
   - Don't start up the ladder until the person in front of you is out of the diving area and on his or her way to the side.

Instructor Note: *If you are teaching small children, stand behind them while they climb up the ladder.*

6. Say "Let's practice climbing up and down the ladder before we try going off the board."

7. Ask "When you're up on the diving board, what should you do? Why?" Answers include the following:
   - Hold on to the guard rails.
   - Walk slowly to the end of the board.
   - Always go straight off the board, never to the side.
   - Curl your toes over the edge of the board so you don't slip.
   - When your toes are at the end of the board, take a big step off the board and jump forward like we did off the side.

8. Ask "After you jump, what do you do?" Answers include the following:
   - Swim up to the surface.
   - Swim directly to the closest side of the pool.
   - Climb out at the ladder.

9. Say "Let's give it a try." Reinforce the diving safety rules before allowing students to try jumping off the board.

Climbing up the diving board ladder

Performance Criteria

The student should:

→ be able to jump into the pool from a one-meter board and swim to the side with or without an IFD.

guppy

Jumping off the one-meter board

Objective: To learn how to in the water, throw and catch a ball, dribble the ball while paddling, pass the ball to a partner, and shoot the ball into a goal

Instructor Note: *Four lead-up skills for water polo are introduced at the Guppy level:*

- *Making a forceful throw (as in making a goal);*
- *Making a soft, accurate throw (as in passing to a teammate);*
- *Catching a pass from a teammate; and*
- *Dribbling the ball out in front while swimming.*

Each skill requires different practice situations, and the two throws and catch require a ball small enough for the swimmer to grip with one hand.

Materials Needed:

balls of various sizes, so students can use a size they can grasp comfortably (a racquetball, a foam ball, a small playground ball, a water polo ball, a mini basketball); water polo caps (recommended for all players, required for the goalie); two cones; flotation belts

Skill Description

To pass the ball while swimming, the student grasps the ball from underneath with a relaxed hand, fingers spread wide. He or she then brings the ball behind the head, with the elbow bent at 90°, to make a good pass. The student can use the opposite hand to assist with balance.

Discussion Guidelines for Instructors

1. Say "Let's see how many different ways you can pick up the ball with one hand. OK, is there any other way?"
2. Say "Let's try it with your other hand. Is there any other way?"
3. Have students match up with partners. Then say "Now let's try to pick up the ball with one hand and throw the ball to a partner. Let's try it another way."
4. Ask "Is it easier to throw the ball from in front of your body or by bringing your arm behind your head? Try both ways."
5. Ask "Is it easier throwing the ball with your arm straight or bent?" (The arm is bent during the backswing and straightens at release only.)

Dribbling

8. When they have succeeded in throwing the ball onto the deck from 20 feet away, have them try it with increasingly larger balls until they are using a ball the same size as a junior water polo ball.

9. Now place cones on the deck 10 feet apart. Say "Now see if you can throw the ball between the cones." Have them try it; then decrease the distance between the cones from 10 feet to 7 feet, and finally to 4 feet.

10. Say "Now let's see if you can dribble the ball and then pick it up with one hand and throw it." Once they are successful, see if they can dribble the ball faster and throw the ball

11. Say "OK, let's see if you can paddle and dribble at the same time."

Instructor Note: *Students may wear flotation belts when they begin working on this skill, then take them off as they become comfortable performing the skill.*

12. Have students pair off again. Then ask "Can you dribble the ball while paddling and pass the ball to a partner? Let's try it a few times." After they try, say "Now let's try dribbling and passing to your partner, then taking turns throwing it into the goal." Have students take turns being the goalie. The goalie tries to stop the ball

Passing the ball

6. Say "Now let's try to throw the ball faster. Which way is faster?"

7. Say "Let's see who can throw the ball out of the pool and onto the deck from 5 feet away." Have them try it at this distance, then from 10 feet away, then from 15 feet away, and so on until they are 20 feet away.

guppy

from going into the goal, by either blocking the ball with the hands or catching the ball.

Performance Criteria

The student should, while in the water,

→ be able to throw the ball with one hand at least 15 to 20 feet and catch a tossed ball with two hands,

→ be able to dribble the ball in front while paddling (with or without an IFD) for at least 75 feet,

→ be able to pass a ball the size of a junior water polo ball to a partner so the partner can catch it,

→ be able to catch a tossed ball the size of a junior water polo ball, and

→ be able to throw the ball between cones 4 feet apart and at least 20 feet away with a 50-percent success rate.

Component 5: Rescue

Objective: To learn more about reaching and throwing assists

Materials Needed:
IFDs; objects that can be used for a reaching assist that are light enough for students to lift and an appropriate size for the students; objects that will float, such as PFDs, kickboards, rubber balls, empty plastic bottles (Soft objects are best.)

Skill Description

Reaching assists are used to help distressed swimmers without endangering the rescuer. Many items can be used to perform a reaching assist: a pole, a towel, a piece of clothing, or a piece of lumber (watch for splinters). A rescuer also can extend an arm or leg. To perform an assist, the student first establishes a firm base of support by lying down or crouching, moving the legs apart to keep the weight low and away from the victim. He or she extends the object within reach of the victim and either slides it under the victim's armpit or presses it against the victim's side. Once the victim has grasped the object, the student maintains position and, with weight shifted away from the victim, pulls him or her in

Reaching assist

slowly, hand over hand. The student also can extend an arm or leg to a victim. The student should communicate with the victim, reassuring the victim as he or she is brought to safety.

At this level, emphasize that students should not get into the water to rescue. Teach students how to grab and hold on to an item extended by a rescuer.

At this level, a throwing assist is performed by tossing a buoyant object out to a distressed swimmer to help him or her stay afloat. (Lifeguards perform assists with a rescue bag, ring buoy, or heaving line or jug, all of which have attached ropes for pulling in the victim.) The student throws the object so it lands close to the swimmer, slightly in front and near the hands.

Throwing assist

Discussion Guidelines for Instructors

1. Review with the students what they learned in the Polliwog level about getting assistance for someone who needs help and about reaching assists. Emphasize that the first thing they should do is to yell for help. Say "Let's try extending something to me. What could you use? What could you do to make sure you didn't get pulled into the water?" Then ask "If you were going to use your arm, how would you extend it to help someone? If you were going to use your leg, how would you extend it to help someone?" Finally, ask "If you needed help, how would you grab the extended object?"

2. Have pairs of students take turns rescuing each other. They can wear an IFD if they like. When students play victims, check that they grab with two hands, try to kick, and do not pull on the object that is extended.

3. Say "If you need help, remember these things:
   - Keep calm—don't panic.
   - Listen to what the rescuer tells you.
   - Keep your head above water by kicking your feet and moving your hands underwater.

   - Let the rescuer grab you to pull you in. If the rescuer holds something out to you, grab it with both hands and kick your feet."

4. Say "Let's look around the pool area. Tell me which things you think will float." After the students tell you, say "Now go get something you think will float." After they have retrieved the objects, have them toss the objects in the water. (If a student's object doesn't float, have him or her pick another object and try again.) Then have them retrieve the objects.

5. Say "If you wanted to help a friend who was in trouble in the water, you could throw a floating object to him or her. How would you throw the object?" Let them try throwing their objects.

6. Ask "What do you think you should try to do when throwing an object to someone in trouble?" (Answers: Get it close to the victim and slightly in front of him or her, near the hands.) Say "Let's try throwing the objects again. I'll pretend to be a victim." Have them practice throwing their objects to you.

7. Ask "Do you think you might need to talk to the person in trouble? What should you say?" (Answer: Things such as "I'm going to help you," "Grab the object," or "Kick your feet.")

Performance Criteria

The student should
- be present for the activity,
- be able to grasp an extended object,
- be able to extend an object to someone,
- be able to identify objects that can be used in a throwing rescue, and
- be able to perform a throwing rescue.

guppy

Objective: To learn about rescue breathing

Materials Needed: a CPR manikin (optional), a pocket mask

Discussion Guidelines for Instructors

1. If possible, demonstrate rescue breathing on a CPR manikin, a student, or an adult, using a pocket mask.

2. Discuss the following topics:
   - How to know when someone needs rescue breathing
   - What to say when you call an emergency medical service
   - Why we do rescue breathing
   - How to do rescue breathing
   - How to protect yourself during rescue breathing by using a pocket mask or other barrier
   - How to become certified in CPR and rescue breathing

3. Teach students the following method of remembering the important points of rescue breathing using the fingers of one hand:
   - Thumb is "Shake and shout." (Touch the person and ask if he or she is OK.)
   - Pointer (index finger) is "Call the emergency number."
   - Tallman (middle finger) is "Look, listen, and feel." (Look for chest movement, listen for breath, and feel for air coming from the mouth.)
   - Ringman (ring finger) is "Two long, full breaths."
   - Pinky (little finger) is "One breath every five seconds."

   Have all students hold up a hand; say each point as they point to each finger on that hand. Demonstrate rescue breathing as students go through the last three phrases; then repeat all the phrases.

4. Tell students that the rescuer must have a barrier between his or her mouth and the victim's mouth. Mention that the number of breaths is different for adults than for children and infants (1:5 ratio for adults, 1:3 for children and infants). Emphasize that they would need to have more training in order to do rescue breathing properly on their own.

Performance Criteria

The student should
   → be present for the demonstration and
   → know the five important points of rescue breathing.

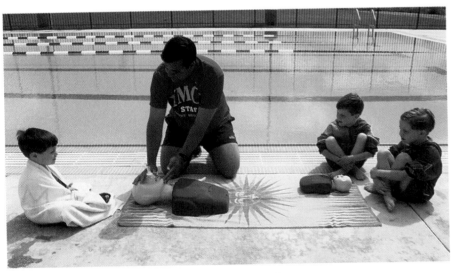

Rescue breathing on a manikin with a pocket mask

Summary

Guppy
Summary of Performance Criteria

Component 1: Personal Safety

- Participate in the discussion of general diving safety rules and be able to name the four most important ones.
- Float on both the front and the back for one minute without wearing an IFD.
- Tread water for 20 to 30 seconds with or without an IFD.
- Select, put on, secure, and take off a PFD. ⛵
- Jump into deep water, paddle stroke 15 feet, roll to a back float for 10 seconds, then return to the side using a paddle stroke without wearing an IFD.
- Maintain the HELP position continuously for two minutes and understand its purpose. ⛵
- Perform 10 bobs in deep water without an IFD, getting a breath each time.
- Get into and out of a boat safely and independently from the side of the pool while wearing a PFD. ⛵
- Actively participate in the discussion and demonstrate the proper way to sit and move around in a boat. ⛵

Component 2: Personal Growth

- Actively participate in the discussion and be able to talk about where dangers are in and around water, follow safety advice, and know how to help in case of a water emergency.
- Share a situation that demonstrates caring, honesty, respect, or responsibility.
- Participate in the discussion and show awareness of safety precautions through discussion in class.

Component 3: Stroke Development

- Swim a front alternating paddle stroke for 25 yards with or without an IFD, using rudimentary rhythmic breathing. Be able to do so with the face in the water, get a breath, and return the face to the water. Arms alternate and can stay underwater or rudimentarily come out on recovery.

- Swim a front symmetrical paddle stroke for 25 yards with or without an IFD. The arms and legs should move symmetrically and simultaneously and should remain underwater.
- Swim a side alternating paddle stroke with or without an IFD. The arms and legs should make alternating motions and remain underwater.
- Swim a back alternating paddle stroke with or without an IFD. The arms and legs should make alternating motions effective enough to go 25 yards.
- Swim a back symmetrical paddle stroke (lead-up for elementary backstroke) for 25 yards with or without an IFD. The arms and legs should move symmetrically and simultaneously and should remain underwater.

Component 4: Water Games and Sports

- Do a front and back somersault in the water with assistance.
- Demonstrate canoe sculling for 30 seconds with or without an IFD.
- Jump into deep water and swim up from at least five to seven feet.
- Perform a kneeling dive with assistance, glide, then paddle 15 feet without wearing an IFD.
- Jump into the pool from a one-meter board and swim to the side with or without an IFD.
- Throw the ball with one hand at least 15-20 feet and catch a tossed ball with two hands, dribble the ball in front while paddling (with or without an IFD) for at least 75 feet, pass a ball the size of a junior water polo ball to a partner so the partner can catch it, catch a tossed ball the size of a junior water polo ball, and throw the ball between cones 4 feet apart and at least 20 feet away with a 50-percent success rate.

Component 5: Rescue

- Be present for the activity, grasp an extended object, extend an object to someone, identify objects that can be used in a throwing rescue, and perform a throwing rescue.
- Be present for a demonstration of rescue breathing and know the five points of rescue breathing.

CHAPTER four

Minnow Level

At this level, students are moving from a beginning to an intermediate skill level.

They are making more decisions, learning about goal setting, and establishing self-discipline. They have learned some fundamentals of swimming strokes and water safety and are continuing to build on them, refining those basic skills.

While enrolled in the Minnow level, the student is

- → provided more information on diving safety and safe boating;
- → helped to learn how to do a resting stroke and to tread water longer;
- → provided with practice in swimming while wearing a PFD and clothing;
- → given an explanation of the dangers of shallow-water blackout caused by hyperventilation;
- → involved in a discussion of the ideas of self-discipline and goal setting and helped to learn how to set some simple personal goals;
- → provided opportunities to demonstrate the core values;
- → given an explanation of the relationship between heart rate and exercise and of how to take a carotid or radial pulse;

- → helped to begin learning the following five rudimentary strokes: front alternating arm stroke with overarm recovery, flutter kick, and rotary breathing; front rudimentary breaststroke (symmetrical paddle stroke with rudimentary circle or whip kick); rudimentary sidestroke with a rudimentary scissors kick; rudimentary backstroke with alternating overarm arm stroke and flutter kick; and rudimentary elementary backstroke with symmetrical arm stroke and circle or whip kick;
- → helped to begin learning some basic synchronized swimming figures, including the circle kick, dolphin, oyster, and waterwheel;
- → helped to learn some basic dives, including a stride dive (from low-stride and high-stride positions), a standing dive, and jumping off a one-meter board with an arm swing;

→ provided with more experiences with wetball, including ones for improving ball passing and scoring skills;

→ provided with practice in throwing and reaching assists; and

→ helped to learn how to perform the conscious obstructed-airway maneuver and rescue breathing.

Prerequisite:

→ Successful completion of the Guppy requirements

Component 1: Personal Safety

Objective: To learn more about diving safety

Discussion Guidelines for Instructors

Review with the students what they learned about diving safety rules at the Guppy level. Start by asking, "What should we always remember about diving into the water?" Targeted answers should include the following:

→ Follow posted diving rules.

→ Dive only in water that is **at least 9 feet deep** when diving from the side and **at least 11½ feet deep** when diving from a one-meter board.

→ Dive with arms extended and hands grabbed.

→ Dive only when you know the water and the bottom are clear of obstructions and other swimmers.

→ Swim directly to the nearest side of the pool after going off the diving board.

→ Use the diving board one person at a time.

→ Don't dive off the board until the person in front of you has swum to the side or has cleared the area.

Instructor Note: *It's dangerous to use starting blocks as diving boards, especially if they are not in nine foot or deeper water. They are intended for competitive swimming purposes only. Check the document "Risk Management Involving Starting Blocks or Platforms, Water Depth, Deep Diving Starts, and Supervision" in* **Principles of YMCA Aquatics** *for more specific guidelines.*

Performance Criteria

The student should

→ participate in the discussion and

→ be able to explain the diving safety rules.

⚓ Objective: To learn more about boating safety

Discussion Guidelines for Instructors

Discuss boating safety tips with students. Include some or all of the following key points:

→ The need to always wear a PFD in a boat

→ Knowing what to do if your boat capsizes (stay with the boat and use it to keep you afloat and out of the water if possible)

→ The need to check the local boating forecast before boating

→ The hazards of drinking alcohol and boating, telling children to remember to not drink and boat and to remind adults of the dangers of drinking and boating (reduced navigation skills, reduced chances for survival in an emergency because of slowed thinking, and vulnerability to hypothermia)

Students in a raft with an instructor spotting

Performance Criteria

The student should

→ participate in the discussion and

→ be able to explain some boating safety tips.

Objective: To learn how to do the resting stroke

Skill Description

The resting stroke is a survival skill that can be used in warm water, in which hypothermia is not a problem. The student begins in a front-float position. When the student needs a breath, he or she exhales slowly while slowly pushing the arms down, kicking the legs once in a scissors, whip, or rotary kick motion, and lifting the head to inhale. After the student takes a breath, he or she relaxes back into the front float.

minnow

Resting stroke

Discussion Guidelines for Instructors

1. Ask "Who remembers how to do a front float?" or "Can anyone tell what a front float is?"

2. Ask "Who can think of a reason why you might have to float for a long time?" (Answers: Getting tired while swimming, falling into deep water, capsizing a boat.)

3. Explain to the students that this technique was used by sailors in World War II to stay afloat for many hours in the Pacific Ocean, when necessary. Emphasize that this skill should not be used in water colder than 70°F because it greatly increases the risk of hypothermia.

4. Say "Let's see you try to float on your front for a minute without moving your arms and legs much. When you need a breath, try to move as little as possible."

5. Say "Let's try again and see if you can get a breath a different way."

6. Ask "Is there something you can do with your hands that might make it easier to get a breath? Let's give your ideas a try. Remember, try not to move too much."

7. Ask "What about your legs? Let's try a few ideas. Try a different one each time you take a breath." After they try, say "Which way made it easier?"

8. Say "Are any of you moving forward slowly as you do this 'resting stroke'? It's all right to move forward very slowly; it's sort of like being in a race to see who can go the slowest. Don't keep your head up or move your arms or legs too much and get tired out."

9. Say "Can you try this for a whole minute without stopping?" Provide assistance and feedback to individual students as needed.

10. Say "Wow, that was pretty good, everybody. We'll keep practicing this every lesson until everybody can do it for a whole three minutes without stopping or getting tired."

Performance Criteria

The student should

→ be able to do the resting stroke (floating with minimum arm and leg movement, keeping the face and head submerged most of the time, and taking a breath as needed) for three minutes.

Objective: To learn more about how to tread water

Discussion Guidelines for Instructors

1. Say "Who remembers what treading water is? Let's try our treading again. Can you show me how you can stand up (be vertical) in the deep water and stay in the same place?"

2. Ask "Can you try again in a different way? Can you do something different with your legs? Is it easier to stay up without sinking or getting tired? Try it."

3. Ask "Is it easier to make bigger movements or smaller movements with your legs? Try it both ways. Why do bigger and slower leg movements work better than small and fast leg kicks?"

4. Say "Now let's think about our arms. Who can show me some different ways of moving them? OK, let's see another way."

5. Ask "Is it easier making them go fast or slow?"

6. Say "Let's try big or little movements. Which of these makes it easier? Why do you think bigger, slower movements seem to work best?"

7. Ask "What happens when you make your arms and legs go the same way? Opposite ways? Is it easy or hard?"

8. Ask "Does it matter if you have the same leg going the same way all the time or if you change them? Let's try it each way and see."

Instructor Note: *Expect different correct answers to the questions in 7 and 8.*

Performance Criteria

The student should

→ be able to tread water for one minute using an effective kick (scissors, whip, or rotary).

Treading water with a scissors kick

minnow

minnow

⚓ Objective: To learn to swim longer on the front and back while wearing PFDs

Materials Needed: PFDs, one for each student

Discussion Guidelines for Instructors

1. Have students select a PFD, put it on, and secure it. Then ask "Can you jump in and paddle the length of the pool on your front? Which way makes it easier to move your arms with your PFD on? Which way makes it easier to kick your legs with your PFD on?" Expect to get several different correct answers to these questions.

2. Ask "Can you jump in, turn over onto your back, and paddle the length of the pool? Which way makes it easier to move your arms with your PFD on?"

3. Have students try putting their lifejackets on while in shallow water. Discuss with students that putting lifejackets on in the water is much harder than when out of the water. Tell them this is why they should always have their lifejackets on before they enter a boat.

Paddling on front   Paddling on back

Performance Criteria

The student should
→ be able to swim 25 yards on the front and 25 yards on the back wearing a PFD using an arm stroke and leg kick of choice.

⚓ Objective: To learn what to do if a boat capsizes

Materials Needed:
PFDs, one for each student; a boat (canoe, rowboat, dinghy, inflatable raft)

Discussion Guidelines for Instructors

1. Review with the students what they learned at the Guppy level about getting into and out of a boat and about how to sit and move in a boat.

2. Say "We're on a boating trip, and the boat tips over because one of the passengers stands up and loses his balance. What should you do?" (Answer: Hold on to the boat.) Ask "How would you hold on to the boat? Let's try."

3. Wearing PFDs, students take turns practicing getting into and out of the boat, sitting and moving in the boat, and holding on to the boat.

Instructor Note: Be sure you have your PFD on whenever you teach boating safety. You must model the behavior you want your students to perform.

4. Turn the boat over and say "Let's see you try to hold on to the boat while it is turned over."

5. Ask "Is there any way to make it easier to hold on to the boat? Let's try at different parts of the boat. Can you tell that holding on to the boat at the middle, not the bow or stern, makes it easier?" (It is appropriate to hold on to any part of the boat that is on the surface of the water.)

6. Talk about what you think it would be like if you really fell into a lake or river.

Performance Criteria

The student should
→ actively participate in the activity and
→ be able to answer some exploration questions appropriately.

Holding on to a capsized raft with instructor assisting

Swimming with clothing on in shallow water

⛵ Objective: To learn how to swim with clothes on

Materials Needed:

Students should wear a clean shirt and pants to class over the swim suit and bring a large plastic bag with their name on it to hold wet clothing.

Discussion Guidelines for Instructors

1. At the previous class meeting, tell students to wear a clean shirt and pants over their swimming suit and to bring a plastic bag with their name on it to hold the wet clothing after the activity. Send home a note with students explaining what the students need to bring to class and why.

2. Say "Most accidents happen when you are not expecting them, right? Many boating and swimming accidents happen when people have their clothes on. What do you think it's like to swim with clothes on—would it be easier or harder? Let's give it a try."

3. Have the students get into the shallow water. Say "Let's practice swimming in the shallow water. Try paddling across the pool on your front and on your back."

4. Have the students get out of the pool. Ask "What was it like? What did the clothes do? How did it feel? Do you think it would be scary now if you had to swim a bit with your clothes on?"

5. Ask "What is easier—swimming on your front, your back, or your side?"

6. Have students get out of the pool, wring out their clothes, and put them in the plastic bag.

Performance Criteria

The student should

→ be able to swim across the shallow end of the pool with clothes on.

minnow

Objective: To learn about shallow-water blackout

Discussion Guidelines for Instructors

1. Ask "Does anybody know what shallow-water blackout is?"

2. Say "If you swam underwater for a long time, you could black out or lose consciousness. Some people also black out if they hyperventilate. Does anybody know what *hyperventilate* means? A person can hyperventilate by taking a number of deep breaths, holding the breath, and then trying to swim underwater longer. If that person doesn't come up to the surface to get air soon enough, even though he or she feels like breathing, that person can black out."

3. Say "Knowing this, what things do you think you should do?" (Answers: Don't swim underwater for long distances; it can be dangerous. Whenever you swim underwater, always have a buddy with you. Avoid doing lots of bobbing continuously.)

Performance Criteria

The student should

→ participate in the discussion.

Component 2: Personal Growth

Objective: To learn the importance of self-discipline and to practice goal setting

Instructor Note: *Self-discipline is crucial to the swimmer who is either competition- or fitness oriented. It also is an important element in learning how to swim, in executing strokes correctly, and in building endurance.*

Materials Needed: copies of a goal-setting form, one for each student

Discussion Guidelines for Instructors

1. Tell the students the following trigger story:

"Susan, a new swimmer, just learned to do a front dive. She also knows how to do the front crawl. But while the rest of her classmates are swimming lengths of the pool, Susan refuses to participate. She's embarrassed because all her classmates can swim more

lengths than she can. When she swam only one length, she became so tired that she wasn't sure she could reach the edge of the pool."

2. Ask the students the following questions to encourage discussion:

• What is a good solution to Susan's problem? If she practices and swims more each day, will she gain the strength and confidence she needs?

• How can you make yourself do something you should do, but may not want to do?

• If you want something badly enough, but know you must practice a lot to be good at it, how do you make yourself practice? Should you practice only when you feel like it or get around to it?

• What do championship athletes or award-winning musicians do to become and to stay good?

• If you wanted to run in a race, what steps would you have to take to build up the skills and energy you would need?

3. Create a goal-setting form like the one in figure 4.1. You can develop it yourself, have students think up additional components, or allow students to create their own form. Distribute the form to your students and explain how to use it.

Performance Criteria

The student should

→ participate in the discussion and

→ be able to achieve one of the goals set.

Objective: To demonstrate caring, honesty, respect, and responsibility

Materials Needed: chalkboard and chalk by the pool

Discussion Guidelines for Instructors

1. Ask "What do the words *caring, honesty, respect,* and *responsibility* mean?"

2. Ask each student to give an example of how he or she demonstrates each of the four values.

Figure 4.1   **Goal-Setting Form**

Name _____ **Age** _____

Swimming level _____

What I want to accomplish in class

In the next class _____

In one week _____

In one month _____

By the end of the session _____

What I want to acomplish in school _____

_____

What I want to accomplish with my hobby _____

_____

What I want to accomplish before my next birthday _____

_____

minnow

3. During each class, point out when someone demonstrates one of the four values. By the end of the session, each student should have demonstrated each of the four values in his or her attitude and behavior.

4. On a chalkboard by the pool, write seven spaces for seven letters. Assign a skill to each student to work on (or have them do it with a buddy). If a student shows you that he or she can do that skill, that student earns a letter and gets to write the letter in the appropriate space on the chalkboard. After the word "respect" has been spelled out, discuss the value of respect.

Performance Criteria

The student should

→ demonstrate caring, honesty, respect, and responsibility in class.

minnow

Objective: To understand heart-rate monitoring

Materials Needed: a clock or watch with a second hand

Discussion Guidelines for Instructors

1. Discuss how activity affects a person's heart rate. Then say "Let's practice taking our own heart rate. You can feel your pulse in two places: Place your index and middle fingers on the side of your neck, just behind your Adam's apple, or place the same two fingers on the inside of your wrist, just below your thumb. See if you can find it." Have students find their pulse. Ask "At which place can you feel it better?" Then say "OK, now I'll time you for 10 seconds. Count the number of beats you feel."

2. Have students swim a length of the pool as fast as they can.

3. As soon as they get out of the pool, say "Now take your pulse again while I time you for 10 seconds." After timing, ask "Is the number different from the first time?"

4. Discuss the difference between resting heart rate and working heart rate.

5. Ask "What are some ways we can get to our working heart rate? How long should we work out at that rate?"

6. Ask "Of the different ways we thought of to reach our working heart rate, which ones do you think you could do longer than the others?"

Performance Criteria

The student should

→ be able to take his or her own heart rate and

→ understand the difference between resting and working heart rate.

Component 3: Stroke Development

Objective: To learn the front alternating arm stroke with overarm recovery and rotary breathing

Skill Description

At this level, students are learning to refine the crawl stroke. Concentrate on helping them add breathing to the stroke and develop coordination of the stroke, both of which can be difficult for many swimmers. Guide your students to find the movement that helps them move more efficiently and increases their comfort level. When you work with students, try not to jump quickly to refining the stroke for them; instead, help each one find his or her own solution.

When students enter this level, their front crawl stroke with rhythmic breathing should look like this:

Arms: The swimmer's arms enter the water fully extended in front of the head (at 11 and 1 o'clock). Thumbs and index fingers enter first. With hand and arm, the swimmer creates a propelling underwater pull/push. The swimmer's hand and arm leave the water fully extended past the hip and thigh. The entire arm and hand recover over the water every stroke.

Kick: The swimmer does a strong flutter kick from the hip, with minimal knee bend and relaxed ankles and toes.

Breathing: The swimmer demonstrates the proper head and body positions while the face is in the water: chin tipped down, water at or slightly above the hair line. He or she attempts rotary breathing (breathing to the side) and definitely demonstrates rhythmic breathing (any type of regular breathing pattern).

By the time students are ready to move to the Fish level, their front crawl stroke should look like this:

Arms: Two phases occur during the arm movement: the underwater pull/push and recovery. In the underwater pull/push, the hand and arm enter the water fully extended (at 11 and 1 o'clock), thumb and index finger entering the water first. With the hand lightly cupped, the hand catches the water; pulls past the nose, chin, and chest; and pushes past the belly, hip, and thigh. The swimmer's elbow is slightly bent through both the pull and the push. After the swimmer finishes the pull/push (past hip and thigh), the hand recovers by leaving the water between thigh and hip. The swimmer's elbow and hand recover high over the water, with the elbow higher than the hand.

Kick: The swimmer performs a strong flutter kick from the hip with minimal knee bend. The ankles and toes are relaxed, and the water should "boil" from the kick.

Breathing: The swimmer performs rotary breathing. He or she exhales when the face is in the water and inhales when the head rolls to the side. The roll of the head is timed with the underwater pull/push. As the hand passes the face and chest, the swimmer rolls the head to the side. As the hand finishes the stroke and exits the water, the swimmer rolls the face back into the water to exhale.

Look for the following points when you observe swimmers:

→ Be sure the swimmer extends at the beginning of the stroke and finishes the stroke past the thigh.

→ See that the swimmer leaves the ear and cheek on the water when he or she rolls the head to the side to inhale. The swimmer should not lift the chin up at any point in the stroke, roll over on the back to inhale, or double pull.

→ Check that the water is at or slightly above the swimmer's hairline. The swimmer should not have a high chin, as it will cause poor body position (low hips and feet) and improper stroke timing.

Discussion Guidelines for Instructors

1. Say "Let's see your crawl stroke across the pool."

2. Say "Let's do it again, but this time stop after 10 strokes. Turn around and head back, and see if you can do something else to help you get back to where you started in nine strokes. Are there other movements you can make with your arms? How about bigger arms, longer arms, or smaller arms? Which one works better for you? Try again."

   Other options students can try include getting the arms out of the water during recovery, reaching farther, and streamlining the body. Continue guiding the students until they work through different ways to make the stroke more efficient, such as streamlining the body or getting the arms out of the water with an overarm recovery.

3. Ask "What happens when you swim across the pool putting your head in different positions? Let's try a few different ways." Point out those students who swim with the face in, the face out, or looking at a shoulder. Ask "What happens to your feet?" Note that when the body is more streamlined, the swimmer has less drag. Ask "Which way is easier?"

4. Say "Getting a breath so you can keep moving is important to

Crawl stroke with rudimentary overarm recovery and rotary breathing

being able to swim long distances. Let's try going across the pool real slow and see if you can get a breath without stopping your arms from moving."

5. Have students continue practicing the stroke. Go to appendix A for stroke drill ideas.

Performance Criteria

The student should

→ be able to swim a front alternating paddle for 25 yards with a rudimentary overarm stroke and rotary breathing.

minnow

Objective: To learn the front rudimentary breaststroke (symmetrical paddle stroke)

Skill Description

At this level, a symmetrical paddle stroke is a rudimentary breaststroke. The arms move simultaneously underwater in the same plane. The heels move symmetrically in the same plane during the kick. The swimmer takes a breath during each stroke cycle.

Rudimentary breaststroke with a water log

Discussion Guidelines for Instructors

1. Say "This time, when you go across the pool, see if you can move on your front with your arms both moving the same arm way and your legs both moving the same leg way and at the same leg speed."

2. Ask "How'd that work? Is there another way to do it? Let's try another." Continue until the students have tried all their ideas.

3. Say "Now, this time, think about your arms. What do you remember about moving with your arms? What do you know?" (Answers: Action/reaction, levers, and Bernoulli's theorem about lift and drag.)

Then say "Let's try some of these ideas with what you are trying to do to see if they will help."

4. Ask "Does it work better with bigger or smaller circles? What else can you do that will help you move better? Do you move your arms at the same speed during the whole cycle? Would it help if you stretched your arms over your head?"

5. Ask "What ways can you move your legs at the same time? How does it affect your moving when your feet are flexed? Pointed? How about moving your legs at different speeds—faster, then slower, or slower, then faster? When would it help to have your legs straight versus bent?"

6. Ask "When is it easier to get a breath while you are doing this movement? Who found it easier to breathe when you began your pull or when your arms were reached over your head? How about if you tried pulling, kicking, and breathing at the same time? Is that hard? How about if you pull, kick, and then breathe? Which way is easier?"

Performance Criteria

The student should

→ be able to swim a front rudimentary (symmetrical) breaststroke for 25 yards. The arms and legs should move symmetrically.

Objective: To learn the rudimentary sidestroke with a scissors kick

Discussion Guidelines for Instructors

1. Ask "Who can swim on the side moving an arm and leg at the same time, although not necessarily the same way, but not together with the other arm and leg?"

2. Say "Let's try it again."

3. Ask "What do you think will happen if you make your movements bigger? Smaller? Try it."

4. Ask "Do your arms move big and your legs move small? Do they need to do the same thing? Try it different ways."

minnow

Rudimentary sidestroke with a scissors kick

5. Say "Let's think about your legs for a while. What are the ways that you can move your legs that make you move forward the best?"

6. Ask "How about your arms? How can you move forward by using your hands? Do both arms have to do the same things at the same time?"

7. Say "Let's try it on your other side. What is it like?"

Performance Criteria

The student should

→ be able to swim a rudimentary sidestroke with a scissors kick for 25 yards. The arms and legs should alternate while the student swims on his or her side.

Objective: To learn the back alternating overarm stroke

Discussion Guidelines for Instructors

1. Say "On your back, how can you get to the other side with your arms moving opposite each other? Let's see."

2. Ask "Does it help to make your arms go higher or lower in the water? How about big or small movements? Try each of the different methods."

3. Say "Let's see how many strokes it takes to get across the pool. Let's see if you can do it again with two less strokes. Let's see who had the least amount of strokes. What did they do that was different from what you did? Try again."

Performance Criteria

The student should

→ be able to swim a back alternating overarm stroke for 25 yards. The arms should alternate and should come out of the water; the legs should do a flutter kick.

Back alternating overarm stroke

minnow

Objective: To learn the back symmetrical stroke

Discussion Guidelines for Instructors

1. Ask "Remember when we swam on our front using both our arms the same way? Can you try doing that on your back now? On your back, your arms should be doing the same thing together, and your legs and feet need to do their same thing together."

2. Ask "Who can do it another way that keeps your arms and legs at the same depth?"

3. Ask "Who can do the stroke real slow? What happens when you try to go fast?"

Back symmetrical stroke

4. Ask "Does it work better with bigger or smaller circles? What about pulling your arms up and out? What about pulling your arms down to the side? What else can you do that will help you move better? Do you move your arms at the same speed during the whole cycle? Is it harder to pull at any point? Why do you think so?"

5. Ask "In what ways can you move your legs at the same time? How does flexing your feet affect your movement? Pointing your feet? How about moving your legs at different speeds—faster, then slower, or slower, then faster? When would it help to have your legs straight versus bent?"

6. Ask "What if you tried pulling and kicking at the same time? Is that hard? Which way is easier? What if you moved faster? Slower? What happens when you glide, legs together and arms at your side?"

Performance Criteria

The student should

→ be able to swim a rudimentary elementary backstroke (back symmetrical) for 25 yards. The arms and legs should move symmetrically and should not break the surface.

Minnow Series Swim Information

Minnow students should swim a length, exit, and walk back, just as they did at the Guppy level. They probably should stay in the first or second lane of the pool. As they progress, they will be able to swim down and kick back, then swim both down and back. Have students stretch before beginning their series swim.

Component 4: Water Games and Sports

Objective: To learn the circle kick

Materials Needed: kickboards or water logs, one for each student

Discussion Guidelines for Instructors

1. Review with the students what they learned at the Guppy level and earlier in this level about treading water.

2. Say "Remember when we were moving the arms and legs the same way on the front? Now I want you to try moving your legs the same way while you are up and down (vertical) in the water." Give each student a kickboard or water log and let the students try.

3. Ask "Does it make it easier if you bring your knees up or your heels up while moving? Let's see you try."

4. Ask "How about moving faster or slower? Try again."

5. Ask "What about your feet? What different things can you do with your feet and toes—point them, flex them, or turn them in or out? What works better?"

minnow

Circle kick while holding on to a water log

6. Say "Now let's try it without a kickboard or water log. What can you do with your hands to help keep your head out of the water?"

Performance Criteria

The student should

→ be able to demonstrate a circle kick for one minute.

Objective: To teach students the dolphin and the oyster

Skill Description: Dolphin

To perform a dolphin, the student moves into a back layout (back float). He or she slides the hands up the sides of the body and over the head. The student arches the upper back and extends the body, with the shoulders pressed down, heels on the surface with the toes pointed, and the head aligned with the shoulders.

The student sculls with hands at the side, fingertips toward the surface. The body moves in a vertical circle. If the circle were a clock face, 12 o'clock would be at the surface, 6 o'clock would hang near the bottom of the pool, 3 o'clock would be the point at which the swimmer moves head-down, and 9 o'clock would mark the point where the swimmer moves head-up again. As the swimmer approaches 4 o'clock, he or she gradually moves the hands back to the sides and starts using a canoe scull. At the 8 o'clock position, buoyancy will raise the body to the surface. As the head starts to rise above the surface, the student turns the hands over. Palms are facedown and fingertips point to the feet as the body emerges. The figure ends as the student returns to the back layout position.

Discussion Guidelines for Instructors

1. Say "Let's see you try your somersaults again. These are ways to do circles in the water. Can you do a forward and a backward somersault?"
2. Say "We are going to try a different type of somersault. Start on your back. Without bringing your knees to your chest, see if you can make a big circle in the water."
3. Say "This time, let's see if you can do it without moving your legs."
4. Say "Try again using your arms moving another way."
5. Ask "Can you make the circle bigger? What would you need to do differently?"

minnow

minnow

Dolphin

Skill Description: Oyster

To perform an oyster, the student starts in a back layout position, hands at the hips. He or she then sweeps the arms, palms up, away from the body until they are over the head. Arms remain fully extended and beneath the surface during the movement. Without stopping, the student keeps the arms straight and brings them toward the surface, reaching for the feet. The arms remain straight, and they are close enough to the head to brush the ears as they go by. At the same time, the student bends sharply at the hips so the feet are brought toward the hands. As the hands touch the tops of the feet, the body descends in the piked position, hips first. The figure is finished when the feet are submerged. The back stays flat and the head stays in line with the trunk throughout the movement.

Discussion Guidelines for Instructors

1. Say "Now we are going to try to be an oyster. Who knows what an oyster is? Where do they live?"
2. Say "We're going to learn names for a few positions. If you are curled up with your knees to your chest or chin, what do you think this position is called?" (Answer: A tuck.) "Now, if your legs are straight, your hands are pointing toward your toes, and your chin is down, what do you think this position is called?" (Answer: A pike.)
3. Say "To look like an oyster, we are going to start in a back float, then move into a pike. Do you remember what a pike position is? The problem is that we need to sink like an oyster to the bottom, with our hands and feet being the last to submerge. Let's see if you can try to do that. Is there another way?"
4. Say "Let's think about it another way. Who knows how to touch their toes on land? Let's see. Fine. Now we want to do that in the water and sink down under the water. Let's see you try. OK, let's see who can get their rear end to the bottom first."
5. Say "Now let's try starting on the back and moving your hands over your head; begin from there. How did that work?"
6. Say "Let's see if we can all go down at the same time."

Performance Criteria

The student should

→ be able to perform a dolphin and an oyster.

minnow

A

B

Oyster

Objective: To learn how to do a waterwheel

Skill Description

To do a waterwheel, the student starts in a back layout. He or she begins the figure with a rotation of the hips to the side so that one hip points up and the other down. Simultaneously the student keeps the shoulders flat and the head aligned with the shoulders. Feet, legs, and hips all stay close to the surface.

(A)

Waterwheel

The student rotates around an axis that is in front of the stomach and perpendicular to the surface. The rotation is created by a pedaling action of the legs and feet. The student extends the ankles as the feet push away from the body and flexes the ankles as the feet move toward the body. After a full revolution, the student rotates the hips back and extends the legs into the back layout position.

The body is propelled only by the legs and feet. Hands can be placed on the hips or one hand on the hip and one on the back of the neck.

Discussion Guidelines for Instructors

Ask the following series of questions:

1. "Has anyone ridden a bike lately? Now we are going to try to ride a bike in the water. Let's see you try."

2. "How many different ways can you ride a bike in the water? What do your hands do when you ride a bike? Let's try putting your hands on your hips. Try again."

3. "Who can try it on the side? What happens when you do it on your side?"

4. "Can you move better by moving your legs bigger or smaller?"

(B)

(C)

minnow

Performance Criteria

The student should

→ be able to perform a waterwheel in each direction.

Objective: To learn how to perform a combination of synchronized swimming skills

Discussion Guidelines for Instructors

1. Review with the students the synchronized swimming skills they have learned so far (sculling, the canoe scull, front and back somersaults, dolphin, oyster, waterwheel).

2. Play Add-On. The first student performs one synchronized swimming skill, then the next student does the first skill plus another one. This continues until all students have had a turn. Then have all the students try the skills together.

Performance Criteria

The student should

→ be able to perform a number of synchronized swimming skills.

Objective: To learn how to do a stride dive from the low-stride and high-stride positions

Skill Description: Stride Dive From Low-Stride Position

To perform a stride dive from the low-stride position, the student begins by assuming a squatting position with one foot forward, one foot back, and arms overhead. The toes of the lead foot are over the edge of the pool. He or she then lifts up so that both knees are flexed and off the ground. The student reaches forward to touch the water with the arms extended and hands grabbed *before* pushing with the feet. While reaching forward, the student lifts the back leg and pushes off the front foot. He or she then glides toward the bottom, then swims up to the surface.

Instructor Note: *When students attempt this dive, spot them at the ankle and hipbone. This should be taught in a minimum of nine feet of water.*

Stride dive from the low-stride position

minnow

minnow

Discussion Guidelines for Instructors

1. Move students to an area of the pool that is at least nine feet deep. Review the progression of diving movements learned at the Guppy level:

   - Surface glide and recover
   - Surface glide to bottom
   - Flying porpoise
   - Headfirst surface dive
   - Kneeling dive

2. Have students start in the kneeling dive position. Say "We want to try to dive in from a little higher. What position would that be? Rise up on the balls of your feet and step back a little with your back foot. Now try again." Say "This is a low-stride dive. When you are ready to go in, what do you need to think about?" (Answers: Focus where you want to enter the water; keep arms extended and hands grabbed.) Ask "Then what will you do?" (Answer: Fall forward to touch the water; then lift the back leg and push off with the front foot forward and downward.)

Instructor Note: *Remind students of the proper position and diving safety rules. This should be taught in a minimum of nine feet of water.*

Skill Description: Stride Dive From High-Stride Position

To perform a stride dive from the high-stride position, the student begins by standing upright with one foot forward and one foot back. Arms are extended and hands grabbed, with the chin down. He or she reaches to touch the surface of the water while lifting the back leg until it is in line with the torso while keeping the forward knee as straight as possible. The student glides toward the bottom with the hands grabbed and arms extended. Once the momentum of the dive has diminished, he or she can swim to the surface.

Discussion Guidelines for Instructors

1. Say "Now we want to try to dive in from a position that's even a little higher. Let's try again. This time we're going to start from a standing position, with one foot front and one foot back. Your arms should be extended and hands grabbed. As you reach toward the surface of the water, lift your back leg. Keep your front leg straight."

Stride dive from the high-stride position with instructor spotting

2. Ask "What do you do after you enter the water?" (Answer: Glide to the bottom.)

Instructor Note: *For safety, establish a set distance between divers of about four feet. You may want to do this by having each student wait for the previous student to dive, then have him or her count up to a certain number before diving, delaying it enough to give the previous student time to move away. This should be taught in a minimum of nine feet of water.*

Performance Criteria

The student should

→ be able to perform a stride dive from a low-stride and high-stride position, glide toward the bottom, surface, then paddle 15 feet.

Objective: To learn how to do a standing dive

Instructor Note: *Move students to water at least nine feet deep for diving activities.*

Skill Description: Squat Dive

This is the first in a series of dives culminating in the standing dive.

To perform a two-foot low-angle takeoff from a squat position, the student begins by assuming a squat position with legs together, arms overhead, hands grabbed, shoulders squeezed against the ears, head neutral (no chin tuck), and knees flexed. He or she grips the edge of the deck with the toes, reaches forward to touch the water with the hands first, then pushes toward the water. As the student dives, he or she focuses the eyes on an entry point and aims the arms and hands at it. Just before entering the water, the student locks the head between the arms, then enters the water as if going through a "hole" in the water. He or she extends the legs in line with the torso and glides toward the bottom, then swims back to the surface.

Discussion Guidelines for Instructors

1. Say "Let's see everyone get into a ready position for diving. What do you do with your arms when you dive? (Answers: Arms are overhead with elbows locked; hands grabbed and thumbs touching; palms facing the water.)

2. Ask "Why is this position important?" (Answers: Helps you control the angle in which you enter the water; reduces the impact of the water on your head; helps protect you from getting hurt.)

3. Ask "When you dive, are your muscles soft or hard?" (Answer: They are hard because they tighten.)

4. Ask "Do you want your body straight or relaxed when you dive?" (Answer: You want your body straight from your hands to your toes.)

5. Say "Let's see everyone squat, then fall forward into the water with hands first."

6. Say "This time when we dive we are going to try it a bit differently. Get into this position: feet together with toes gripping the edge. Squat down, with hands over head, hands together, and shoulders squeezed against the ears."

minnow

Squat dive

7. Say "When it is your turn, I want you to lean forward and reach for the water with your hands first; then push into the water. Straighten your legs and glide toward the bottom; then swim to the surface."

Skill Description: Long Shallow Dive

To perform a long shallow dive, the student assumes the same squat position as in the two-foot low-angle takeoff from a squat position. This time he or she dives to enter the water farther out each time, entering at a low angle to add distance rather than depth to the dive. The student focuses the eyes on an entry point and aims the arms and hands at it, moving hands to a streamlined position. Just before entering the water, he or she locks the head between the arms, then enters the water as if going through a "hole" in the water. Once in the water, the student angles the hands up toward the surface to slow downward motion. He or she stays in a streamlined position, hands in front, until he or she starts to slow down. The student always should remember to keep the arms extended and the

hands grabbed. Once the student has mastered this dive, he or she can start the dive with a back and forth arm swing to gain momentum.

Discussion Guidelines for Instructors

1. Say "This time when we try a dive, you are going to do the same thing we did before, but try diving a little farther out. This helps you go out farther and not go as deep. Remember, you glide in a streamlined position, surface, then swim.

Instructor Note: *This movement has been commonly referred to as a long shallow dive. It means the dive is shallow, not going deep into the water; it does **not** mean that this dive can be performed in shallow water. It is the lead-up skill to starts, which we will do more of in later levels.*

2. Once students have mastered this skill, have them try to use their arms to get farther out. Ask "How can using your arms help you get farther out on your dive?" When students are in the squat position, they should start moving their arms back, then swing the arms

Long shallow dive

forward as they begin pushing off with their legs. They should enter the water with their arms extended and hands in a streamlined position.

Skill Description: Forward Fall-in Pike

To perform a forward fall-in pike, the student stands at the side of the pool, toes over the edge, arms extended, and hands grabbed (a forward entry position). He or she bends forward at the hips so that the upper body points to the entry point on the water. The student tucks the chin into the chest, raises up on the toes, and locks knees straight. He or she falls forward, pushing the hips straight until the legs are in line with the trunk. The student glides toward the bottom and rolls in place when the feet submerge with arms extended and hands grabbed. This should be taught in a minimum of nine feet of water.

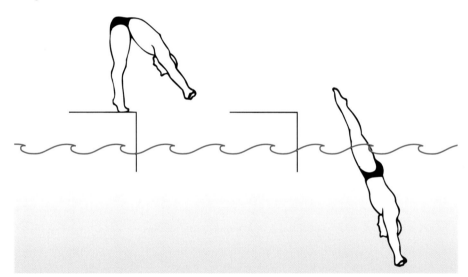

Forward fall-in pike

Discussion Guidelines for Instructors

Say "Let's try another type of standing dive. This time we are going to add a roll after you enter the water. Remember how to do a somersault? Well, this is like a half a roll. This standing dive is trying to go deep again. First, get into the starting position (toes over the edge, hands over the head). Bend forward at the hips, tuck your chin. Next, raise up onto your toes

and fall forward. Then push with your legs so you straighten your body as you enter the water. Glide toward the bottom and then roll over and swim to the surface."

Skill Description: Front Standing Dive With a Jump

To perform a front standing dive with a jump, the student first takes a practice jump on the side, then jumps feetfirst into the water. He or she keeps the arms overhead with hands grabbed and centers the weight over the balls of the feet. (No arm swing is used at this time.)

From an upright starting position, he or she jumps into the dive. Without falling, the student maintains the weight over the balls of the feet while the knees bend. His or her hips move forward and upward during knee extension to achieve the appropriate amount of angle on the last push with the feet. The diver should be able to control the weight over the

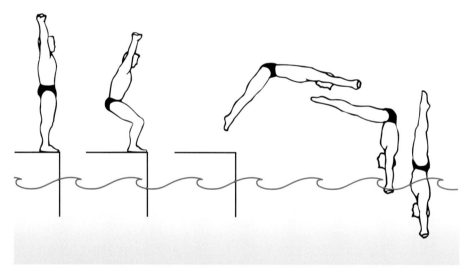

Front standing dive with a jump

balls of the feet during the beginning of the dive. He or she should enter the water, hands first, in a near vertical position with arms extended and hands grabbed, glide toward the bottom, and roll in place underwater when the feet submerge. This should be taught in a minimum of nine feet of water.

minnow

Discussion Guidelines for Instructors

1. Say "Now we are going to do something just a bit different, putting all your previous dives together. Try the standing dive with a jump, so that you can get your hips high and straighten your legs before you enter the water." Instructors place their arms by divers' knees. "You want to dive over my arm and aim for your water entry by the lane marking on the bottom of the pool. Start in your starting position with your arms over your head and hands grabbed, squeezing your shoulders, and toes over the edge. Get a good jump by bending your knees. Aim for your target. When your feet enter the water, do your roll, and then swim to the surface."

Instructor Note: *If your pool doesn't have lane markings on the bottom, provide students a target for diving, such as a hula hoop on the water's surface.*

2. Have students refine their dive by working on their form or improving their near-vertical entry by getting their hips up or getting their legs together and toes pointed.

Performance Criteria

The student should

→ be able to perform the progression of dives up to and including the standing dive off the side.

Objective: To learn to jump off a one-meter board using an arm swing

Materials Needed: gym mats (optional)

Skill Description

To perform the forward jump straight, the student first puts the arms overhead with hands together and feet together. He or she then swings the arms backward and down until the hands pass the hips and bends the knees. He or she continues the arm swing, moving forward and up as the arms rise, the legs straighten, and the feet push off the board or deck.

Instructor Note: *When using the one-meter board, the water depth should be at least 11½ feet.*

Forward jump straight

Discussion Guidelines for Instructors

1. Review with the students the diving safety rules and the rules about using the diving board from the Guppy level and earlier in this level.

2. Have students practice jumping off the board and swimming to the side. Before each student can jump, he or she has to tell you one of his or her daily responsibilities. Follow this activity with a discussion of the value of responsibility.

3. Ask "If you wanted to go higher off the board and straighter into the water, what could you do?"

4. Teach the forward jump straight using the following steps:

   • Have students practice the arm motion in slow motion while on the deck. Then have them practice in slow motion with the eyes closed. Call "stop" at the critical positions, at which they should freeze, open their eyes, and check their body alignment. They should feel the arms stop overhead before the knees and hips are completely extended and before the heels leave the ground in the jump phase. Then have them practice the leg and arm motions together.

- Have students practice the drill at normal speed while on the deck. With their eyes closed, students should feel first the arms and then the legs move from slow to fast in the descent and the ascent phases, respectively. With their eyes open, they should say "slow, fast, stop" to themselves as their arms circle. They should then clap their hands together overhead before their heels leave the ground.

5. Have students practice the jump on deck. As another activity, have them try the jump onto a mat. (Be careful spotting as they jump and land to make sure the mat doesn't slip or students don't lose their balance.)

6. Teach the forward jump straight on the one-meter springboard using the following steps:

- Have students practice coordinating the arm swing and the squat with the board's depression. Students should raise their heels up as their arms lift to a **Y** position. As their arms begin a backward and downward swing to shoulder level, they should bend into the squat. They pull the hands toward each other to facilitate the swing as much as possible and speed up the arms as the feet flex up toward the shins and the knees and hips flex into the lowest position. They freeze the legs in the lowest position and continue to circle the arms overhead. They remain in the squat until the arm swing is completed overhead.

- Have students practice jumping off the board while coordinating the arm swing and squat with the board's depression and recoil during takeoff. The starting position should be with the toes at the tip of the board.

- Have students practice jumping for height. The fulcrum should be all the way forward to make the recoil of the springboard quicker and easier to control. Students should jump for height, but should still maintain body control.

Instructor Note: *Children weigh less than adult-sized divers, so regardless of the fulcrum setting, the board will oscillate faster for a child than for an adult-sized diver at the same setting.*

- Have students practice jumping for accuracy. Students should perform a forward jump straight, entering the water three to four feet from the end of the board.

Performance Criteria

The student should

→ be able to jump into the pool from a one-meter board feetfirst, vertically, three to four feet from the end of the one-meter board using an arm swing and swim to the side.

Objective: To improve the ball-handling skills of dribbling and passing while swimming and throwing a ball into a goal with one hand

Materials Needed:

various sizes of balls; IFDs; four or six cones (set up cones as a goal, two to a goal) or wetball or water polo goals; wetball caps, one for each student (optional)

Instructor Note: *If students are not wearing wetball caps with ear guards, you may want to use bigger, softer balls so there is less chance that a thrown ball can hurt students.*

Discussion Guidelines for Instructors

1. Review with students the wetball skills they previously learned.
2. Have students dribble the ball across the pool while running.
3. Have students dribble the ball while paddling. For the first few tries, allow students to wear IFDs if needed.
4. Pair up students with partners. Then have students swim in pairs and try to pass the ball between them using one hand as they swim.
5. Have students line up in two lines. Tell them to pass the ball with one hand and catch with two. Say "Let's see how many passes we can make in one minute."

minnow

Dribbling and passing with a partner

6. Break up the class into smaller groups, one group to a goal. At a point 10 feet out from a goal, have the students take turns shooting at a goal with one hand. Once students succeed in getting the ball into the goal or between the cones 10 times, have them try again, throwing the ball harder.

7. Once they are successful at making a goal 10 times in a row, move the cones closer together to make the goal space smaller or divide the goal in half horizontally. See if they can get the ball into the smaller space or the same side 10 times in a row. If it is divided in half, have them then try to hit the other side 10 times in a row.

Performance Criteria

The student should

→ be able to dribble and pass the ball while swimming, and shoot the ball into the goal using one hand.

Objective: To learn how to play wetball

Materials Needed:
8″ foam ball, beach ball, or small playground ball; wetball caps with ear guards (at least two, one for each of the goalies; the other students can wear bathing caps if wetball caps are not available); four cones (use two cones for each goal)

Instructor Note: If the students can throw the ball well, you may want to use a bigger, softer ball in play so there is less chance that a thrown ball can hurt players.

Discussion Guidelines for Instructors

1. In shallow water, have students put on wetball caps and place students in game positions. Explain the game to them (see appendix B for wetball rules). Have them walk through a few sample plays. At this stage, students should play by walking and running instead of trying to swim.

2. Have students play a wetball game for five minutes.

Instructor Note: Once the game is over, rinse the wetball caps in fresh water. This will help extend the life of the caps.

Performance Criteria

The student should

→ participate in a five-minute wetball game in shallow water (walking or swimming without an IFD).

Component 5: Rescue

Objective: To practice throwing and reaching assists

Materials Needed:
objects that will float, objects that can be extended to a victim, a large plastic hoop

Discussion Guidelines for Instructors

1. Review with the students what they learned about throwing and reaching assists at the Polliwog and Guppy levels.

2. Have students pair up to practice doing a throwing and a reaching assist. They can take turns at being the victim and rescuer and try using different pieces of equipment.

3. To increase students' accuracy and distance in performing a throwing assist, set up a large plastic hoop in the pool about 10 feet away from the edge as a target. Then have students throw a number of

minnow

buoyant objects for practice. When they have successfully thrown the objects into the hoop 10 times in a row, move the target five feet farther and have them try again.

Instructor Note: *Let students try different objects to find out which objects are easier and harder to throw.*

Performance Criteria

The student should

→ be able to demonstrate the proper technique for a throwing- and a reaching assist.

Objective: To learn the conscious obstructed-airway maneuver (Heimlich maneuver)

Discussion Guidelines for Instructors

1. Ask "Has anyone ever choked on a piece of food? What happened?" (Answer: The food came out.)

2. Say "When people choke on food, they can't breathe. When they can't breathe, they will put their hands up to their neck and hold it. If you see this, you should ask 'Are you OK?' Go for help by calling the emergency number. If no one is around, you can reach around the person and put your fist right above the person's tummy, thumb side into the stomach. Then pull in and up (pulling in is called an abdominal thrust) until the object works its way out. If not, you can repeat the process until it works or the person passes out."

Performance Criteria

The student should

→ participate in the discussion.

Objective: To learn more about rescue breathing

Materials Needed:
CPR manikin, a pocket mask, alcohol wipes or rubbing alcohol, and cotton swabs

Discussion Guidelines for Instructors

1. Have a CPR manikin available to demonstrate rescue breathing.

The Heimlich maneuver

2. Review with the students what they learned at the Guppy level about what to do when they see someone in trouble and rescue breathing.

3. Show students how to use the manikin, talk about barrier protection (show a pocket mask), and demonstrate rescue breathing.

4. Let each student try doing rescue breathing on the manikin. Clean off the manikin's mouth and the pocket mask with alcohol or an alcohol wipe after each student tries.

Performance Criteria

The student should

→ be able to demonstrate the steps of rescue breathing.

minnow

Summary

Minnow

Summary of Performance Criteria

Component 1: Personal Safety

- Participate in the discussion and be able to explain some diving safety rules.
- Participate in the discussion and be able to explain some boating safety tips.
- Do the resting stroke, floating with minimum movement, take a breath, and continue floating for three minutes.
- Tread water for one minute using a scissors kick.
- Swim 25 yards on the front and 25 yards on the back wearing a PFD.
- Be present for the boat capsizing activity.
- Be able to swim across the shallow end of the pool with clothes on.
- Participate in the discussion on shallow-water blackout.

Component 2: Personal Growth

- Participate in the discussion of goal setting and achieve one of the goals set.
- Demonstrate caring, honesty, respect, and responsibility in class.
- Take own heart rate and understand the difference between resting and working heart rate.

Component 3: Stroke Development

- Swim a front alternating paddle for 25 yards with a rudimentary overarm stroke and rotary breathing.
- Swim a front rudimentary (symmetrical) breaststroke for 25 yards. The arms and legs should move symmetrically.
- Swim a rudimentary sidestroke with a scissors kick for 25 yards. The arms and legs should alternate while the student swims on his or her side.
- Swim a back alternating overarm stroke for 25 yards. The arms should alternate and should come out of the water; the legs should do a flutterkick.

- Swim a back symmetrical rudimentary elementary backstroke for 25 yards. The arms and legs should move symmetrically and should not break the surface.

Component 4: Water Games and Sports

- Demonstrate a circle kick for one minute.
- Perform a dolphin and an oyster.
- Perform a waterwheel in each direction.
- Perform a number of synchronized swimming skills.
- Perform a stride dive from a low-stride and high-stride position, glide, then paddle 15 feet.
- Perform the progression of dives up to and including the standing dive off the side.
- Be able to jump into the pool from a one-meter board feetfirst, vertically, three to four feet from the end of the one-meter board using an arm swing and swim to the side.
- Dribble and pass the ball while swimming, and shoot the ball into the goal using one hand.
- Participate in a five-minute wetball game in shallow water (walking or swimming without an IFD).

Component 5: Rescue

- Demonstrate the proper technique for a throwing- and a reaching assist.
- Participate in the discussion of the conscious obstructed-airway maneuver (Heimlich maneuver).
- Demonstrate the steps of rescue breathing.

minnow

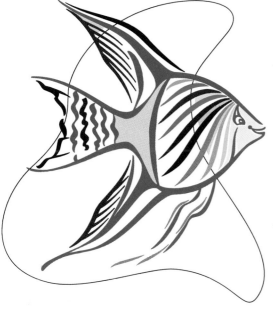

CHAPTER five

Fish Level

As the name implies, Fish are swimmers. At this level, students perfect their skills and acquire new ones, from the elementary backstroke to basic skin diving skills.

First-aid orientation also becomes more sophisticated at this level. The Fish level concentrates on teamwork, going beyond swimmers' previous individual involvement.

While enrolled in the Fish level, the student is

→ helped to learn about skin diving safety and safety in currents;

→ provided more practice in floating, treading water, and swimming wearing a PFD and clothes;

→ helped to learn about the huddle position, boating safety, sun safety, and leg cramps;

→ given opportunities to develop teamwork;

→ helped to refine the crawl stroke with rotary breathing, the breaststroke, the elementary backstroke, the back crawl stroke, and the sidestroke;

→ helped to learn the breaststroke and breaststroke start and turn, and the butterfly stroke;

→ helped to learn synchronized swimming movements, including additional types of sculling, the plank, and stroke variations;

→ helped to improve wetball skills, including ball handling, directional swimming, dribbling, throwing, shooting goals, rotary kicking, and playing the game of wetball;

→ helped to learn the standing dive from a one-meter board and the headfirst and feetfirst surface dives;

→ introduced to using a mask and fins; and

→ helped to learn more about rescue and first aid, including throwing assists, preventing accidents, performing rescue breathing, and providing first aid for wounds.

Prerequisite:

→ Successful completion of the Minnow requirements

Component 1: Personal Safety

Objective: To learn about skin diving safety

Discussion Guidelines for Instructors

1. Ask "What is skin diving? If you wanted to swim underwater or go farther underwater, what do you think you might want to remember before you try it?" Discuss the following skin diving safety rules:

   • Always skin-dive with a buddy. One buddy dives while the other stays on the surface. It's much more fun and much safer than diving alone.

   • Skin-dive only when you are feeling healthy. Colds and the flu do better on land than in or under the water.

   • Always look up, hold one hand above your head, and do a 360° turn when you surface.

   • Use a float or boat and a diver's flag to show where you are swimming.

   • Skin-dive in the pool or at the beach only when you have had time to practice under an instructor's supervision.

   • Know the area. Prepare in advance for your dive.

2. Discuss the phenomenon of *ear squeeze,* pain in the ear caused by water pressure on the outer ear. The pressure causes the eardrum to stretch inward and hurt. This problem can be remedied by pinching the nose and closing the mouth, then blowing through the nose gently to equalize the pressure inside the ear. This should be done early and often during descent or whenever it feels necessary to relieve pain or discomfort. Equalizing the pressure prevents rupturing the eardrum. Congestion from a cold, the flu, or sinusitis can make it difficult to equalize pressure, putting the diver at risk of ear injury. Remember to equalize early and often.

3. Tell students that they should equalize the pressure inside the ear right after performing a surface dive.

4. Discuss the phenomenon of *sinus squeeze,* sharp pain in the sinuses during descent. Students may experience this as pain in the forehead, cheeks, or teeth when submerging underwater. Such pain is caused by the sinuses being closed due to congestion from a cold or allergies. As the sinuses cannot be equalized under these conditions, students shouldn't go underwater when congested.

5. Two other situations that skin divers should avoid are mask squeeze and eye squeeze. With *mask squeeze,* water pressure against the mask compresses the air in the mask, which causes a vacuum. If the air pressure is not equalized, blood is drawn toward the surface of the skin, causing discoloration. Pressure can be equalized by exhaling gently through the nose into the mask. This should be done any time pressure is felt.

   Eye squeeze is caused by wearing goggles below the surface of the water. The water pressure compresses the air inside the goggles, creating a vacuum. If the swimmer wearing the goggles goes too deep, blood is drawn toward the surface of the eyeballs, causing the white of the eye to turn bright red. This is known as a conjunctival hemorrhage. As goggles cannot be equalized, the only way to avoid this type of injury is to not descend too far while wearing goggles.

   Swim goggles should not be worn by swimmers who are swimming underwater. Dive masks are designed for underwater swimming, not goggles.

Performance Criteria

The student should

→ participate in the discussion.

Objective: To learn about swimming in currents

Discussion Guidelines for Instructors

1. Have students form a circle and hold hands in a corner of the shallow end of the pool. Tell them to move around in a circle, all in the same direction, and gradually increase speed until they get a signal from you. On that signal, they should let go of each other and float, letting the current carry them away.

2. Discuss with students how they felt when they let go. Relate that feeling to water safety and to swimming in a current.

3. Have the students try the circle activity again, except instead of letting go and floating, have them try to walk in a circle in the direction opposite to the current. Then discuss how hard it is to move against the current.

4. This time make two circles, an inner circle and an outer one. Have one circle move clockwise while the other moves counterclockwise. Discuss what happens.

5. Discuss with students what they can do if they are caught in a current. Ask "Where could you find currents?" Talk about how currents can be very strong and can take you where you do not want to go. Then ask "If you find yourself in a current, what can you do to be safe? Let's hear some ideas." Include the following among the ideas:

   • Turn onto your back and float feetfirst downstream. (Ask them why this would be a good idea.)

   • To swim across a current, move upstream higher than where you want to get out and swim diagonally.

Performance Criteria

The student should

   → participate in the activity and discussion and

   → describe what to do if he or she were ever caught in a current.

Objective: To practice floating longer

Discussion Guidelines for Instructors

Have the students do a float they've already learned at previous levels for six minutes without an IFD. They may do a combination of the resting stroke, front float, or back float with minimum movement.

Performance Criteria

The student should

   → be able to float for six minutes with minimum movement on the front or back without an IFD.

Objective: To improve treading skills

Materials Needed: water logs

Discussion Guidelines for Instructors

1. Review with the students what they learned at the Guppy and Minnow levels about treading water. Have them tread water as you discuss a situation in which someone isn't treated nicely. Ask them if they know someone who usually isn't treated nicely and discuss what they can do to be nicer to that person. Students should try to not touch the side of the pool at all during the discussion.

2. Have them try the breaststroke kick (circle kick, symmetrical). Allow students to use a water log when practicing to refine the kick. Then have them try again without it.

3. Do the same when working on single (same leg forward) and double scissors (alternating) kicks.

4. Have students practice treading while playing a game or singing songs.

Treading water using the breaststroke kick

Treading water using a scissors kick

Performance Criteria

The student should

→ be able to tread water in deep water for three minutes using a combination of single and double scissors kicks and circle kicks.

⛵ Objective: To improve endurance while swimming wearing a PFD and clothing

Materials Needed:
Students should wear a clean shirt and pants to class over the swim suit and bring a plastic bag with their name on it to hold wet clothing; PFDs, one for each student.

Discussion Guidelines for Instructors

1. At the previous class meeting, tell students to wear their clothing over their swimming suit and to bring a plastic bag with their name on it to hold the wet clothing after the activity. The clothes should be a clean shirt and pants. Send home a note with students explaining what the students need to bring to class and why.

2. Have the students put on PFDs and swim the front and back crawl for 25 yards with their clothes on.

Performance Criteria

The student should

→ be able to swim 25 yards on the front and back without stopping while wearing a PFD and clothes.

fish

Swimming with clothes on while wearing a PFD

The huddle position with instructor spotting

⚓ **Objective:** To learn about the huddle position

Materials Needed: PFDs, one for each student

Discussion Guidelines for Instructors

1. Review with the students what they learned at the Guppy level about the HELP position.

2. Begin a trigger story about a boating trip with family and friends. You and three friends fall overboard. You need to wait for help to arrive, and the water is cold. Ask "What can you do to be warmer?" Have students put on PFDs and try a few ideas. Guide them to find the proper position of huddling in a circle facing each other with their arms around each other.

3. Explain that the huddle position conserves body heat by sharing heat and covering heat loss areas. Tell students that, if a child is in the water, he or she should be placed in the middle of the huddle. Children are more susceptible to heat loss than adults when immersed.

Performance Criteria

The student should

→ participate in the activity.

⚓ **Objective:** To learn more about boating safety

Discussion Guidelines for Instructors

1. Say "Let's pretend that we're going to go on a boating trip. For us to be safe, we need to do careful planning. What do we need to know about?" Make sure students include the following ideas:
   - PFDs for each person
   - A weather forecast to avoid stormy weather
   - Extra gear such as first-aid supplies, a visual distress signal and sound-producing devices, in case of emergencies
   - Leaving instructions with someone as to who is going on the trip, where you're going, and how long you plan to be gone, in case an accident occurs or you get lost
   - Staying dry and warm to avoid hypothermia
   - Keeping fishing and other equipment clean and well-packed so it is ready when needed

2. Ask "If we decide to change seats while we're in the boat, how do we need to move and why?" (Answers: Stay low and near the center of the boat, so we don't capsize the boat. Maintain three points of contact. One person should move at a time.)

3. Say "Now we know some things about boating safely. If you and your family boat often, you might also want to take a boating safety course."

Performance Criteria

The student should

→ participate in the discussion and

→ be able to name some safe-boating tips.

⚓ **Objective:** To learn how to get into a boat after falling overboard and how to get into and out of a swamped boat

Materials Needed:

boat (canoe, rowboat, dinghy, inflatable raft); PFDs, one for each student

Skill Description: Getting Into a Boat After Falling Overboard

To get back into a canoe after falling overboard, the student should remain calm, stay with the boat, and try to reenter the craft. From the side of the canoe, he or she holds on to the gunwale (top edge of the craft) with one hand and the thwart (the center seat) with the other. (See illustration showing parts of boat in the Polliwog level.) The student kicks hard and fast, trying to get the hips to the gunwale and keeping weight on the hands. He or she rotates the hips to sit on the inside of the canoe's hull, then brings the legs in. The student then moves slowly and regains position.

To get back into a rowboat after falling overboard, the student should remain calm and maneuver to the transom (the flat end at the back of the boat). He or she places the hands on the transom and kicks hard and fast to raise the hips while keeping the weight on the transom. The student rotates the hips to sit on the stern (back of the craft) or stern seat. He or she brings the legs around to sit properly in the boat.

The biggest danger in falling out of a rowboat is being struck in the head by the boat as it turns over. If the boat cannot be righted, the student should climb onto the hull (main body of the boat) and signal for help.

Discussion Guidelines for Instructors

1. Say "Let's talk a few minutes before we try these new skills. If you fell overboard, what do you think you should do?"

2. Ask "You need to try to get back into the boat. How do you think you can do it? Let's try a few of your ideas." Place the boat in the pool and have students get into the water (do not practice falling

Getting back into a raft

overboard) and try to get into the boat. Assist students while they are trying their ideas. After they have tried a few ideas, guide them to the right position, and when necessary, assist students into the boat.

3. After each student has tried getting into the boat, discuss their experiences. Include the following questions:

- What is easy or hard about getting into the boat from the water?

- What do you think it would be like in a lake or river? Would it be easier or harder?

- What are some things you should do before you really go boating? (Answers: Practice self-rescue skills; prevent accidents by following the boating safety rules previously discussed.)

fish

Getting into a swamped raft

Skill Description: *Getting Into and Out of a Swamped Boat*

To get into a swamped canoe or rowboat that is upright, the student should remain calm and then turn the boat toward shore. He or she maneuvers so he or she is lying across the middle of the boat to keep it from rolling sideways. When the boat is stable, the student turns over and moves into a sitting position on the bottom of the boat, then hand paddles to safety.

Discussion Guidelines for Instructors

1. Say "Let's think about how a boat can swamp. It can be pretty scary. We need to talk about it so if it happens, you will know what to do."

2. Ask "Why is it important to stay with the boat if it is swamped?" (Answers: It's easier for rescuers to find you if you stay with the boat. Also, the boat provides you with buoyancy and can sometimes allow you to climb out of the cold water.)

3. Have the boat at the side of the pool and swamp the boat. Then ask "What happens to the boat? Where does it stay in the water? Do you think you can get into and out of it?" Have students swim into and out of the swamped boat. Keep part of the boat low enough in the water that students can get in more easily. Tell students to lie across the middle of the boat to keep it from rolling side to side. Once the boat is steady, they can turn over and move into a sitting position.

4. While talking, have students try sitting in the swamped boat. Ask "What should you reach for?" (Answer: In the middle of the boat, reach over the side for the bottom of the boat.) Then ask "What do you think you could do to help yourself get on to the boat? "Let's try it, now. Everybody get out of the boat, then try to get in again."

5. Ask "Do you think the boat can move? How can you get it to move? Let's see your ideas." Have students try sitting in the boat and paddling with their hands, then try paddling with oars.

Performance Criteria

The student should

→ know how to get back into a boat after falling overboard and

→ know how to get into and out of a swamped boat.

Objective: To teach students more about sun safety

Discussion Guidelines for Instructors

1. Review with the students what they learned at the Polliwog level about sun safety.

2. Tell students "It's important to follow sun safety rules because the invisible ultraviolet light from the sun damages skin cells. This damage can accumulate over time and cause skin cancer as you get older."

3. Ask "If you're wearing sunscreen, how often should it be applied?" (Answer: Frequently, and always after swimming.) "How can you tell if you're beginning to be sunburned?" (Answer: The skin becomes reddish or discolored, with mild swelling and pain.) "What can you do to prevent further damage once you've sun-

burned?" (Answer: Stay out of the sun, put a T-shirt or long pants on, always wear a sunscreen when you go outside.)

4. Ask "When do you think the sun's rays are most intense?" (Answer: The sun's rays are most intense between 11 A.M. and 3 P.M. during the summer, when it's Daylight Savings Time, and 10 A.M. to 2 P.M. when we use Standard Time.) Ask "Why do you think it's important to know this?" (Answer: We should try to avoid being out in the sun for long periods of time during these hours to avoid sunburn.)

Performance Criteria

The student should

→ participate in the discussion and

→ understand the importance of protecting the skin from the sun.

Objective: To teach students how to treat leg cramps

Discussion Guidelines for Instructors

1. Say "Cramps occur most frequently in the legs or feet. If they occur while you are swimming, you can use one of the two following remedies:
   • In the pool, swim to the side, climb out, knead and stretch the cramped muscle, and try to walk to release the cramp.
   • In open water, when you are far from shore, try to knead and stretch the cramped muscle while you are in the resting stroke position."

2. Have students role-play releasing cramps, and discuss the situations.

Performance Criteria

The student should

→ be able to demonstrate (by role playing) how to treat cramps.

Component 2: Personal Growth

Objective: To help learn teamwork

Materials Needed: balls or T-shirts, depending on the games you choose

Discussion Guidelines for Instructors

1. Discuss with your students that teamwork is a group effort to achieve goals that an individual either could not achieve or would have difficulty achieving alone. Improving the ability of an individual to work well in a group is an important goal in all YMCA activities. Ask "Why do you think teamwork is an important goal?"

2. Say "Your first encounter with the learning process is as an individual. Gradually you may find that to get things done it takes more than just you. Can you give me some examples of when you need others to get something done? How could swimming do this?" (Answer: At its most dramatic, swimming has an impact in rescue. The safety of others may depend not only on your skill but on your knowledge of rescue techniques and your willingness to help someone in a difficult or life-threatening situation.)

Massaging a cramped leg muscle

fish

3. Ask "Where, besides in this class, is teamwork important?" (Answer: At home, at school.)

4. Say "When you work well in a group, you help yourself and others. You often gain more and have more fun. Can you think of some games to show how this works? How about water polo or wetball, water volleyball, water basketball, T-shirt relays? OK, let's play."

Performance Criteria

The student should
→ participate in the discussion and the games.

Objective: To learn to reinforce others for displaying positive values

Materials Needed:
diving rings in the four value colors (caring is red, honesty is blue, respect is green, and responsibility is yellow or gold)

Discussion Guidelines for Instructors

1. Review with the students the four core values, then say "Let's try to tell each other when we see one of us using one of the four values. If someone is doing something good, let him or her know about it."

2. During the class, praise those students who recognize other class members for demonstrating caring, honesty, respect, and responsibility.

3. Try this activity: Throw diving rings into the pool and ask students to dive and retrieve them. As each swimmer brings a ring up, he or she must make a statement about the value corresponding to the color of the ring.

Performance Criteria

The student should
→ reinforce other class members for demonstrating one of the four core values in class.

Objective: To learn safety and cooperation through games

Discussion Guidelines for Instructors

Give students instructions on how to play the following games and play one or more of them:

Frogmen

Material: bright objects heavy enough to sink, one for each team
Divide the class into teams of equal numbers. Have players line up single file in chest-deep water facing the far side of the pool. Place a bright object at the feet of the first player on each team. At the signal *Go,* the first player goes underwater and, without coming up, moves the object toward the far side of the pool as far as he or she can go. The next player goes underwater at the location of the object and moves the object farther toward the far side of the pool. Then the third player takes a turn, and so on. The first team to get its object to the far side of the pool wins. The game should be played across the width of the pool rather than the length of the pool.

Fan race

Material: fans, one for each student
Divide the class into teams and have players line up at the starting line. Each player has a fan. At the word *Go,* the first player on each team swims to the finish line on his or her back, holding the fan out of the water. Players may use any kick they wish or any kick you say they should. When the first player reaches the other side of the pool, the next player starts. The first team to get all players to the other side of the pool wins.

Other team races

A T-shirt relay, baton relay, and any other relay races are appropriate teamwork games. Students can create their own team races. (See appendix A for more game ideas.)

Performance Criteria

The student should
→ learn safety and cooperation through playing games.

fish

Component 3: Stroke Development

Objective: To refine the crawl stroke with rotary breathing and to learn open turns

Discussion Guidelines for Instructors

1. Continue to work on refining the crawl stroke using the drills in appendix A based on the individual needs of your students. Pay particular attention to refining students' rotary breathing.

2. Say "We want to change directions at the end of the pool (either widths or lengths). What can you do to change directions faster? Anybody have any ideas? Let's try a few of them out." (For descriptions of open turns, see chapter 7 of *Teaching Swimming Fundamentals.*)

3. Ask "When you get close to the wall, what do you think you can do?"

4. Ask "Should you use one or two hands? What happens when you use one? Two?"

5. Say "Let's try some things with our feet. Show me some of your ideas. Is it easier if your legs are straight or tucked?"

Performance Criteria

The student should

→ be able to swim the crawl stroke with rotary breathing for 50 yards with open turns.

Crawl stroke with rotary breathing

Objective: To refine the breaststroke and to learn starts and open turns

Skill Description

In the underwater stroke on the start and turn, the student pulls the arms through to the hips. Once the body is under the surface and momentum from the dive or push-off has begun to subside, he or she pulls out until shoulder level and then pushes back parallel with the sides, then with the hips. As the student recovers the arms, he or she kicks. (See chapter 7 of *Teaching Swimming Fundamentals* for more detail.)

Discussion Guidelines for Instructors

1. Continue to work on refining the breaststroke using the drills in appendix A based on the individual needs of your students.

2. Say "We want to change directions at the end of the pool (either widths or lengths). What can you do to change directions faster? Anybody have any ideas? Let's try a few of them out."

3. Ask "When you get close to the wall, what do you think you can do?"

4. Ask "Should you use one or two hands? What happens when you use one? Two?"

5. Say "Let's try some things with our feet. Show me some of your ideas. Is it easier if your legs are straight or tucked?"

6. Say "Let's work on our starts. We know how to dive in. Let's see."

7. Say "To continue the breaststroke from a dive, we want to make use of the momentum from our dive. How can we keep the speed going longer? Any ideas?"

8. Point out those who are trying an underwater pull and who, when the speed slows, start a strong kick, then pull, then begin the stroke. This is called an underwater pullout. After a start or turn, the swimmer can do one full pull down to the legs and one kick underwater before surfacing.

9. Have students try the underwater pull with the turns as well as after the start.

fish

fish

Performance Criteria

The student should

→ be able to swim the breaststroke for 50 yards with a pull, kick, and glide with open turns.

Objective: To refine the elementary backstroke

Discussion Guidelines for Instructors

1. Ask "What stroke on our back looks like the breaststroke on our front? Let's see yours."

2. Continue to work on refining the elementary backstroke using the drills in appendix A based on the individual needs of your students.

Performance Criteria

The student should

→ be able to swim the elementary backstroke for 50 yards with a glide.

Elementary backstroke

Objective: To refine the back crawl stroke and learn open turns

Discussion Guidelines for Instructors

1. Continue to work on refining the back crawl stroke using the drills in appendix A based on the individual needs of your students.

2. Say "We want to change directions at the end of the pool (either widths or lengths). What can you do to change directions faster? Anybody have any ideas? Let's try a few of them out."

3. Ask "When you get close to the wall, what do you think you can do?"

4. Ask "Should you use one or two hands? What happens when you use one? Two?"

5. Say "Let's try some things with our feet. Show me some of your ideas. Is it easier if your legs are straight or tucked?"

6. Ask, "If you are swimming on your back, how do you know when it's time to turn?" (Answer: Count your strokes. Watch for the backstroke flags.)

Performance Criteria

The student should

→ be able to swim the back crawl for 50 yards with a roll and bent arm with open turns.

Objective: To refine the sidestroke

Discussion Guidelines for Instructors

1. Continue to work on refining the sidestroke using the drills in appendix A based on the individual needs of your students.

2. Have them try open turns with the sidestroke, using the concepts they learned from performing other open turns.

Performance Criteria

The student should

→ be able to swim the sidestroke for 50 yards with a regular scissors kick with glide.

Objective: To learn the butterfly stroke

Materials Needed: fins

Discussion Guidelines for Instructors

Instructor Note: Refer to chapter 7 in **Teaching Swimming Fundamentals** *for a detailed description of the butterfly stroke. At this level the priority is to have students get the idea of the two-beat rhythm and to move their arms and legs simultaneously. It's not necessary to emphasize two kicks per stroke at first; one is OK. Begin in shallow or waist-deep water.*

1. Say "Now we are going to try another stroke in which we use both our arms and legs the same way while we're on our stomach. Let's see what you can come up with. Let's see another way."

2. Say "Let's try to kick like a dolphin. What would that look like? Let's see."

3. Ask "Can you try to kick like that underwater for a few seconds? It's OK if your knees bend."

4. Ask "Can you push off the side and glide for a count of two, then try moving your arms like you do in the crawl stroke, just once, then glide again, then stop. Try this again."

5. Say "This time, push off the side, glide, arm pull, then kick once as the hands enter, glide, then stop. Try this sequence a few times."

6. Say "Do the same thing, but this time instead of stopping, try another stroke, kick, glide, then stop."

7. Ask "Do you ever feel that your body is up higher in the water than another time? That's right, during the last part of pulling your arms down, your body is lifted. Well, when you feel that upward movement, lift your chin, take a breath of air, and put your chin back down when your arms reenter the water. Let's try the strokes again and try to get a breath."

8. Ask "When should you exhale your air?" (Answer: Exhale near the end of the glide and during the first half of your arm pull.)

9. Say "Try the stroke again two times." Watch students for the single kick, the glide, and for trying to get the rhythm. With the single kick, there is no kick during the pull. On beat one, the swimmer glides; on beat two, the pull, arm recovery, and breathing occur.

10. Say "Try again, getting a breath every second stroke."

11. Say "Now try going across the pool."

12. Once students have accomplished this much of the stroke, work on endurance until they can complete 25 yards comfortably. The rhythm and basic arm and leg movements are the parts that should be completed at the Fish level.

13. Let students try using fins for the kick as they work on building endurance.

Performance Criteria

The student should

→ be able to swim the butterfly stroke 25 yards with fins and 15 yards without fins.

Fish Series Swim Information

These experienced swimmers can swim lengths back and forth, although for some activities you may want them to swim down and walk back. You may want to use IFDs for working on some skills. Students usually use the middle lanes of the pool. You will usually be on deck to be able to observe better. Have students stretch before beginning their series swim.

fish

Component 4: Water Games and Sports

Objective: To learn more about sculling

Skill Description

To perform headfirst or eel sculling, the student angles the palms up from the wrist with the fingers pointing up so that pressure is applied against the water. This moves the student through the water headfirst. He or she holds the body in a streamlined position, with the toes remaining at the surface. If the body or toes sink, the student is not applying enough pressure downward against the water to support himself or herself. He or she must angle the palms to provide maximum support and propulsion according to his or her individual buoyancy.

To perform feetfirst or reverse sculling, the student moves the same as in the headfirst or eel scull except for angling the palms down from the wrists with fingers pointing down. This should reverse the direction of movement, moving the student in a feetfirst direction.

Feetfirst sculling

Discussion Guidelines for Instructors

1. Say "Let's see what you remember about sculling."
2. Ask "If you wanted to move while sculling, what could you do? Show me your ideas."

3. Ask "What do you need to do differently to move headfirst?"
4. Ask "What if you wanted to move feetfirst—what would you need to do? Let's see if you can come up with some ideas."
5. Say "When you move while sculling headfirst, it is called headfirst or eel sculling. When you scull feetfirst, it is called feetfirst or reverse sculling."
6. Ask "Is there any other way you can move while sculling? Let's try."
7. Try the following exercise. Have students form two lines facing each other and do a back layout with toes touching. Tell them to scull away from their partners for 10 counts, do a tub around in a circle for 4 counts, face their partner in a layout position for 2 counts, then scull for 10 counts. Then have them return to the original position, touching their partner's toes.

Performance Criteria

The student should
→ be able to perform headfirst and feetfirst sculling for 45 feet each.

Objective: To learn how to do the plank

Skill Description

The plank is a synchronized swimming figure that requires two partners. Both start in a back float position, the head of one touching the feet of the other. The swimmer in front (the one whose head is touching the other partner's feet) grabs the ankles of the partner and holds them together, pulling the partner's body forward. This action submerges the front partner, who keeps the body straight and glides backward underneath the back partner. The partners end up in reversed positions. The front partner may need to scull backward after the pull to come back to the surface.

Discussion Guidelines for Instructors

1. Ask students to find a partner. Then say "I'm going to give you and your partner a problem, and I want to see if you can figure out a way to do this."
2. Say "Both of you should do a back float, one in front of the other, toe to head. Now, here is the problem. How can you change places without swimming any strokes?"

fish

The plank

3. See what the students come up with. Then suggest one person pull the partner over and the other go under. See what happens and guide them to performing the skill correctly.

Performance Criteria

The student should
- → be able to perform the plank.

Objective: To learn stroke variations used in synchronized swimming

Materials Needed:

tape or CD player and music tapes or CDs (optional)

Discussion Guidelines for Instructors

1. Say "Let's see if we can come up with some new strokes. First try some on your front, then some on your back."
2. Say "Get a partner and show your stroke to him or her. Then try to do the stroke together, synchronized."
3. Say "Now have your partner show you his or her stroke, then try to do it together."
4. Have each of the partners show their strokes to the rest of the class, synchronized.
5. Try some other stroke variations, as described here, and then try to get the class to perform a variety of them in a synchronized fashion.

Front crawl variations

The following is a modification of this stroke:
- → Keep the head, held steady, out of the water, watching the person swimming next to you out of the corner of your eye in order to stay in line;
- → lower the kick so the feet do not splash water; and
- → use the hands in a sculling movement as they pull through the water to give more lift and support.

Many arm variations can be used to keep time with the music. Suggest a theme and synchronize with others. Two of the more frequently used movements are the straight-arm recovery and the accent high-elbow recovery.

For the straight-arm recovery, lift the arm out of the water after the pull phase without bending the elbow. The arm will be close to the ear as it moves forward and enters the water held straight. The count might be *1, 2, 3,* lift right arm, *4, 5, 6,* lift left arm.

'Have students first practice the straight-arm recovery alone, then synchronize with a partner. Tell them to use their eyes to watch the partner, not to turn the head. They can watch a swimmer on the left, straight ahead, or to the right without turning the head.

Have students do the following front crawl exercises:

→ Swim the pool length in pairs or threes. As the first line starts the third stroke, the next line joins them. All use the swimmer directly in front as a guide, keeping in line.

→ Practice formation swimming on the deck first. Swimmers form lines of four or six, one behind the other. The first swimmer on the far right in the first line is the leader. Each swimmer "guides" right, watching the swimmer on the right only. The swimmer on the right end of each line guides straight ahead, watching the swimmer in front only. The lines will then be synchronized with the leader.

→ When changing direction, as the lines turn to the right, the swimmer on the end of the last line becomes the leader. All swimmers continue to guide right without turning their heads. This can be done with all strokes, any number of swimmers, and any number of counts.

Other stroke variations

Breaststroke: Keep the head out of the water, the legs lower in the water, and the arms recovering over the water.
Backstroke: Kick underwater, sculling to support hand actions such as slaps and waves with the opposite hand.
Sidestroke: The top arm recovers over the water and the bottom arm recovers out of the water; both arms alternate.

Other variations

Try other variations such as these:

→ Do two somersaults in a row, forward or backward, without stopping.

→ Combine strokes such as two front crawl strokes and rolling to the back on the third, or two back crawl strokes, rolling to the front on the third.

→ Keep count and perform to music with a partner or group.

→ Try a Hawaiian stroke (using arm and hand in a waving motion) or a marching stroke (quick, sharp, high-elbow crawl stroke).

If you like, try these additional exercises (with music when possible) to help swimmers practice sculling and other synchronized swimming movements:

→ Have students practice sculling the width of the pool.

→ Form relay teams with half the team at each end of the pool and have them race each other using sculling only.

→ Select five judges. Then have each of the other class members choose a synchronized swimming skill with which to compete. The skill will be judged on correctness, effortless performance, control, and strength. Each student performs the chosen skill and is judged on a scale of 1 to 10. The judges may hold up fingers or cards with numbers. Scores are recorded, the high and low scores dropped, and the remaining three totaled. The top three scores can be announced. (This is an orientation to competitive synchronized swimming.)

→ Ask students to think of what else they can do using sculling and the movements previously learned.

→ Split the class into teams of three and have them develop their own routines.

Performance Criteria

The student should

→ participate in the activity and

→ be able to perform a variation of the crawl stroke, backstroke, breaststroke, and sidestroke.

Objective: To learn to perform a front dive with a spring in the tuck and pike positions

Instructor Note: *If your pool has only shallow water, no diving board, or water not deep enough for the student to be considered to be in deep water (at least 9 feet for dives from the side and at least 11½ feet for dives off a board), use this time to review general diving safety rules from previous levels.*

Discussion Guidelines for Instructors

1. Review the diving safety rules from previous levels.

2. Have students review the dives leading up to and including the standing front dive into deep water from the deck.

3. Divide the students into pairs of diving buddies. Explain to the students how to critique each other tactfully. Then have them practice dives off the side with their buddies. After one student dives, the other tells the diving student a good thing about what she or he did and suggests one aspect to improve upon.

4. Say "On the one-meter board, try your standing dive with one foot forward and the other one back." Check that students are focusing on their entry point until their hands enter the water; that they have arms extended and hands grabbed; that students don't move their heads, which may cause the body to arch or bend, or lift their chins, which may cause a belly flop; and that they keep their bodies streamlined and tight. Once they are comfortable with this dive, move to the next one.

5. Say "Stand in the ready position at the end of the board. (Some students may need you to stand behind them to help support the proper position.) Then raise your heels and balance on the balls of your feet. Keep focused on your entry point and fall forward, pushing your hips straight and keeping your legs in line with your torso. Extend your body from a pike position to a straight position for the entry." Let them practice.

6. Say "Now we are going to try the front dive in a tuck position. How do you think the tuck position may help you with diving?" (Answers: Better control of the body in flight; helps develop timing.) "Now let's see how much you remember about the tuck position." Ask students to perform a forward jump in tuck position off the side.

7. Then have students dive off the board. Say "When you get on the diving board, get into the ready position. Raise your heels and balance on the balls of your feet. As you begin your jump, focus on the entry point (this helps keep the head in proper position), push your hips up, and let your head go down, focusing on your entry point. Pull your knees to your chest and grab your legs into a tuck position (the body rotates forward). Keep your focus on the entry point as you come out of the tuck. As you enter the water, extend your legs and point your toes. Keep your arms extended and hands grabbed." Let students practice this.

8. Say "Now let's try your jump off the board with the arm swing." Once students have practiced doing this, move to the standing front dive, tuck position with arm swing and spring.

9. Say "Let's see if you can try your dive with a double footed jump and arm swing now. This time when you do it, step back one step from the tip of the board. Raise up on your toes and bring your arms above your head in a **Y** position. Begin your arm swing and squat. This will help as you take your jump. As you land from your jump, your arms rise for take off. The spring from the board will give you the lift to perform your dive into the water. Focus on your entry point as you bring your knees up into a tucked position. As you reach your arms toward the entry point and you feel your body rotate, extend your body. Straighten your legs and extend your arms and grab your hands as you begin to enter the water." Allow the students to practice a few times. Once the students feel comfortable with this dive, move on to the next dive.

10. Have students repeat the previous jump with arm swing and the dive with arm swing and spring, only using the pike position instead of the tuck. Mention to students to keep their legs straight and just bend at the hips. Once they touch their toes, they should extend the arms laterally in preparation for the entry.

Performance Criteria

The student should
→ be able to perform a front dive with a spring in the tuck and pike positions

Objective: To improve ball-handling skills, learn more about dribbling, improve throwing skills, and learn how to shoot at the goal

Materials Needed:
balls of various sizes, two cones set up to form a goal 10 feet wide

Discussion Guidelines for Instructors

As the students work on ball handling and other wetball skills, remind them that keeping the ball under control and throwing accurately are preferable to doing things too fast.

Ball handling

1. Have students practice the ball-handling skills from the Minnow level. Increase the difficulty by adding distance and speed to the movements.

2. Ask students to see if they can juggle the ball with one hand while kicking on their back. Add quick changes in direction as they swim.

Dribbling

1. Have the students dribble a ball across the pool while swimming.

2. Have a relay race to help increase the speed at which the students can dribble. They can run as well as swim while dribbling.

Throwing skills and shooting goals

1. Have students dribble and try to shoot the ball into the goal. You can play goalie and block shots.

Dribbling a ball while swimming

2. Let students dribble and pass to a partner and then try to shoot the ball. Allow students to walk, run, or swim. This and the preceding activity help students build strength and endurance, ball-handling skills, throwing for accuracy, and teamwork.

Instructor Note: *Review goal practice safety tips with students:*

- *Don't shoot the ball until the goalie is ready.*
- *If you are the goalie, wear ear guards.*
- *Review the rules before playing.*
- *Always make sure the goalie knows whose turn it is to throw the ball so it won't surprise him or her.*
- *If you are the goalie, signal readiness before a player shoots.*

Performance Criteria

The student should

→ be able to kick across the pool on the back while juggling a ball,

→ improve ball passing and catching skills,

→ be able to swim across the pool while dribbling, and

→ participate in an activity that improves throwing skills and teaches how to shoot at the goal.

Objective: To improve directional swimming

Discussion Guidelines for Instructors

Have students swim the crawl stroke halfway across the pool, then, on a signal, start swimming the back crawl. Before they reach the side of the pool, give another signal for them to begin swimming the crawl stroke again. This exercise builds endurance and the ability to change direction quickly, which helps in playing wetball.

Performance Criteria

The student should

→ be able to change from the crawl stroke to the back crawl quickly.

Objective: To learn how to rotary kick

Materials Needed: ball, water logs or flotation belts

Discussion Guidelines for Instructors

1. Have students get into a circle, tread water, and pass the ball to each other. Students can use a water log or float belt for support, as the exercise emphasizes working on the legs.
2. Take the ball away and have the students try doing the circle kick (taught at the Minnow level).
3. Ask "Can you alternate using each leg in your circle kick?" This is the rotary kick.
4. As they become able to do the rotary kick, have them form a circle and tread water using the rotary kick, then pass the ball around the circle.

5. Continue using this exercise until they can tread water using the rotary kick and pass the ball for two minutes without additional support.

Performance Criteria

The student should

→ be able to tread water using the rotary kick while passing a ball around a circle for two minutes without additional support.

Objective: To play wetball and have fun

Materials Needed:

ball; four cones (use two cones for each goal) or wetball or water polo goals; wetball caps with ear guards, one for each student (at least two, one for each of the goalies; the other students can wear bathing caps if wetball caps are not available); flotation belts or water logs

Rotary kick

fish

fish

Wetball

Discussion Guidelines for Instructors

1. Review the wetball game rules with the students, then divide them into two teams. (Rules for wetball can be found in appendix B.)
2. Play wetball in the deep end going across the pool. Students can use flotation belts or water logs to help support them.

Performance Criteria

The student should
→ participate in a five-minute wetball game in deep water with or without an IFD.

Objective: To learn the headfirst and feetfirst surface dives

Skill Description: Headfirst Surface Dive

The headfirst surface dive is performed in deep water. The student starts with a surface glide with arms overhead. He or she then takes a breath, tucks the chin, and reaches toward the bottom, lifting the legs and gliding. The student exhales slowly and gently during the descent and ascent. He or she should equalize the pressure in the ears as needed.

Discussion Guidelines for Instructors

1. Move students to water that is chest deep or higher. Ask "Who can do a front somersault in the water?"
2. Move students to shallow water. Ask "Who can do a front glide, then a handstand?"
3. Move students to deep water. Ask "Who can do a half front somersault to a handstand, then pull themselves underwater?"
4. Finally, have students attempt to do a headfirst surface dive and swim down six to eight feet in deep water.

Skill Description: Feetfirst Surface Dive

The feetfirst surface dive is useful for searching in murky water. In a vertical position, the student takes a deep breath, does a big scissors kick, and pushes downward with both hands. This raises the body up out of the water. He or she then points the toes and raises the hands in an upward scooping action above the head, which helps the student descend. The student then tucks and reaches forward and begins swimming underwater.

Discussion Guidelines for Instructors

1. Discuss the concept of a streamlined body position, with legs straight and arms at the sides.
2. Ask "Who can jump in from the pool deck and sink to the bottom in six or seven feet of water without using a single stroke?"
3. Have students execute a feetfirst surface dive from sculling or treading water
   • by stroking and kicking (large scissors kick) downward to raise the body as high as possible out of the water,

- by sinking below the surface with the body streamlined, and
- after the downward motion subsides, by lifting and pushing the water upward with the hands.

4. Ask "Who can reach the bottom in six to eight feet of water with one arm stroke?" To return to the surface from this dive, a swimmer should reverse the arm motion. When he or she reaches the bottom, the arms will be fully extended above the head. The palms should be turned away from each other and press the water down

Headfirst surface dive

Feetfirst surface dive

until the arms are along the sides. The swimmer can add a kick to the surface if needed.

Performance Criteria

The student should

→ perform a headfirst and feetfirst surface dive and swim down six to eight feet.

Objective: To be introduced to using a mask and fins

Materials Needed:

different types of face masks, one for each student; pairs of fins, one for each student

Discussion Guidelines for Instructors

Say "As your swimming and diving skills grow, your confidence in and under the water will increase. With this new-found confidence, you'll want some exciting activities to enjoy. One activity is skin diving. Since ancient times, people have dived and explored underwater for sport or gain. To explore the underwater world, whether you dive for food, treasure, or fun, you will need the proper equipment."

Mask

1. Have a number of different types of face masks available for students to see and try on.

2. Tell students the mask is designed so that a layer of air between the eyes and a transparent lens lets swimmers see what they are doing underwater.

3. Explain that masks should be made only of tempered or safety glass and that plastic face plates should be avoided because they can splinter or cause injury if shattered.

4. Show that masks come in a variety of shapes and sizes. Explain that a properly fitting mask fits over the eyes and nose and allows the swimmer to inhale and exhale through the mouth without dislodging the mask or creating leaks.

5. Then help students choose the face mask most suitable for their face. The mask should seal properly and be comfortable. Hold the mask in your hand and place it on the student's face without the strap. Tell the student to breathe in through his or her nose and momentarily hold his or her breath; you check whether the mask stayed in place.

6. Assist students in putting the mask on correctly. Check it for proper fit. Show students how to keep the mask from fogging up by spitting into it, swirling the spit around the window of the mask, then rinsing it, or by using a defogging solution. Tell them to brush their hair away from their face, then wet the face and place the mask on the face, and, finally, pull the strap over the head.

7. Remind students that the masks should not be placed on the forehead when not in use. If the mask is held on the forehead, it may fall off and be lost in open water.

8. Give students the following directions to clear the mask underwater in shallow water:

   • Hold the side of the mask closest to the surface of the water firmly against your face.

   • Tilt your head back and look up. Place two fingers in the middle of the top edge of the mask while blowing out slowly through your nose. This will force the water out.

Instructor Note: If your students have difficulty clearing their masks, check the straps; they may be too tight.

Fins

1. Tell students that fins can help them kick stronger and faster. Have a number of pairs of fins of various sizes available for them to see and to try on. Say "When choosing fins, make sure you pick a pair that will stay on your feet without cramping your feet."

2. Let students try them on and choose the fins that are most comfortable for them.

3. Help swimmers put on and use the fins properly. Give students the following directions on how to put on the fins:
   - First, wet your feet.
   - Then wet the fins.
   - Push your foot into the pocket firmly as you hold the fin blade.
   - Then pull the back of the foot pocket or strap into position. Turning the heel inside out should help.
   - Once your foot is in the pocket, pull the heel part carefully back into place.

4. Explain to students that fins are not designed to be walked in and that, whenever possible, they should put the fins on at the edge of the pool. If they do need to walk a short distance in them, they should walk backwards slowly or step sideways, being careful not to step on the fin, to avoid tripping.

5. Then have swimmers practice small flutter kicks, large flutter kicks, and the dolphin kick while wearing the fins and mask. Have the swimmers try kicking on their front, side, and back, first with a flutter kick, then with a dolphin kick. Tell them to keep the ankles loose and toes pointed and to kick slowly, with the arms at the sides. Make sure enough practice time is available so everyone has a turn.

Instructor Note: Fins should not come out of the water when doing the kick.

Putting equipment away

After this activity, have students rinse the masks and fins in fresh water. Do not allow students to walk on the deck wearing fins. Tell them it is important to care for the masks and fins properly so the equipment can last a long time. Disinfect the masks for the next class using a solution of 1:10 chlorine (bleach) and water, and put them away.

Performance Criteria

The student should
- → be able to put on a mask and fins properly and
- → be able to demonstrate the proper use of a mask and fins.

Wearing a mask and fins

fish

Component 5: Rescue

Objective: To practice throwing assists

Materials Needed:
a plastic hoop, floating objects big enough to use for a throwing assist

Discussion Guidelines for Instructors

1. Place a plastic hoop in the pool. Have students practice throwing floating objects that could be used for a throwing assist into the hoop.

2. Pair up students, one on the deck and one in the water, and have the one on the deck practice throwing an object to the partner. Have the partner try to grab on to the object and assist in his or her own rescue by kicking.

Performance Criteria

The student should
→ be able to toss an object that could be used in a throwing assist into a target.

Objective: To learn about preventing accidents

Discussion Guidelines for Instructors

1. Ask "To help keep anyone from being hurt, what are some things we can do?" (Answers: Follow rules, put things away after using them, tell adults if you see something wrong.)

2. Say "Let's look around the pool area. Do you see anything that can help prevent accidents?" (Answers: Lifeguards, signs about rules, safety equipment, safety strips on steps.) "Do you see anything we could do something about that could prevent an accident?" (Answers: Equipment out in the middle of the deck; another child not following the rules.)

3. Say "I want you to let me know if you see anything that may cause an accident so we can do something about it."

4. Discuss rescues and values beginning with a trigger story. Here is a sample scenario you can use:

"A small group of kids was playing in the grassy area by the pool. The ball fell into the pool. One of the kids jumped into the pool to try to retrieve the ball and started having trouble. One of the other

fish

kids ran over. She yelled for help, gave a pole to the kid in the pool, and brought him in."

Talk about how performing the rescue showed caring. Ask the questions "How did it really happen?" (talk about honesty); "What rule was broken?" (talk about respect); and "What steps can be taken so it doesn't happen again?" (talk about responsibility).

Performance Criteria

The student should

→ participate in the discussion.

Objective: To learn more about rescue breathing

Instructor Note: As you are keeping your CPR and first-aid certifications current, inform your class participants of any revisions in procedures as soon as you learn of those changes.

Materials Needed:

pocket masks (either have one for each student or have materials to disinfect a single one between uses), alcohol wipes or rubbing alcohol and cotton swabs, a CPR manikin (If a manikin is not available, you may substitute a CPR training video.)

Discussion Guidelines for Instructors

1. Say "Your brain must be furnished at all times with blood containing oxygen. If it goes without such blood for more than three or four minutes, your brain can be permanently damaged. A few minutes more than that and you may die. When someone has stopped breathing because of drowning or some other cause, rescue breathing should be started right away. Seconds count."

2. Ask students to tell you the steps of rescue breathing as you demonstrate them. Then let students try each of the following steps:

a. Tilt the victim's head back with one hand so that the chin points straight up. This will help clear an airway for the victim.

b. Look for the chest to rise. Listen and feel for air coming from the victim.

c. If there is no air, then pinch the victim's nostrils and at the same time keep pressure on his or her forehead with one hand. This prevents the victim's tongue from falling back and blocking the airway.

d. Place a pocket mask over the victim's mouth and hold it securely. Then take a breath, open your mouth, and place it over the mask valve. Blow two full breaths into the victim's mouth. This should be done so as to saturate the victim's blood with oxygen.

fish

e. After each time you blow into the victim's lungs, take your mouth away from the mask to allow air to escape. Listen for air coming out of his or her lungs and look for his or her chest to fall. Establish a rhythm. Blow once every 5 seconds or about 12 to 15 times a minute for adults and once every 3 seconds for infants and children. This is how many times you yourself breathe.

3. Disinfect the single mask between each use, or, if each student has his or her own mask, disinfect all masks after students have used the masks.

Performance Criteria

The student should
→ be able to demonstrate the steps of rescue breathing on a manikin.

Objective: To learn some basic first aid

Instructor Note: *As you are keeping your CPR and first-aid certifications current, inform your class participants of any revisions in procedures as soon as you learn of those changes.*

Materials Needed: dressings, bandages, red sticker, latex gloves

Discussion Guidelines for Instructors

1. Choose a student to be the "victim." Mark a "severe wound" on the arm or leg with a red sticker. Provide dressings, latex gloves, and bandages.

2. Have the students role-play the following situations:
   • Sending someone for help
   • Putting on gloves, then applying direct pressure to the wound, preferably with a sterile dressing or other clean cloth
   • Elevating the limb
   • Applying pressure to the brachial or femoral pressure points

3. Talk with students about blood-borne pathogens and how diseases can be spread through contact with blood. Explain that wearing gloves helps prevent the spread of disease and protects you when you help others.

Performance Criteria

The student should
→ be present for the basic first-aid presentation and
→ participate in role playing.

Summary

Fish

Summary of Performance Criteria

Component 1: Personal Safety

- Participate in the discussion on skin diving safety.
- Participate in the activity and discussion on currents and describe what to do if caught in a current saying "What I would do is . . ."
- Float for six minutes with minimum movement on the front or back without an IFD.
- Tread water in deep water for three minutes using a combination of single-, double-, and circle kicks.
- Swim 25 yards on the front and back without stopping while wearing a PFD and clothes. ⚓
- Participate in the huddle-position activity. ⚓
- Participate in the discussion about safe boating and be able to name some safe-boating rules. ⚓
- Know how to get back into a boat after falling overboard and know how to get into and out of a swamped boat. ⚓
- Participate in the discussion on sun safety and understand the importance of protecting the skin from the sun.
- Demonstrate (by role playing) how to treat cramps.

Component 2: Personal Growth

- Participate in the discussion on teamwork and participate in the games.
- Reinforce other class members for demonstrating one of the four core values in class.
- Learn safety and cooperation through playing games.

Component 3: Stroke Development

- Swim the crawl stroke with rotary breathing for 50 yards with open turns.
- Swim the breaststroke for 50 yards with a pull, kick, and glide with open turns.
- Swim the elementary backstroke for 50 yards with a glide.
- Swim the back crawl for 50 yards with a roll and bent arm with open turns.
- Swim the sidestroke for 50 yards with a regular scissors kick with glide.
- Swim the butterfly stroke for 25 yards with fins and 15 yards without fins.

Component 4: Water Games and Sports

- Perform headfirst and feetfirst sculling for 45 feet each.
- Perform the plank.
- Participate in the activity and perform a variation of the crawl stroke, backstroke, breaststroke, and sidestroke.
- Perform a front dive with a spring in the tuck and pike positions.
- Kick across the pool on the back while juggling a ball, improve ball passing and catching skills, swim across the pool while dribbling, and participate in an activity that improves throwing skills and teaches how to shoot at the goal.
- Change from the crawl stroke to the back crawl quickly.
- Tread water using the rotary kick for two minutes while passing a ball around a circle.
- Participate in a five-minute wetball game in deep water with or without an IFD.
- Perform a headfirst and feetfirst surface dive and swim down six to eight feet.
- Put on a mask and fins properly and demonstrate the proper use of a mask and fins.

Component 5: Rescue

- Toss an object that could be used in a throwing assist into a target.
- Participate in the discussion on preventing accidents.
- Demonstrate the steps of rescue breathing on a manikin.
- Be present for the basic first-aid presentation and participate in role playing.

fish

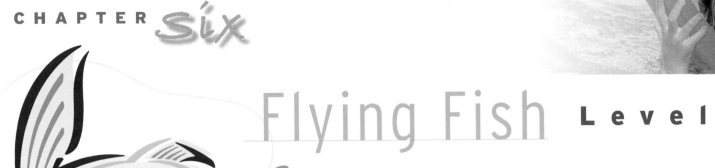

CHAPTER Six

Flying Fish Level

By this level, the swimmer has advanced to a high level of comfort with and confidence in the water.

Determination, caution, patience, self-discipline, and teamwork have been a natural progression for students who have mastered a variety of strokes, basic dives, and safety and rescue techniques.

At the Flying Fish level, the student is ready for additional challenges. He or she will work to refine the strokes learned at the earlier levels. New underwater swimming skills and an introduction to snorkeling add to the fun and sense of adventure.

At this level, skills are practiced and perfected with patience and guidance, encouragement, and positive reinforcement.

While enrolled in the Flying Fish level, the student is

→ helped to learn backyard pool, waterpark, and boating safety;

→ helped to develop the ability to float and tread water longer;

→ given reinforcement for good fitness and personal health habits and taught more fitness concepts;

→ helped to understand the concepts of adventure and risk taking and develop personal ground rules;

→ helped to set personal goals;

→ helped to learn the crawl stroke with bilateral breathing and open turns, and the butterfly stroke;

→ helped to refine the following strokes and increase his or her endurance: breaststroke, elementary backstroke, back crawl stroke, and sidestroke;

→ helped to learn more synchronized swimming skills such as underwater swimming; stroke variations; figures, including the sailboat, ballet leg, and kip; and to combine figures into a routine;

→ helped to learn how to perform a front dive off the one-meter board using a three-step approach;

→ given practice in wetball skills such as shooting and blocking, ball handling, and rotary kicking while treading, as well as building endurance;

→ helped to learn how to use a snorkel and how to do front (flip) turns for the crawl stroke and back crawl; and

→ helped to learn more about rescue skills such as reaching- and throwing assists, paddle rescues, and rescue breathing.

Prerequisite:

→ Successful completion of the Fish level

Component 1: Personal Safety

Objective: To learn about backyard pool safety

Discussion Guidelines for Instructors

1. Say "A backyard pool is fun to have. It also can be very dangerous if it's used without any responsibility for its safety for people and animals, its cleanliness, or its appropriate use."

2. Ask "How many people have a dog or cat at home that they are responsible for? What are your responsibilities for your pet? Do you have to feed your pet? Keep it safe? How? Do you have to make sure your friends play safely around your pet?"

3. Say "Having a backyard pool is a lot like owning a pet! You have certain responsibilities to carry out if you and your friends are going to play in the pool safely." Ask "What are you responsible for doing when your friends go home?" (Answer: Closing and locking the gate, picking up toys and equipment off the deck.) "What should you be responsible for when your friends come over to swim? Should you have a clean pool? Should you always swim with a buddy? Do you think you should have an adult around? What should you do if the adult has to leave the pool area to answer a phone or a knock at the door?" Even if students do not have a pool, they should understand the responsibilities involved with having a pool.

4. Review the responsibilities they have when friends come over to swim. Tell them that, even if they don't own a pool, they need to know what to ask if they visit someone else's pool. Say, "First, you need to tell your friends the rules." Rules might include the following:

   • Always walk, don't run.
   • Never have anything in your mouth when you swim, such as food or gum.
   • Never dive in shallow water; it should be at least 9 feet deep for diving from the deck and $11\frac{1}{2}$ feet for diving from a diving board.
   • Never dive into an above-ground pool or an in-ground pool less than 9 feet deep.
   • Always have an adult at the pool when you swim.
   • Always swim with a buddy, never alone.
   • Bring drinks in unbreakable containers.
   • Never push each other or hold each other's heads under the water.
   • Always keep the gates locked.
   • When you're playing outside, if a ball or toy lands in someone's pool area, always ask permission before going in to retrieve it.
   • Always get out of the pool if there's a thunderstorm, because lightning could hit you.

5. Say "Second, you need to show your friends the deep end and the shallow end and explain who is allowed to swim at either end. Third, if you have a pool cover, tell your friends that no one should swim under the pool cover or step on it, and that pets shouldn't be allowed around the pool when the cover is on, as they could get trapped under it. And finally, show them where the rescue equipment is kept and where the phone is in case of an emergency. If you are visiting someone else's pool, make sure you ask someone to give you this information."

flying fish

Performance Criteria

The student should

→ participate in the discussion.

Objective: To learn about waterpark safety

Discussion Guidelines for Instructors

Ask "Are there any other places where you can swim that we haven't talked about yet? Has anyone ever been to a waterpark? What are some of the things you should do when you are in a waterpark?" Review the following tips:

→ Stay with your parents or group; don't run off by yourself.

→ Arrange a spot to meet if family members get separated.

→ For all rides, make sure you are in the proper position to avoid injury.

→ Follow the rules of the ride. If you are too big or too little to be allowed on a ride, it's because it would be dangerous for you to ride it.

→ Ride the slides feetfirst only, never headfirst.

→ Don't take a dare in the water. It's braver to say *no* than to take a foolish risk.

→ Walk, don't run.

→ Listen to and obey the lifeguards.

→ Put on sunscreen regularly.

→ In a wave pool, know how deep the water is before the waves start. Watch for rafts and inner tubes. Listen for the signal that the waves are starting so you can be ready.

Performance Criteria

The student should

→ participate in the discussion.

Objective: To develop the ability to float longer

Materials Needed:

Students should wear a clean shirt and pants to class over the swim suit and bring a plastic bag with their name on it to hold wet clothing.

Discussion Guidelines for Instructors

1. At the previous class meeting, tell students to wear a clean shirt and pants over their swimming suit and to bring a plastic bag with their name on it to hold the wet clothing after the activity. Send home a note with students explaining what the students need to bring to class and why.

2. Ask "Why do you think we are going to practice floating in our clothes? Why is doing this important?"

3. Encourage students to choose one floating method (front or back) and maintain that for as long as possible before switching to a second or third method. Tell students they can only move minimally. Do this for six minutes.

Performance Criteria

The student should

→ be able to float for six minutes on the front or back with clothes on.

Objective: To develop the ability to tread water longer

Materials Needed: a ball

Discussion Guidelines for Instructors

1. Have students get into a circle in the water and tread water. Give them a ball and have them pass it around. As they do, call out a kick to be used in treading water and one of the character development values. As the ball is passed around, the student with the ball must yell out a way in which that value can be demonstrated. Every minute or so, change the kick and the value. Do this for six minutes.

2. Another treading activity involves having the students tread water while you call out statements such as "I don't care if my brother gets dessert as long as I get mine" or "It doesn't matter what a person looks like, but rather what kind of person he or she is inside."

flying fish

If the statement is a caring statement, students should tread with their thumbs up and out of the water. If the statement is not a caring statement, students should put their thumbs down in the water.

Performance Criteria

The student should

→ be able to tread water for six minutes using all four kicks: single scissors kick, double scissors kick, circle kick, and rotary kick.

⛵ Objective: To learn what to do if a boat capsizes

Materials Needed: a rowboat or canoe; PFDs, one for each student

Discussion Guidelines for Instructors

1. Ask "What does it mean if a boat capsizes?" (Answer: It's turned over.) Say "OK, let's see about this. Let's capsize our boat and let's figure out what we can do." Capsize the boat, then have all students and you get into the water, all wearing lifejackets. Have them stay close enough to the boat so that they can participate in the discussion and activity.

2. Ask "If you are ever in a boat that capsizes, what do you think you should do? Let's hear your ideas." Guide students to understand the importance of staying with the boat and not trying to swim to shore unless the boat is being moved into a dangerous situation by the wind or currents. Tell them to check that everyone who was aboard is OK.

3. Ask "OK, do you think the boat will sink when it is overturned? Why do you think so?" (Answer: The boat will probably not sink because it is made of materials that float.)

4. Ask "Should we leave the boat overturned, or should we try to turn it over (right the boat)? Let's see what we can do if we leave it overturned. What can you tell me about the boat now? (Answers: It's still floating; there is some air underneath; it is buoyant, but not very stable; it might be harder to move or steer it to shore if it's not righted.)

5. Ask "Do you think we could hang on to it? How could we do it?" (Answer: Passengers get on opposite sides of the craft, grab each other's wrists, and hold on over the bottom [keel]. They can take turns holding on to each other as they get tired, or if they think it will be a long time before help arrives, they can tie their wrists together with a rope, belt, or strap. A lone passenger may be able to kick up and get a portion of his or her weight across the hull and hold on to the boat that way.)

6. Ask "Do you think we could turn the boat over? Let's see if we can do this. Any ideas?" This is a better option than hanging on to the capsized boat.

7. Ask "If the boat is full of water, do you think it will still support you? How could you get in?"

Have them try their ideas. Here are some ways that a canoe or rowboat can be righted and brought to shore.

A canoe: If the canoe capsized in quiet water, roll it back upright. If two people were aboard, one way for them to get back into the boat is to swim or maneuver from opposite sides of the canoe toward the middle, then move at the same time to slide over the side of the canoe and roll in, seat first. Another way is for one person to stay low in the water and steady the canoe by holding on to the gunwale as the other person gets in. The person in the canoe can then lean to the opposite side to balance the canoe as the person in the water gets in.

Once in, each person should sit flat on the bottom, directly over the keel, with legs spread wide to get the center of gravity low enough to keep the canoe from rolling over. They should sit facing each other with their feet near the center and backs against the paddling seats. Bail or splash out the water. They can then use a paddle or their hands to move toward shore, one person paddling forward and the other, backward. They should watch for oncoming craft as they move.

A rowboat: Here are several ways to right a rowboat: Lift up at the gunwale so the boat rolls over on its own; swim, pushing the gunwale ahead to roll the boat up under you; or push down on the gunwale while pulling the keel toward you and, as the boat begins to roll toward you, hand-walk across the bottom to the gunwale on the far side, bringing it over.

If two people were aboard, one can hold down one side while the other person pulls up over the other side of the boat by pushing down on the gunwale with both hands. Once her hips are level with the gunwale, she can roll over into the bottom of the boat, landing on her seat. She can then lean to one side as the person in the water gets in.

flying fish

flying fish

Once in the boat, both people should sit as low as possible directly over the keel. One should sit on the bottom just ahead of the transom, with her legs against or over the middle seat; the other should sit with his head at the bow and feet against or over the bow seat. They then can use a paddle or their hands to move toward shore, one person paddling forward and the other, backward. They should watch for oncoming craft as they move.

Instructor Note: *Supervise your students closely as they try these skills. It will take balance, teamwork, and practice for them to perform these skills successfully. Point out to your students that it is best to know how to get out of trouble before you undertake any adventure or risk so you are equipped to handle whatever happens.*

Performance Criteria

The student should
→ know what to do when a boat capsizes.

Objective: To reinforce healthy lifestyle habits

Discussion Guidelines for Instructors

1. Encourage students to remember to use the bathroom before swimming and discuss why.
2. Ask "Why do we take a cleansing shower before swimming?"
3. Ask "Why is food prohibited in the gym and pool areas?"
4. Remind students to swim only at adult-supervised pools and never to swim in a private pool unless invited.
5. Define the Golden Rule and have students give examples of it.
6. Discuss how good health is important to each of us. Exercising sound judgment is particularly important when we are with large groups of people in public places. Good personal health habits are important for ourselves and for others.
7. Ask "Other than physical activity, what are other things that relate to a healthy lifestyle?"
8. Ask "What is the difference between eating a good food and one that is not?"
9. Ask "What are some good foods you should eat everyday?"
10. Ask "Why are sleep and rest important?

Performance Criteria

The student should
→ be able to say why having good personal health habits is important to others and
→ be able to describe what he or she could do to have a healthier lifestyle.

Objective: To learn more about personal health

Discussion Guidelines for Instructors

1. Ask "What are some things that can affect someone's health?" (Answers: What you eat, amount of physical activity, stress, personal hygiene, drugs/smoking/alcohol, amount of rest or sleep, seeing a doctor regularly for a checkup.)
2. Say "Let's see how much you know about each of these. For instance, what good things can happen to you and your body when you eat properly? What can happen if you don't?" Ask similar questions for all of the different factors.

Performance Criteria

The student should
→ participate in the discussion and
→ demonstrate an understanding of the importance of personal health.

Objective: To learn more about fitness concepts

Discussion Guidelines for Instructors

1. Say "Physical fitness means being healthy and having enough energy to move all day without becoming too tired. Physical fitness involves several different types of fitness. These are called health-related components, because the better you are in each component, the less likely you are to become sick. The four health-related components are these:

- *Cardiorespiratory endurance,* which is the ability of the circulatory system to provide oxygen-rich blood for energy. A person who can run several miles without stopping has good cardiorespiratory endurance.
- *Muscular endurance,* which is a muscle's ability to repeat a movement many times. A person who can do many sit-ups has good muscular endurance of the stomach muscles.
- *Flexibility,* which is the amount of motion in a joint. A person who can do a backbend has back flexibility.
- *Body composition,* which is the amount of fat and lean tissue in your body."

2. Say "We need to choose different types of exercise to improve each of the four components, and we should include exercises for all four components." Ask students to provide examples of which kinds of exercise might improve each of the four components.

3. Say "You should try to exercise moderately once or more during each day for an amount of time that adds up to 30 minutes or more daily."

Performance Criteria

The student should

→ be able to describe the four components of health-related fitness.

Component 2: Personal Growth

Objective: To understand the concepts of making personal ground rules and risk taking

Discussion Guidelines for Instructors

1. Ask "Before we take a risk, usually we think about whether or not we want to or should. What are some ground rules you use yourself before you decide to do something risky?"

2. Ask "What is it that makes you come up with those rules?"

3. Ask "Can you give an example of when you used those rules to decide what you were going to do?"

4. Ask "Have you had any friends who challenged those rules when they wanted to do something that you didn't think was a smart idea?"

Performance Criteria

The student should

→ be able to give an example of personal ground rules that he or she follows and

→ be able to describe what a risk is.

Objective: To understand the concepts of adventure and risk taking

Discussion Guidelines for Instructors

1. Ask "What does the word *adventure* mean?" (Answer: An exciting experience that involves some risks.) "What is *risk taking*?" (Answer: Putting yourself in a situation in which you may be in danger.)

2. Ask "When is it smart to look for adventure? When is it not smart?"

3. Ask "What is the difference between taking a chance and looking for trouble?"

4. Ask "What do you do if one of your friends wants to do something you feel is risky?" Ask students the different things they can say to resist pressure from their friends.

5. Ask "Are there different ways of saying things that affect people differently? How can you tell?" Say "How we communicate with people affects how others perceive and treat us. You can say the same words in different ways and give them totally different meanings. The tone of your voice, your facial expressions, and your body language all affect the way people see you. People often ask us to do things we don't want to do. Saying no should be easy, but for a lot of reasons, it's often difficult. What are some situations in which this can occur?" (Answer: A friend wanting to do something that is risky or something that you know you are not supposed to do.) Say "It's important to communicate in the way you mean to communicate. It takes skill to stick up for your rights without interfering with other people's rights. Sometimes, it is hard to say no, but saying no often

makes the difference between acting in a way that helps you and acting in a way that hurts you."

Performance Criteria

The student should

→ understand the meanings of *adventure* and *risk taking,*

→ discuss possibilities for adventure and establish ground rules to limit riskiness,

→ enforce his or her own rules, and

→ understand peer pressure.

Objective: To learn about personal goal setting

Materials Needed:
an envelope with the class name, day, and time on it; paper and pencils

Discussion Guidelines for Instructors

1. Say "We've been talking about the values of caring, honesty, respect, and responsibility. Now what I want you to do is to think of times when you didn't demonstrate those values in the way you now think you should have. The important thing now is for you to come up with what you can do to help yourself the next time you are confronted with that type of situation."

2. Say "Think of three things you can do to improve yourself by the time this session of lessons is over. Write those down. If you need help in writing them, I'll be glad to help you. At the end of the session, I'll open this envelope and return your paper to you. At that point we'll see who has achieved his or her goals."

Performance Criteria

The student should

→ set three goals for self-improvement related to caring, honesty, respect, or responsibility.

Component 3: Stroke Development

Objective: To learn the crawl stroke using bilateral breathing with open turns

Discussion Guidelines for Instructors

1. Say "As a competitive swimmer, you would need to know what was happening on both sides of you. How would this help you? How could it be done? Let's try."

2. Say "Let's see if you can swim 50 yards with open turns using bilateral breathing, which is breathing to both sides." Once they can do this, have them try to swim 100 yards.

Instructor Note: *Remind students to be sure to breathe and to avoid taking multiple strokes without breathing. Have them try breathing one width or length on the left side and the next span on the right side, or breathing to the right one stroke cycle, then left one stroke cycle.*

Performance Criteria

The student should

→ be able to swim the crawl stroke with bilateral breathing for 100 yards with open turns.

Objective: To refine the breaststroke and improve endurance

Materials Needed:
stroke observation checklist from *Teaching Swimming Fundamentals*

Discussion Guidelines for Instructors

Observe students' performance of the breaststroke. Determine which areas of their stroke need refinement by using the stroke observation checklist. Use drills from appendix A that you believe can help your students improve their stroke and build their endurance.

Performance Criteria

The student should

→ be able to swim the breaststroke for 100 yards with open turns.

flying fish

Objective: To refine the elementary backstroke and improve endurance

Materials Needed:

stroke observation checklist from *Teaching Swimming Fundamentals*

Discussion Guidelines for Instructors

1. Observe students' performance of the elementary backstroke. Determine which areas of their stroke need refinement by using the stroke observation checklist. Use drills from appendix A that you believe can help your students improve their stroke and build their endurance.

2. Have students perform an elementary backstroke kick with arms extended, hands just above the surface of the water. This increases the difficulty of the stroke and builds leg strength.

3. Ask "How can you tell when you should stop at the end? You don't want to hit your head." (Answer: By looking for the backstroke flags or another landmark (poster, ladder point on ceiling) that will warn you that you are getting close to the wall and counting the strokes you need to get from there to the wall.)

4. Ask "How can you turn effectively when doing the elementary backstroke? Let's see if you can come up with some ideas."

Performance Criteria

The student should

→ be able to swim the elementary backstroke for 100 yards with a glide.

Objective: To refine the back crawl stroke and improve endurance

Materials Needed:

stroke observation checklist from *Teaching Swimming Fundamentals*

Discussion Guidelines for Instructors

Observe students' performance of the back crawl stroke. Determine which areas of their stroke need refinement by using the stroke observation checklist. Use drills from appendix A that you believe can help your students improve their stroke and build their endurance.

Performance Criteria

The student should

→ be able to swim the back crawl for 100 yards with open turns.

Objective: To refine the sidestroke and improve endurance and to learn the lifesaving sidestroke

Materials Needed:

stroke observation checklist from *Teaching Swimming Fundamentals*

Discussion Guidelines for Instructors

1. Observe students' performance of the sidestroke. Determine which areas of their stroke need refinement by using the stroke observation checklist. Use drills from appendix A that you believe can help your students improve their stroke and build their endurance.

2. Describe the lifesaving sidestroke to students and discuss when this stroke would be used. Tell students to use an inverted scissors kick (top leg back, bottom leg forward simultaneously, then scissor together). The body may be rolled slightly on the back. The top hand should remain at the side or be held out of the water to simulate pulling a victim as a lifeguard would do with a rescue tube. The bottom hand does short, choppy arm pulls, pushing water toward the feet. Students should perform the stroke on both sides. Have the students try to swim the lifesaving sidestroke for 50 yards.

Performance Criteria

The student should

→ be able to swim the sidestroke for 100 yards (alternating 25 yards each on the left and right sides) using the regular kick, and

→ be able to swim the lifesaving sidestroke for 50 yards.

flying fish

Objective: To refine the butterfly stroke

Materials Needed:

pairs of fins, one pair for each student; stroke observation checklist from *Teaching Swimming Fundamentals*

Discussion Guidelines for Instructors

Observe students' performance of the butterfly stroke. Determine which areas of their stroke need refinement by using the stroke observation checklist. Use drills from appendix A that you believe can help your students. Have students begin practicing wearing fins, then practice later without them.

Performance Criteria

The student should

→ be able to swim the butterfly stroke with fins for 50 yards and without fins for 25 yards.

Flying Fish Series Swim Information

These experienced swimmers can swim lengths back and forth, although for some activities you may want them to swim down and walk back. You may want to use IFDs for working on some skills. Students usually use the middle lanes of the pool. You will usually be on deck to be able to observe better. Have students stretch before beginning their series swim.

Component 4: Water Games and Sports

Objective: To learn about underwater swimming

Materials Needed:

pairs of fins and masks of various sizes, one for each student

Discussion Guidelines for Instructors

1. Say "Good swimming skills are essential for swimming underwater effectively. Why do you think that's true? Underwater swimmers should strive for the best results and the most fun while using the least amount of energy. Is that a good idea?"

2. Say "Expert underwater swimmers usually can propel themselves very efficiently using only fins. Many of them use either a dolphin or a flutter kick. To do a good flutter kick, you should hold your legs straight from the foot to the hip with the toes pointed, although they shouldn't be so stiff that it's uncomfortable. A steady, alternating up-and-down movement works well. Keep your arms at your sides."

3. Say "When you're not wearing fins, use a modified breaststroke kick, scissors kick, or combination to swim underwater. A dolphin kick also will work well. The arm stroke for underwater swimming is often a modified breaststroke." In the modified breaststroke for underwater swimming, the pull is lengthened and the hands push past the hips, arms recovering as the legs kick; the chin is kept toward the chest to maintain depth.

4. Explain to students the importance of keeping one arm extended in front of the head when swimming, ascending, or descending in murky water.

Wearing a mask and fins swimming underwater

5. After students have had some experience with the fins and masks, have them do the following in pairs with one buddy on the surface observing the other buddy underwater:
   - Wearing fins and a mask, swim underwater using the flutter kick.
   - Swim underwater using the dolphin kick.
   - Now, wearing a mask but no fins, try the paddle stroke while completely submerged.
   - Wearing a mask but no fins, use the scissors kick.
   - Experiment to find which kick is most comfortable for you.

Instructor Note: Don't allow extended underwater swimming. Dives and activities should always be done in pairs with one buddy underwater and one buddy on the surface watching his or her buddy.

6. Have students get out of the water and take off the masks and fins. Then have them stand on the pool deck with their hands stretched overhead.

7. Say "Tighten your buttocks and stretch your body. Feel that? That is the feeling you want when you're gliding underwater."

8. Have students practice pushing hard off the wall in the shallow end of the pool and traveling toward the deep end, staying as close to the bottom as possible. Say "Remember to tighten your buttocks and to stretch your bodies."

9. When they begin to slow down, explain that the breaststroke is the most popular underwater swimming stroke. Tell them to do one long breaststroke pull (arms pull to the hips before recovery) and one breaststroke kick.

10. After the first stroke, have students continue to swim underwater, using the breaststroke adaptation.

11. Have students practice pushing off the swimming pool wall and swimming underwater. Remind them that they should avoid hyperventilating before they swim underwater (first mentioned in the Minnow level). Extended underwater swimming can be dangerous.

12. Make a game of underwater swimming. Let the students establish the rules and decide the goals. *Emphasize the buddy system.*

13. After this activity, have students rinse the masks and fins in fresh water. Do not allow students to walk on the deck wearing fins. Tell them it is important to care for the masks and fins properly so the equipment can last a long time. Disinfect the masks for the next class using a solution of 1:10 chlorine (bleach) and water, and put them away.

Performance Criteria

The student should
→ be able to cover three to four body lengths entirely underwater and
→ be able to use the modified breaststroke underwater to keep the momentum going.

Objective: To learn how to perform a sailboat

Skill Description

To perform the sailboat, the student assumes the back layout position, keeping the legs straight and the toes pointed on the surface. He or she bends one knee slowly, drawing the foot along the inside of the straight leg to the knee. The hands perform a sculling movement against the water. The student moves headfirst by angling up the wrists and fingertips and moves feetfirst by bending the wrists downward and pressing the fingers back against the water.

Sailboat

flying fish

Discussion Guidelines for Instructors

1. Teach students how to do the sailboat.
2. Have students try the following combinations:
   - Do a sailboat moving in a headfirst position, alternating legs.
   - Do a sailboat moving in a feetfirst position, alternating legs.
   - Sailboat side by side with a partner using first one leg, then the other.
   - With a partner, sailboat headfirst for 12 counts.
   - With a partner, sailboat feetfirst for 12 counts, with the right leg bent.
   - With a partner, sailboat headfirst for 12 counts, alternating legs.
   - Sailboat with another pair, headfirst, one pair behind the other, pairs side by side.
   - Make up a routine using strokes and the tub, somersault, and sailboat. If you like, set it to music.

Performance Criteria

The student should

→ be able to demonstrate the sailboat with variations.

Objective: To learn how to perform a ballet leg

Skill Description

For the single ballet leg, the student starts in a back layout position. Doing a stationary scull, the student draws one leg up the inside of the other leg until it is in a bent knee position. The thigh should be perpendicular to the surface. From this position, the student lifts the bent leg until it is fully extended to a vertical position from the hip. The thigh is kept still while the lower leg is drawn up. The movement from the bent knee to the fully extended position should be slow, controlled, and continuous.

The figure ends by reversing the procedure. The student flexes at the knee and returns the lower leg to the bent knee position. The movement is entirely in the lower leg; the thigh remains still. The swimmer then slides the foot back along the extended leg and returns it to the horizontal position, finishing in the back layout. Lowering the leg should be a slow, controlled, continuous motion.

Single ballet leg

For the alternate ballet leg, the student starts with a single ballet leg. As soon as the student finishes the single ballet leg, he or she performs the same figure with the leg that had been horizontal, with no pause between the two figures.

Discussion Guidelines for Instructors

1. Ask "Who can put one leg in the air?"
2. Ask "What about the other leg? Both legs?"
3. Say "With one leg, try to do it another way. There's got to be another way to do it, so try again."
4. Begin pointing out students who are close to doing it correctly, and have the students try it again. Point out one thing at a time. Choose those who are on their back; sculling close to the hips; bringing their knees up first; developing stability in that position; straightening the leg in the air over the hips.

Performance Criteria

The student should

→ be able to perform a ballet leg and hold it in the air for 10 seconds.

Objective: To learn to perform a kip

Skill Description

To do the kip, the student first assumes a back layout position. He or she then draws the knees to the chest into a tub position, keeping the knees and toes at the surface. Without stopping, the student gets into a tight tuck by pressing the knees to the forehead and the heels to the buttocks while executing a partial back tuck somersault. The swimmer can use one of three arm actions to execute the partial back tuck somersault:

1. Move the hands level with the head with the palms facing the surface, pull through in small circular motions from over the head to the hips, and stop circling and start sculling when halfway over.

Kip

2. Keep the hands at the hips with the palms facing the bottom of the pool, press down, and continue in a circular movement over the head. Return the hands to the hips and start sculling when halfway over.

3. Scull strongly behind the hips with the palms facing the bottom of the pool and the wrists sharply flexed, lift the hips, and press the body backward. When the partial roll is complete, slide the hands forward close to the body with the fingers leading and scull, keeping the hands close to the legs between the knees and ankles and the palms facing the bottom of the pool.

When the student reaches the vertical tuck position with shins perpendicular to the surface and shoulders and back of the head facing the bottom of

flying fish

D

Kip

the pool, he or she stabilizes. The student maintains the tight tuck while performing a flat scull close to the ankles, hands parallel to and just beneath the surface. The elbows should be close to the body, with the hands flat and in line with the forearms. While continuing to execute the scull in this manner, the student extends the legs to a vertical position by lifting the heels from the buttocks and knees from the chest in a fluid and continuous motion. The trunk, legs, and head should reach full extension all at the same time.

Once in the inverted vertical position, the student should hold the position momentarily by performing a support scull. Then the student gently moves the arms to an overhead position and makes the descent. The descent is controlled by the overhead scull. The figure is complete after the student's toes submerge.

Discussion Guidelines for Instructors

1. Ask "Who can do a back somersault? Show me."
2. Ask "Who can do a half of a back somersault? Where would you end up?" (Answer: With the head underwater.) "Give it a try."
3. Say "This time, when you do the somersault and you think your head is aimed at the bottom of the pool and your feet are on the surface, do a handstand and finish off with a headfirst surface dive. Who thinks they can give it a try? Spread out a bit."
4. Say "Try it again. Would it help trying faster or slower? Let's see."
5. Ask "Would it help to have a partner? Would it help if we tried it in the shallow end first?"
6. Begin pointing out students who have the idea of the figure. Indicate what part they have right. Let the students watch and have them all try again.

Performance Criteria

The student should

→ be able to perform a kip.

Objective: To practice stroke variations

Discussion Guidelines for Instructors

Review with students some of the more commonly used adaptations of strokes for synchronized swimming:

Front crawl variations

The following is a modification of this stroke:

→ Keep the head, held steady, out of the water, watching the person swimming next to you out of the corner of your eye in order to stay in line;

→ lower the kick so the feet do not splash water; and

→ use the hands in a sculling movement as they pull through the water to give more lift and support.

Many arm variations can be used to keep time with the music. Suggest a theme and synchronize with others. Two of the more frequently used movements are the straight-arm recovery and the accent high-elbow recovery.

For the straight-arm recovery, lift the arm out of the water after the pull phase without bending the elbow. The arm will be close to the ear as it moves forward and enters the water held straight. The count might be *1, 2, 3*, lift right arm, *4, 5, 6*, lift left arm.

For the accent high-elbow recovery, hold the elbow high during recovery. Then straighten the arm out before it reenters the water.

Have students first practice the straight-arm recovery alone, then synchronize with a partner. Tell them to use their eyes, not to turn the head to watch the others. They can watch the swimmer on the left, straight ahead, or to the right without turning the head.

Have students do the following front crawl exercises:

→ Swim the pool length in pairs or threes. As the first line starts the third stroke, the next line joins them. All use the swimmer directly in front as a guide, keeping in line.

→ Practice formation swimming on the deck first. Swimmers form lines of four or six, one behind the other. The first swimmer on the far right in the first line is the leader. Each swimmer "guides" right, watching the swimmer on the right only. The swimmer on the right end of each line guides straight ahead, watching the swimmer in front only. The lines will then be synchronized with the leader.

When changing direction, as the lines turn to the right, the swimmer on the end of the last line becomes the leader. All swimmers continue to guide right without turning their heads. This can be done with all strokes, any number of swimmers, and any number of counts.

Other stroke variations

Breaststroke: Keep the head out of the water, the legs lower in the water, and the arms recovering over the water.

Backstroke: Kick underwater, sculling to support hand actions such as slaps and waves with the opposite hand.

Sidestroke: The top arm recovers over the water and the bottom arm recovers out of the water; both arms alternate.

Other variations

Try other variations such as these:

→ Do two somersaults in a row, forward or backward, without stopping.

→ Combine strokes such as two front crawl strokes and rolling to the back on the third, or two back crawl strokes, rolling to the front on the third.

→ Keep count and perform to music with a partner or group.

→ Try a Hawaiian stroke (using arm and hand in a waving motion) or a marching stroke (quick, sharp, high-elbow crawl stroke).

Discussion Guidelines for Instructors

Introduce the following new stroke variations to students:

Hand position

On the Over-the-Waves Breaststroke, instead of recovering out of the water with the thumb edges of the hands touching, do one of the following:

→ Place the palm of the right hand over the back of the left hand.

→ Place the palms together.

→ Have the palms facing up with edges of the little fingers touching.

Use different hand positions to change the character and expressiveness of strokes. Experiment with a variety of different positions with any stroke in which the hand comes out of the water.

Combining strokes

Breaststroke/Butterfly: Follow one breaststroke with one butterfly and repeat.

Breaststroke/Sidestroke: Do one breaststroke. Start a second breaststroke but end in the glide position. Do one sidestroke. Start a second sidestroke but finish in the front glide position.

Crawl/Back Crawl (waltz crawl): Do three back crawls, rolling onto the face on the third stroke, and do three front crawls, rolling onto the back on the third stroke. You may also do this using four front crawls and four back crawls.

Revolving Crawl: Turn on each arm stroke so that the body revolves while doing the crawl and back crawl.

flying fish

flying fish

Using a roll

Corkscrew: Begin in a back layout position. Then rotate to one side and extend the arm over the head. (This is the same position you are in when you are gliding during the sidestroke.) Continue the figure by pressing the head against the extended arm while rolling onto the face. Then lift the side of the body (the side on which the arm is extended) and press down with the other side of the body. Continue this movement until you have made a full horizontal rotation. You must keep all your muscles tight in order to make the body roll as a unit in the fully extended position. *Breaststroke Roll:* Do a breaststroke, and when in the glide position, make a complete roll. Repeat.

Adding movements to out-of-water recovery

→ Clap the hands.

→ Snap the fingers.

→ Tap the water with the hand or fingers. This may be done on the back crawl and crawl strokes. As one arm finishes the pull, tap the water, then raise that arm overhead and begin to pull with the opposite arm. An additional variation is to do the back crawl, cross the arm over after the pull, and tap the water on the other side before raising the arm overhead for the pull.

→ Cross the arms on the recovery. Do the double-arm backstroke: Cross the arms just above the surface after the pull, then open them and bring them just above the surface to the **V** position and repeat the stroke.

→ On the crawl with the head out, swish the surface of the water with the fingertips or the palm of the hand with the wrist bent, in recovery, while bringing the arm forward. The arm can be bent or straight.

→ Execute a swish (as described just before) but spin the body in the direction the arm is moving. The swish spin can stop at any point desired, such as the quarter, half, three-quarter, or full circle.

→ Do the breaststroke, and, on the glide, raise the arms just above the surface and move them backward and then forward to the glide position. Keep the legs together while the arms move backward and forward.

Changing head position

→ Use the head to complement the stroke by focusing on the hand and following it with the head.

→ Use sharp focus and head changes to contrast to the movement of the arms. The head position can change at any time during the stroke and can dramatically alter the effect of the stroke.

Discussion Guidelines for Instructors

Have students choose stroke variations for the crawl, back crawl, breaststroke, and sidestroke and give them time to practice.

Performance Criteria

The student should

→ be able to demonstrate stroke variations with the crawl, back crawl, breaststroke, and sidestroke.

Objective: To learn to combine skills into a routine

Discussion Guidelines for Instructors

1. Quickly review with students the different figures that they have learned: sculls, tub, somersaults, back dolphin, kip, sailboat, ballet leg, plank, and stroke variations.

2. Ask the students to come up with a quick routine that uses three figures and two stroke variations. Give them a couple minutes to practice on their own.

3. Have each student perform his or her routine.

4. Divide students into groups of three or four, and have each group come up with a routine that they perform together, using the same criteria. Let them practice, and then have them perform.

Performance Criteria

The student should

→ participate in developing and performing a routine of his or her choosing that uses three figures and two stroke variations.

Objective: To learn how to perform a front dive off the one-meter board using a three-step approach

Instructor Note: *Classes taught in pools with only shallow water, no diving board, or water not deep enough for the student to be considered to be in deep water (at least 9 feet for dives off the side and at least 11½ feet for dives off a one-meter board), should review the general diving safety rules from previous levels.*

Discussion Guidelines for Instructors

1. Have students review previously learned diving skills from the deck and off the board.
2. The front approach requires a minimum of three steps and a hurdle. Explain that the drills on the deck represent the diving board.
3. Say "Show me four normal walking steps." Tell them to repeat the steps and return to their starting point.
4. Say "This time, hop forward on your third step and land on two feet."
5. Say "Now, go up a little higher on your third step and land on two feet. What did you do with your arms to make you go higher on your last step? Can you use your arms to lift your body during the last step (hop) and again on the jump? Try again. This time clap your hands over your head on the last jump."
6. Have students measure their steps and hurdle by starting at the end of the board and going back toward the starting place. Stress natural walking steps and a hop forward. Keep the landing spot in mind so students know where to begin.
7. Tell them to first practice on the pool deck and then on the diving board until both feet land on the end of the board, then to jump into the water. (The surface for landing must be a nonslip surface.)
8. Have the students walk through the entire approach until they can jump off the board and into the water without losing their balance.
9. Have them try this with a front dive tuck and pike.

Front dive with a three-step approach

flying fish

Performance Criteria

The student should
→ be able to demonstrate the three-step approach, hurdle, and front dive off a one-meter board.

Objective: To learn how to shoot the ball

Materials Needed:
various sizes of balls, a pair of cones for the goal, or wetball or water polo goals; wetball caps

Discussion Guidelines for Instructors

1. Demonstrate and explain how to do an overhand shot. Hold the ball in the palm of one hand and extend your arm behind your head. The other hand should scull slightly in front of the body, with the shoulder of that arm pointed toward the goal. As you throw the ball forward, the shoulders should rotate until the shoulder on the throwing arm is facing the goal. As you let the ball go, you snap your wrist and your hand follows through, moving toward the goal.

2. Have students practice shooting in a variety of different ways:
   • Using an overhead shot, shoot while stationary
   • Shoot from a dribble
   • Shoot after receiving a pass

3. Remember the progression that is used for building accuracy and power in the throwing:
   • Begin with a large goal and help students develop accuracy in getting the ball into the goal.
   • Help students increase their speed and power in getting the ball into the goal.
   • Divide the goal in half and do the same thing to each side of the goal.
   • Divide the goal into fourths and do the same thing for each section of the goal.

This process takes a long time; try not to rush your students through the process. Developing good basics in throwing will help them in the long run.

Performance Criteria

The student should
→ be able to shoot the ball into a wetball goal.

Objective: To learn how to block a ball

Materials Needed:
ball; a pair of cones for the goal or wetball or water polo goals; wetball caps

Skill Description

To block with two hands, the student watches the ball and stretches the arms and head toward the ball, turning the hands slightly downward. This stops and drops the ball in front of the student, who then picks up the ball and passes it back out.

To block with one hand, the student watches the ball and extends one arm and the head toward the ball. One-handed blocking should be used only when two-handed blocking is not possible, as it does not control the drop of the ball as well.

Discussion Guidelines for Instructors

1. Have students take turns being the goalie. The other students form a semicircle around the goal and try to shoot a goal one at a time. The goalie uses a two-handed block to stop the ball and then passes it to the next player. Once each player has shot, the goalie becomes a player and one of the players becomes the next goalie. Repeat until everyone has had a chance to be a goalie.

2. As players get better, have them try to swim in and shoot the ball. Let one student be the goalie and have the others line up about 30 feet from the goal. The first player swims in and shoots. The goalie blocks it with a two-handed block and passes it as fast as possible to the next player, who then starts dribbling the ball in. Continue until all players have shot, then have one of the players become the goalie and the goalie become a player. Repeat until everyone has had a chance to be a goalie.

3. This time, choose one player to be the goalie and have the others form a semicircle around the goal. Have the goalie stay in the middle of the goal. Ask the players to try to shoot the ball into the goal

Blocking the ball

by aiming at the high corners. The goalie should leap to the side to do a one-handed block, then retrieve the ball, pass it to the next player, then return to the center of the goal. Allow all players to have a chance to be the goalie.

Performance Criteria

The student should

→ be able to block a ball being shot into a goal.

Objective: To develop endurance and ball-handling skills, while having fun

Materials Needed: balls of various sizes; wetball caps

Discussion Guidelines for Instructors

Divide the class into two teams for relays across the pool. Have them perform one or more of the following activities while doing the crawl stroke, breaststroke, or back crawl:

→ Dribblinxg across the pool

→ Dribbling and passing to a partner

→ Juggling the ball while swimming on the back

Performance Criteria

The student should

→ be able to combine ball-handling skills with a stroke and

→ participate in the relays.

Objective: To improve the rotary kick while treading

Materials Needed: water logs or kickboards, ball (optional)

Discussion Guidelines for Instructors

1. Review with the students the sculling arm motion for treading.
2. Review the rotary kick (see the Fish level). With the students on the edge of the pool, explain that the alternating breaststroke kicking motion of the legs gives the kick an eggbeater effect.

flying fish

Rotary kick

3. Have students practice the kick in the water. They may hold on to a water log or kickboard for buoyancy.
4. Start with the students practicing the rotary kick, then have them try treading water, alternating between using the arms only and the legs only.
5. Have students practice various activities during treading such as throwing a ball around, talking to each other, or holding their arms up to develop the leg kick.
6. Have students experiment and learn how to move forward, sideways, and backward by slightly tilting the body angle while treading.

Performance Criteria

The student should

→ be able to rotary kick and

→ try to move forward, backward, and side to side while treading.

Objective: To improve endurance while playing wetball in deep water

Materials Needed:

ball; four cones (use two cones for each goal), or wetball or water polo goals; wetball caps with ear guards, one for each student is recommended with a minimum of one for each goalie

Discussion Guidelines for Instructors

Divide the class into two teams and have them play a five-minute wetball game in deep water, using the width of the pool.

Performance Criteria

The student should

→ participate in playing a wetball game in deep water.

Objective: To learn how to use a snorkel

Materials Needed:

masks, pairs of fins, snorkels, one for each student; objects that sink

Discussion Guidelines for Instructors

1. Review with the students the information about using masks and fins from the Fish level.

2. Say "Now let's learn about the snorkel. The snorkel helps you breathe with your face in the water." Show students how the snorkel works and how it is used. Put the mouthpiece in your mouth and grip it with your lips.

3. Give each student a mask and snorkel. Attach the snorkel to the mask or slip it under the strap of the mask. The tube should be pointing up. Let the students try them surface swimming. Tell students to breathe in slowly and out with a little more force.

4. Show students how to clear the snorkel of water. They can either blow out forcefully when they surface or tilt the head so the snorkel is at a 45° angle as they surface and exhale gently through the mouth beginning about two feet from the surface. The next breath should be small so they don't breathe in any leftover water. The face should remain in the water.

5. Review ear squeeze and mask squeeze with students (see Fish level). Remind them not to rest their masks on their foreheads.

6. In shallow water, have the students do the following:
   - Sit on the side of the pool and slip on fins, then get into the water.
   - Put a mask on with two hands.
   - Try breathing with the snorkel with the face in the water.
   - Practice finning (kicking while wearing fins) holding on to the side of the pool and breathing.
   - Try finning across the pool.

7. Have students try surface dives while wearing this equipment. Remind them to clear their ears. When they surface, have them give the OK signal with their fingers to let you know they are OK.

Clearing the snorkel

8. Drop into the pool some objects that will sink. Have students swim underwater for three to four body lengths and recover an object while wearing the equipment.

9. Drop students' masks and snorkels into the water. Then ask the students to try to recover and clear their mask and snorkel in six to eight feet of water in one breath.

10. Say "Pretend you are all dolphins, playing in the water. Try to swim underwater and do stunts." Some of the stunts they might try include forward and backward somersaults or swimming on the back or side.

flying fish

Instructor Note: *After use, the snorkels should be washed in fresh water and disinfected before being used by anyone else.*

Performance Criteria

The student should

→ be able to demonstrate the use of a snorkel while swimming and

→ be able to clear the mask and snorkel.

Objective: To learn how to do front (flip) turns for the crawl stroke and back crawl stroke

Skill Description: Front Flip Turn

To do the front flip turn, the student approaches the wall, lowers one shoulder, and "rolls" on that shoulder, throwing the feet to the wall. The legs should bend as if they were jumping on land. He or she extends the arms over the head into a streamlined position, with the back of the head tightly against the upper arms, and pushes hard with the legs off the wall. As the student's body slows down, he or she begins the kick, then starts with two strokes before the first breath.

Discussion Guidelines for Instructors

1. Review front somersaults with students.

2. Say "This time, when you try a somersault, do only three-quarters of a turn and layout and stop." Have them try, then ask "Where did you end up?"

3. Say "Try swimming across the pool three or four strokes and begin the flip and turn (without reaching the wall), then swim three or four strokes again, then flip and turn."

4. As students get the idea of the turn, have them move to the wall. Have them try to swim to the wall and stop before the last pull, do their turn, push off the wall, swim two or three strokes, and stop. Repeat until the students can do the turn without hesitating before performing it. When you observe the students' performance, help them with the finer points of the turn as described in the skill description.

5. When students perform their series swim and refine their strokes during practice, have them always include the front flip turn.

Skill Description: Back Crawl Flip Turn

To do the back crawl flip turn, the student turns over to the stomach after the last stroke and executes a somersault, throwing the feet to the wall and pushing off on the back into a streamlined position. The student kicks first, then pulls. When racing, the student needs to count the number of arm strokes between the backstroke flags and the wall in order to know when to stop stroking and to turn on to the stomach to perform the flip turn.

Front flip turn

flying fish

Discussion Guidelines for Instructors

1. Review front somersaults with students.

2. Review the corkscrew swimming activity done in the stroke variations activity in this level.

3. Have students swim three or four backstroke cycles, roll over to the crawl stroke, and then roll over again onto the back. Have them repeat a few times.

4. Have students swim three to four backstroke cycles, roll over to the crawl stroke, and then try the front flip turn without using the wall. Have them repeat a few times.

5. Have students move out four backstroke cycles from the wall, then swim in on the back and, before the last stroke before getting to the wall, roll over to the crawl stroke and try the front flip turn. Then, before the first stroke, roll over again onto the back and continue backstroking. Have them repeat a few times.

6. Repeat this activity until the students can do the turn without hesitating before performing it. When you observe the students' performance, help them with the finer points of the turn as described in the skill description.

7. When students perform their series swim and refine their strokes during practice, have them always include the back crawl flip turn.

Performance Criteria

The student should

→ be able to demonstrate a front (flip) turn for the crawl stroke and backstroke

Component 5: Rescue

⚠️ Objective: To learn more about reaching assists and the paddle rescue

Materials Needed:
objects that could be used for a reaching assist, boat, paddles, lifejackets (If possible, have additional assistants and boats available for this activity in order to minimize waiting time for students.)

Discussion Guidelines for Instructors

1. Review with the students how to do reaching assists (see Polliwog, Guppy, and Minnow levels).

2. Demonstrate reaching assists with items such as poles, towels, and ropes.

3. Ask "How should you position yourself when you do a reaching assist?" (Answer: Lie down flat and spread your legs.)

4. To help demonstrate why it's important to stay low, you role-play being the rescuer and let one of the students be the victim. Show them that you can fall in if you are not staying low when the victim is pulling against you, and stress the need to stay low.

5. Have a student demonstrate the correct position for performing a reaching assist. The student should be prone, legs spread out, with the hand grasping the edge of the pool.

6. Have students role-play being rescuers and victims, with the rescuer performing a reaching assist.

7. Ask "Under what circumstances should you use a reaching assist?" (Answer: When someone needs help and is not far from the side of the pool or dock or is close to the shore.)

8. Ask "What could you use to perform a reaching assist if you were in a boat?" (Answers: A pole, an oar, a stick.)

9. Review boating safety tips and skills already learned. Then tell a trigger story about being out boating and coming upon someone in the water who needed help.

10. Ask "What could you do to help this person?"

11. Say "Extend the handle of your paddle to the swimmer. Stay low in the boat and slowly pull the paddle and swimmer to the boat."

12. Ask "How would you help a victim into the boat?" (Answer: Once the victim has been pulled to the side of the boat, help him or her to hold onto the boat. Keep your weight low. If it is a rowboat, assist the victim to the end of the boat and, if he or she is capable of doing so, have the victim pull himself or herself up on the side of the boat, then lift one leg over the side. Help balance the boat by being on the other end.)

flying fish

13. Have each student practice a paddle rescue and assisting a victim into the boat. You should play the victim. As students practice by being in the boat, discuss issues that they need to be concerned with like balancing in the boat and trying to assist the victim in the pool without capsizing the boat.

14. Tell students about lifesaving strokes and approaches for situations involving a victim who is unable to hold on to an extended object. Discuss the consequences of jumping into the water to assist a drowning person. Emphasize using reaching and throwing assists as alternatives to jumping into the water. Talk about YMCA Lifeguard training and the Aquatic Safety courses offered by the YMCA.

15. Make sure students are aware of emergency procedures. Check that they know how to call for help from an emergency medical service (EMS), and discuss the need to think about how to obtain help in case of an emergency whenever they visit a new swimming facility (for example, look for where the phones are located and where the lifeguard stations are).

Reaching assist with a paddle with instructor spotting

Performance Criteria

The student should

→ participate in the reaching-assist practice,

→ be able to demonstrate a paddle rescue in a boat, and

→ be aware of emergency procedures.

Objective: To improve distance and accuracy at throwing assists

Materials Needed: ring buoy (or similar object), plastic hoop

Discussion Guidelines for Instructors

Place the hoop in the water 15 feet away from the side of the pool. Have students practice throwing a ring buoy (or similar object) into the hoop. See who can get the buoy into the hoop most often. Then move the hoop 20 feet away to repeat, then 25 feet away.

Performance Criteria

The student should

→ be able to throw a ring buoy (or similar object) into a hoop 7 out of 10 times at 15, 20, or 25 feet from the side of the pool.

Objective: To refine rescue breathing techniques

Materials Needed:
a CPR manikin, pocket mask(s), rubbing alcohol, cotton swabs

Discussion Guidelines for Instructors

1. Review with students how to do rescue breathing (see Guppy, Minnow, Fish levels).

2. Practice each step, perfecting the technique. Also demonstrate how to decontaminate the manikin by wiping rubbing alcohol over the face of the manikin with cotton swabs.

Performance Criteria

The student should

→ be able to demonstrate the steps of rescue breathing on a CPR manikin (and how to decontaminate the manikin).

Summary

Flying Fish
Summary of Performance Criteria

Component 1: Personal Safety

- Participate in the discussion of backyard pool safety.
- Participate in the discussion of waterpark safety.
- Float for six minutes on the front or back with clothes on. ⚠
- Tread water for six minutes using all four kicks: single, double, circle kick, and rotary kick.
- Know what to do when a boat capsizes. ⚠
- Say why having good personal health habits is important to others and make a self-critique of personal health habits with ideas for achieving a healthier lifestyle.
- Participate in the discussion of personal health and demonstrate an understanding of the importance of personal health.
- Describe the four components of health-related fitness.

Component 2: Personal Growth

- Give a true-life example of having followed personal ground rules and describe what a risk is.
- Understand the meanings of *adventure* and *risk taking,* discuss possibilities for adventure and establish ground rules to limit riskiness, and enforce these personal rules.
- Set three goals for self-improvement related to caring, honesty, respect, or responsibility.

Component 3: Stroke Development

- Swim the crawl stroke with bilateral breathing for 100 yards with open turns.
- Swim the breaststroke for 100 yards with open turns.
- Swim the elementary backstroke for 100 yards with a glide.
- Swim the back crawl for 100 yards with open turns.

- Swim the sidestroke for 100 yards (alternating 25 yards each on the left and right sides) using the regular kick, and swim the lifesaving sidestroke for 50 yards.
- Swim the butterfly stroke with fins for 50 yards and without fins for 25 yards.

Component 4: Water Games and Sports

- Cover three to four body lengths entirely underwater and use the modified breaststroke underwater to keep the momentum going.
- Demonstrate the sailboat with variations.
- Perform a ballet leg and hold it in the air for 10 seconds.
- Perform a kip.
- Demonstrate stroke variations with the crawl, back crawl, breaststroke, and sidestroke.
- Participate in developing and perform an original routine that uses three figures and two stroke variations.
- Demonstrate the three-step approach, hurdle, and front dive off a one-meter board.
- Shoot the ball into a wetball goal.
- Block a ball being shot into a goal.
- Combine ball-handling skills with a stroke, and participate in the relays.
- Rotary kick and try to move forward, backward, and side to side.
- Participate in playing a wetball game in deep water.
- Demonstrate the use of a snorkel while swimming, and be able to clear the mask and snorkel.
- Demonstrate a front (flip) turn for the crawl stroke and back crawl stroke

Component 5: Rescue

- Participate in the reaching-assist practice, demonstrate a paddle rescue in a boat, and be aware of emergency procedures.
- Throw a ring buoy (or similar object) into a hoop 7 out of 10 times at 15, 20, or 25 feet from the side of the pool.
- Demonstrate the steps of rescue breathing on a CPR manikin (and how to decontaminate the manikin).

flying fish

CHAPTER *Seven*

Shark Level

At the Shark level, students learn the relevance of swimming skills, lifesaving techniques, conditioning, and decision making. Service to others is fostered through teamwork.

Improved conditioning and the refinement of new water skills build on the students' already well-developed understanding of their potential for learning new things.

While enrolled in the Shark level, the student is

→ helped to learn safety precautions for rafting and tubing and for swimming in open water;

→ helped to learn about target heart-rate range;

→ encouraged to serve others and to think about the four core values;

→ helped to improve endurance and refine the following strokes, including starts and turns: crawl stroke, breaststroke, inverted breaststroke, back crawl stroke, butterfly stroke, and individual medley strokes;

→ provided with the opportunity to perform synchronized swimming skills, figures, formations, and routines with others;

→ helped to learn how to do a front walkover in the water and how to do the trudgen crawl and overarm sidestroke;

→ helped to improve his or her wetball skills such as swimming a water polo medley, ball handling, and playing the game;

→ helped to refine his or her competitive starts;

→ given more experience in using skin diving gear; and

→ helped to learn more about rescue skills, such as ice rescues, first aid for heat and cold disorders, recognizing and treating shock, and performing rescue breathing and opening an obstructed airway for an unconscious victim.

Prerequisite:

→ Successful completion of the Flying Fish level

Component 1: Personal Safety

⚓ Objective: To learn safety precautions for rafting and tubing

Discussion Guidelines for Instructors

1. Discuss with the students safety when rafting and tubing. Bring up the following guidelines:
   - Each person should wear a Coast Guard–approved PFD.
   - Prepare before going by learning about the area—its dangers and calm spots.
   - Know and follow the local laws regarding rafting and tubing. If you don't know them, contact the local conservation or park department.
   - Be trained to handle the raft or tube safely. If you have never rafted or tubed before, meet with an experienced person before starting your expedition. Many park districts and outdoor or wilderness stores offer training or can recommend effective training programs.
   - Check your equipment before entering the water.
   - Be aware of other watercraft in the area.
   - Carry bailers, sponges, extra paddles, a throw bag for rescues, a first-aid kit in a dry bag, and other safety items.
   - Avoid rafting or tubing after a heavy rain.
   - Avoid alcohol. You need your best judgment to remain safe.

2. Talk about what to do if you fall into river rapids. Remain calm. Roll onto your back and float downstream feetfirst to protect yourself from head injury and to see where you are heading. Never stand up because if your foot becomes entrapped in rock debris, the current will force you forward. Once you have passed the rapids, swim to shore. You may have to swim diagonally with the current, rather than directly against it.

Performance Criteria

The student should
   → participate in the discussion.

Objective: To learn about open-water safety

Discussion Guidelines for Instructors

Ask "How many of you have ever been to the beach? When you go to the beach, there are some special dangers to watch for. Can you think of some?" Mention the following precautions:
   → Watch out for dangerous marine life.
   → Swim close to shore; don't swim out too far.
   → If you are caught in a current, don't fight it or swim against it. Instead, gradually swim away from it.
   → Don't dive into the waves.
   → Don't jump or dive from piers or rock jetties.
   → Keep your arms out in front of you when body surfing.

Performance Criteria

The student should
   → participate in the discussion.

Objective: To experience swimming in rough water

Materials Needed: kickboards, one for each student

Discussion Guidelines for Instructors

1. Give each student a kickboard, then have students form two parallel lines about five feet apart and face each other. Each student should hold the kickboard vertically in the water and push it back and forth, creating waves. Make sure students do not hit each other with the kickboards.

2. Have students take turns trying to swim in between the two lines.

3. After all students have had a turn, discuss how this is similar to swimming in rough water or with waves. Ask how it affected their swimming. Was it easier or harder to swim? Was it faster or slower?

shark

What do they think they might have to do in order to swim in water like this for a long time?

Performance Criteria

The student should

→ participate in the activity and discussion.

Objective: To learn about target heart-rate range

Materials Needed:

a clock or watch with a second hand, a target heart-rate range chart for swimming that covers the ages of your students

Discussion Guidelines for Instructors

1. Say "Let's practice taking our own heart rate. You can feel your pulse in two places: Place your index and middle fingers on the side of your neck, just behind your Adam's apple, or place the same two fingers on the inside of your wrist, just below your thumb. See if you can find it." Have students find their pulse.

2. Say "Now let's see how many times your heart beats in 10 seconds. Start counting on a beat, and count that beat as zero." Have students count their 10-second pulse. Say "Take the number of beats and multiply it by six to find your beats per minute, or heart rate. Remember that number." Have each student determine his or her heart rate.

3. Say "Now let's try swimming across the pool and back. As soon as you get back, take your heart rate, and remember that number." Have students swim and take their heart rate.

4. Say "This time, try swimming across and back again as fast as you can, then take your heart rate as soon as you get back." Have students swim fast and take their heart rate.

5. Show students a target heart-rate range chart and say "The reason we check our heart rate is to measure how hard we are working when we exercise. To get the most benefit, we should work out at a heart rate that is between 65 and 85 percent of our maximal heart rate, the fastest that our heart can beat. This is called a target heart-rate range, and it varies somewhat for different ages. Compare your

heart rate when swimming to the target heart-rate range for your age. Is it higher or lower? If it's lower, you need to work harder; if it's higher, you need to work less."

Figure 7.1	Heart Rate Range Chart	
Ages	65%	85%
7-8	138	181
9-10	136	179
11-12	135	178
13-15	133	176

Performance Criteria

The student should

→ be able to take his or her own heart rate and

→ be able to swim within his or her target heart-rate range.

Component 2: Personal Growth

Objective: To consider being of service to others and building a better world

Discussion Guidelines for Instructors

1. Start a discussion by asking the following questions:
   • How can we build a better world?
   • Is volunteering a good idea?
   • How can you help out at home, in school, or in this class?

2. Briefly discuss the possibilities for volunteering locally through the YMCA and other public or private agencies.

3. Continue the discussion by asking the following questions:
   • How does learning and improving swimming and rescue skills involve others?
   • Can new skills usually be learned better alone or with help?

shark

• Does working together make the class better? The neighborhood better? The world better?

4. Ask the students to talk to their parents about getting permission to volunteer at the YMCA for an hour one day. Once they have permission to do so, ask the students what they would like to do or what kinds of activities they would like to be involved in, then work with the aquatic director to arrange a schedule for the students to volunteer. Send home reminder cards of what students' responsibilities will be and the day and time they are supposed to come.

Performance Criteria

The student should

→ participate in the discussion,

→ be able to give three examples of how to serve others to build a better world, and

→ perform one volunteer assignment of his or her choice for the YMCA.

Objective: To learn more about the four core values

Discussion Guidelines for Instructors

1. In each class, highlight one of the four core values. Ask students what they think are the advantages of accepting and demonstrating that value. Then ask what they feel might be a disadvantage or a reason why they might not want to accept and demonstrate the value.

2. Allow students time to think about this during their series swim. After their series swim, ask them again, and see if they have any new responses about the advantages. See if they can think of what they might say if they were challenged or pressured by one of their friends not to demonstrate the value. Give an example and ask how they might respond.

3. Another activity you can try is bringing the class to a Polliwog or Pike class for part of the class period and having them be "big buddies" to the children, helping teach one-on-one.

4. In another class you can have a lifeguard visit your students. Have the lifeguard discuss what his or her responsibilities are around the pool. Have the lifeguard ask the students "Why do you think I have these responsibilities?" or "What can you do to make it easier for me to accomplish my responsibilities?" Allow students time to ask questions.

5. Before one class, assign each student to teach part of the next class. Give students time to ask you questions. Tell them that it is their responsibility to practice before class so that the other students will learn and have fun. At the next class, allow each student to teach. Direct and help students as necessary.

Performance Criteria

The student should

→ be able to describe the advantages and disadvantages of being caring, honest, respectful, and responsible.

Component 3: Stroke Development

Objective: To refine the crawl stroke, including starts and turns, and improve endurance

Materials Needed:

crawl stroke observation checklist from *Teaching Swimming Fundamentals,* mat (optional)

Skill Description

To perform a front start, the student begins by standing at the front of a block or the edge of the pool in a relaxed position. He or she places the feet shoulder width apart and curls the toes over the edge, then bends the knees and waist slightly, keeping the head down. Keeping the weight of the body on the balls of the feet, the student leans forward with the arms outstretched in front of the body, thumbs down and elbows up.

Discussion Guidelines for Instructors

1. Say "Let's play 'Count That Stroke.' Count the number of strokes you make in one width (or length); then try to do one less the next time. Use bilateral breathing."

shark

2. Continue practice until they have reduced the distance per stroke by 20 percent. Using the stroke observation checklist to guide you, choose drills from appendix A that you believe can help your students improve their stroke and build their endurance.

3. Continue refining students' flip turns from the Flying Fish level.

4. Move students to water that is at least nine feet deep to teach the front start. Review the front standing dive from the Minnow level.

5. Have the students practice their starting position, demonstrating their stance on the deck without falling forward.

6. Then have the students do a long shallow dive. (The entry should be in the following sequence: hands, arms, torso, and legs. Emphasize practicing this in water no less than nine feet deep.)

7. Ask "If you wanted to get a good start, getting out as far and as fast as possible, what could help you?" (Answer: Your arms and legs.) "How could your legs help?" (Answer: The legs and feet could push hard off the deck.) Have students try jumping up from the deck. Then say "When you push down hard with your legs like that against the floor, it pushes your body up. That push is called thrust." Next, ask "How could your arms help?" (Answer: The arms could be moved to provide momentum. They could circle up, around, and out and be thrown forward.) "How could your body start? Finish?" (Answer: The body coils and springs forward and is relatively straight as it enters the water.)

8. Have students demonstrate the start from the edge of the pool and then, once the start is mastered and they are able to control their dive, from the starting blocks in deep water.

Instructor Note: *Make sure that students maintain body control while demonstrating.*

9. Discuss the proper commands for starts:
   - *Step up*—standing position (both feet equal distance from starting edge)
   - *Take your mark*—starting position (one foot forward with toes curled over edge)
   - *Gun sound, whistle, or Go*—take off

10. Emphasize diving safety rules such as checking the water depth before diving.

Performance Criteria

The student should
- → be able to swim the crawl stroke for 100 yards, streamlining efforts and cutting the distance per stroke by 20 percent and
- → be able to perform a front start and front flip turn.

Objective: To refine the breaststroke, including starts and turns, and improve endurance

Materials Needed: cone or other marker

Discussion Guidelines for Instructors

1. Say "When you start with the breaststroke, you are allowed to do one pull and one kick underwater before you surface. If you wanted to make the most of it with distance and speed, what do you think you could do? Let's give your ideas a try." Have students try their starts off the blocks or from the deck in a minimum of nine feet of water. Mark their distance using a cone or other marker. See if they can improve their distance.

2. Help students improve their distance by using an underwater stroke on the start and turn. Their arms should pull through to the hips in both the start and turn. Once the body is under the surface and momentum from the dive or push-off has begun to subside, they should pull out until shoulder level and then push back parallel with the sides, then with the hips. As the arms recover, they should kick. (See chapter 7 in *Teaching Swimming Fundamentals* for more detailed instructions.)

3. Have students practice the breaststroke turn with push-off (see the Fish level or chapter 7 in *Teaching Swimming Fundamentals* for more details).

shark

Performance Criteria

The student should

→ be able to swim the breaststroke for 100 yards with a pullout (a transitional movement from the wall), starts, and turns.

Objective: To learn the inverted breaststroke

Skill Description

The inverted breaststroke is a combination of the elementary backstroke and the breaststroke. The student glides on the back in a streamlined position, with the arms extended overhead and the legs straight. The elementary backstroke kick is used. The student's arms start straight overhead, then press outward and down toward the feet until the palms are along the thighs. The arms then immediately recover along the body to the armpits, palms turn up, and hands go over the shoulders, slide under the ears, and return to the extended glide position.

The student recovers the legs as the hands move under the ears. He or she kicks as the arms reach the thighs. The student inhales during the arm recovery and exhales during the kick.

Discussion Guidelines for Instructors

1. Ask "How can you do the breaststroke on your back? Let's see."
2. Point out those students who are using proper techniques, then have students try again.
3. Observe students and help them improve their stroke and increase their distance per stroke.

Performance Criteria

The student should

→ be able to swim the inverted breaststroke for 50 yards.

Objective: To help students refine the back crawl, including starts and turns, and improve their endurance

Materials Needed:
back crawl stroke observation checklist from *Teaching Swimming Fundamentals*

Inverted breaststroke

Skill Description

To do the start, the student curls loosely at the starting block or pool side with knees flexed and feet positioned on the wall one slightly above the other, just below the surface. The hands grip the starting block or pool side, shoulder width apart.

At the command *Take your mark,* the student draws closer to the wall in a coiled position, pulling the body out of the water. He or she lowers the head toward the knees and keeps the feet submerged.

At the command *Go,* the student releases his or her grasp and uncoils in a back extension. He or she throws the head back between the outstretched arms while thrusting the legs from the wall. The body is streamlined and arches clear of the water's surface, enters, and straightens out about eight inches below the water's surface. Excessive arching will force the swimmer deeper. The student holds the head well back and exhales forcefully through the nose. He or she extends the arms in a glide. The free arm remains in momentary extension above the head. The student should take the first kick and arm pull on the same side.

Discussion Guidelines for Instructors

1. Show students the starting position for the back crawl.

2. Ask "What do you think you can do to help your start be more effective?" (Answers: Give a good push with the legs, be streamlined.)

3. Say "Let's see how you can try to do that." Point out students who are effective and see if they can tell you what helped them to be so.

4. Once students have mastered this part of the start, talk about how they can improve their speed by using the dolphin kick prior to surfacing on the transition from the start and their first stroke.

5. Refine stroke performance by observing students, using the skill observation checklist to help you analyze their stroke. Assign them appropriate back crawl drills from appendix A to practice to improve their stroke, increase distance per stroke, and build their endurance. Encourage students to use their back crawl flip turns when they make turns.

6. Have students practice the back flip turn. See the Flying Fish level or chapter 7 of *Teaching Swimming Fundamentals* for a description of the back flip turn.

Performance Criteria

The student should

→ be able to swim the back crawl for 100 yards and perform transitions with a dolphin kick, streamlining, starts, and turns.

Objective: To learn the overarm sidestroke

Skill Description

The body position, kick, lower arm action, breathing, and rhythm of the overarm sidestroke is the same as the sidestroke. The arm variation is that the top arm recovers out of the water with the elbow high as the hand enters the water just in front of the face. The top hand enters the water as the lower arm finishes its pull.

Discussion Guidelines for Instructors

1. Say "We are going to do something a little different with your sidestroke. Your top arm is going to pull down like you are used to, but instead of recovering underwater, it is going to recover by coming out of the water and reaching overhead, entering just past your head. The rest of the stroke remains the same. Let's see you try it."

2. Once the students have mastered the stroke on one side, have them try it on the other side.

3. Help students improve their stroke and build their endurance.

Performance Criteria

The student should

→ be able to swim the overarm sidestroke for 50 yards (25 yards each on the left and right sides).

Objective: To refine the butterfly stroke, including starts and turns, and improve endurance

Materials Needed:

butterfly stroke observation checklist from *Teaching Swimming Fundamentals*

shark

Overarm sidestroke

Discussion Guidelines for Instructors

1. Using the stroke observation checklist to guide you, assign students to practice drills from appendix A that you believe can help them improve their stroke, distance per stroke, and build their endurance. Starts should be done in a minimum of nine feet of water.

2. Have students practice their starts. Let them know that they can improve the effectiveness of their start by using the one underarm pull as in the breaststroke and the dolphin kick until they surface with their first arm cycle.

3. Have students work across widths so they can practice performing their turns and transitions.

Performance Criteria

The student should

→ be able to demonstrate the butterfly stroke for 25 yards, streamlined and using a push-off with starts and turns.

Objective: To learn how to do the trudgen crawl

Skill Description

The trudgen crawl combines a scissors kick with a front crawl. The kick is shortened and a greater body roll is added. To perform the trudgen crawl, the student does a scissors kick during the final phase of the arm stroke on the breathing side and adds two or three flutter kicks in between. He or she uses a slower front crawl arm stroke in order to allow for more body roll to the breathing side as the scissors kick is executed. The student kicks the leg on the breathing side as the arm on the breathing side finishes the pull. He or she inhales as the breathing arm starts to recover.

Discussion Guidelines for Instructors

1. Say "We're going to try something a little different. I want to see you combine the crawl stroke and sidestroke and make it into a new stroke. What would yours look like? Let's see."

2. Ask "Are there any other ways? What parts did you keep from each of the strokes to make your new one?"

3. Say "OK, I want you to try this idea. Kick and pull like the crawl

shark

Trudgen crawl

shark

stroke, but when you need a breath, kick and breathe on your side. What does this feel like? This is called the trudgen-crawl stroke. It is used as a resting stroke."

4. Help students with their trudgen-crawl stroke and help them build endurance.

Performance Criteria

The student should

→ be able to swim the trudgen crawl for 50 yards.

Objective: To refine each of the strokes in the individual medley (IM)

Discussion Guidelines for Instructors

1. Have students practice swimming 50 yards, with starts and turns, for each of the strokes in the medley.

2. Time students and see if they can decrease their time during the session. Time them for the 100 IM and the 200 IM for comparison.

Performance Criteria

The student should

→ be able to swim the individual medley for 200 yards: the butterfly stroke, backstroke, breaststroke, and freestyle with starts and turns.

Shark Series Swim Information

These experienced swimmers can swim lengths back and forth, although for some activities you may want them to swim down and walk back. You may want to use IFDs for working on some skills. Students usually use the middle lanes of the pool. You will usually be on deck to be able to observe better. Have students stretch before beginning their series swim.

Component 4: Water Games and Sports

Objective: To learn how to do a front walkover in the water

Skill Description

To do a front walkover, the student first assumes a front layout position, then pulls down into a front pike. As the body reaches 90°, the student lifts one leg and keeps it extended while he or she moves it in an arc over the water. To move the leg, the student can press the hands toward the bottom of the pool, keeping the palms flat. (Other arm movements are also acceptable.) The hips should remain in a relatively stationary position during the arc. When the leg finishes the arc, the student will be in an inverted split position.

After holding the inverted split momentarily, the student lifts the leg extended in front to meet the leg extended behind. The student can perform the lift by returning the hands to a position beside the knees with the palms facing the pool bottom and pressing down and backward to a position behind the head.

As the second leg passes the vertical point, the student should hold the trunk in a maximum arched position. As the leg completes the arc and joins the first leg, the student should position the hands over the head and perform an overhead scull to prevent the body from moving footfirst too much. The student controls the ascent of the body by continuing the scull until the head surfaces and the body reaches a back layout. The body should travel only enough so that the head finishes in the position in which the hips started.

Discussion Guidelines for Instructors

1. Ask "Who knows what a front walkover is? Does anybody know how to do one on land? Do you think it would be harder or easier in water?" (Answer: A little bit of both.) "What would be easier? (Answer: The water holds you up so you don't need as much arch in your back.) "What would be harder?" (Answers: Staying near the surface, and not getting water up your nose.)

2. Ask "Who thinks they would like to try one? Show me."

3. Tell students how to perform the front walkover:
   - Say "Start on your stomach and begin it like a front surface dive. Stop when your head is pointing to the bottom. Scull with your palms flat toward the bottom. This will help to keep you from sinking too deep."
   - Then say "Now lift one leg over your head and let it fall over, and then follow with the other. Try not to roll over. Scull over your head and bring your body up to the surface on your back."

4. Let the students try it. As they get the idea, try to help them improve their form: legs straight, toes pointed, keeping hips at the surface.

Performance Criteria

The student should
   → participate in learning how to do a front walkover in the water.

Objective: To get the opportunity to perform skills, figures, and formations with more than one person

Skill Description: Chain

Instructor Note: *Before trying activities that involve contact with other people, make sure your students feel secure in the water. The use of water logs or another IFD may help students increase comfort and success when they are first attempting these skills.*

Two swimmers, Swimmers 1 and 2, stand in shallow water, Swimmer 2 behind Swimmer 1. Both bend their knees and submerge to shoulder level, then lean back, looking up until their ears are underwater. Swimmer 2 places the right foot on the right shoulder of Swimmer 1, with toes touching just under Swimmer 1's ear, staying low in the water. Then Swimmer 2 assumes a back float position and places the left foot over Swimmer 1's left shoulder. Swimmer 2 gently squeezes the feet to hold

shark

Front walkover

Swimmer 1's head securely. Swimmer 1 slowly assumes a back float. Swimmer 2 uses standard sculling to pull Swimmer 1. Both swimmers should now have their knees straight and be in a streamlined position. Both should scull.

Discussion Guidelines for Instructors

Have swimmers practice until they can do a chain in the position of either Swimmer 1 or 2 for a pool length. Then have them try the following:

→ Form a chain with another pair.

→ Form a chain and move in a circle.

→ Add as many people as you can to your chain.

→ Form a chain of many people, form a circle, and move the circle around.

→ Practice doing other things with the chain.

The chain

Skill Description: Tandem

Two swimmers, Swimmers 1 and 2, stand in shallow water, both facing the same way. Swimmer 1 is in front of Swimmer 2. Swimmer 1 lies facedown, while Swimmer 2 places Swimmer 1's feet on both hips and also stretches out prone. Both swimmers should do the breaststroke arm movement.

The tandem

Discussion Guidelines for Instructors

Tell swimmers to do the following:

→ Add two more swimmers.

→ Add as many swimmers as you can.

→ Do the tandem on your back.

→ Turn from front to back and back to front while in tandem.

→ Try other figures in tandem.

Performance Criteria

The student should

→ participate in performing synchronized swimming skills that involve more than two people.

Objective: To give students the opportunity to perform formations with others

Discussion Guidelines for Instructors

Divide the class into teams of two to four people. Have each team try to create an accordion and a star.

Accordion

Accordion patterns: Swimmers lie next to each other, alternating head-down/feet-up and feet-down/head-up. They touch each other's feet with their hands. They can then either open their arms and legs (as in a jumping jack) or extend the inside arms straight at shoulder level. Other variations for four or more people include these:

→ Two people who are head-down hold hands and touch the feet of the alternating person whose feet are down, and two people who are feet-down hold hands and touch the feet of the alternating person whose feet are up.

→ Two people who are head-down use their hands to touch the feet of the two people who are feet-down, and vice versa.

shark

Accordion pattern

Star

Star pattern: Swimmers lie in back float with toes touching. Together, they separate their legs, and then hold that position momentarily. Then, they bring their legs together again.

Performance Criteria

The student should
→ participate in creating synchronized swimming pattern formations with others.

Star pattern

Objective: To get the opportunity to develop a routine with others

Discussion Guidelines for Instructors

Divide the class into teams. Ask each team to develop a routine that includes two strokes, five figures, and at least one formation that they have learned. Everyone on the team should participate and the skills should be synchronized.

Performance Criteria

The student should

→ participate as a team member and perform the team's routine.

Objective: To develop endurance and watermanship

Discussion Guidelines for Instructors

Have students try the following stroke variations for water polo: head-up butterfly stroke with a rotary kick, head-up backstroke with a rotary kick, rotary kick forward with the hands in the water, and head-up freestyle (widths).

Performance Criteria

The student should

→ be able to swim the water polo medley: head-up butterfly stroke with a rotary kick, head-up backstroke with a rotary kick, rotary kick forward with the hands in the water, and head-up freestyle (widths).

Objective: To improve ball-handling skills

Materials Needed: balls of various sizes, one for each pair of students

Discussion Guidelines for Instructors

Pair up students. Have the partners practice passing the ball, alternating between using the left hand and the right hand, while swimming and dribbling across the pool. Start in shallow water; then move to deep water.

Performance Criteria

The student should

→ be able to pass the ball alternating the right and left hands (first in shallow water, then in deep).

Objective: To improve endurance by playing a five-minute wetball game in deep water

Materials Needed:

ball; four cones (use two cones for each goal); wetball caps with ear guards, one for each student

Discussion Guidelines for Instructors

Divide the class into two teams and have the students play a five-minute wetball game in deep water.

Performance Criteria

The student should

→ participate in a five-minute wetball game in deep water.

Objective: To don skin diving equipment in deep water and to surface dive to retrieve an object on the bottom of the pool and return it to the side of the pool.

Materials Needed:

masks, fins, snorkels, one for each student; a number of objects that sink

Discussion Guidelines for Instructors

1. Ask students to don masks, fins, and snorkel in deep water and swim across the pool.

2. Pair students up into As and Bs so that each student has a buddy. Have students kick with arms at sides, then have all the A students surface dive when you signal. Their buddies should watch for any trouble. When the A students come to the surface signal the B students to surface dive while their buddies watch.

3. Throw a number of objects that sink into the pool. Have first the A students, then the B students surface dive. Students should try to retrieve the objects from the bottom of the pool and carry them to the side of the pool.

4. Create an obstacle course.

Instructor Note: *Remember to always have students dive in buddy pairs. Remind students to equalize their ears and to perform proper ascents.*

Performance Criteria

The student should

→ be able to don skin diving equipment in deep water with ease,

→ perform a surface dive, and

→ retrieve an object from the bottom of the pool, clear the snorkel as he or she comes up, and return the object to the side of the pool.

Component 5: Rescue

Objective: To learn about ice rescues

Materials Needed:
a long object such as pole, oar, stick, or ladder (optional)

Discussion Guidelines for Instructors

1. Ask "What are some reasons that we might want to go out on the ice in wintertime?" (Answers: To play hockey or other ice games; to skate; to ice fish; to take a shortcut.) Ask "How can we know when is it safe to be out on the ice?" (Answer: When the town or city has posted a sign saying that it is safe. Stay off ice if you don't know the thickness or if you see water on the ice, slush, crackles or holes, or gray or dirty veins in the ice.)

Instructor Note: *Ice that is six inches (15 cm) thick should be safe for one or two people, and if it is eight inches (20 cm) thick it should be safe for group activities.*

2. Say "Let's see how much you know about ice:

• Is ice uniformly thick everywhere on the body of water? (Answer: Ice rarely forms with uniform thickness; it can vary a lot.)

• Does snow on top of ice make it stronger and make it freeze faster? (Answer: Snow acts as an insulating blanket. The ice under the snow will be thinner and weaker. A snowfall can also insulate, warm up, and melt existing ice.)

• Is the strength the same for all types of ice at the same thickness? (Answer: Different types of ice can have different strengths at the same thickness. Clear blue, black, or green ice is the strongest; six inches should support one or two people. White opaque ice should be twice as thick to safely support the same number of people. Snow ice or spring ice cannot be trusted to support anyone.)

• If it is really cold outside, will the ice be safe and thick? (Answer: A cold snap with very cold temperatures quickly weakens ice and can cause large cracks within half a day. A warm spell will take several days to weaken the ice.)

3. Say "Sometimes people fall through the ice. What kinds of problems can be encountered in ice rescues?" (Answers: Freezing temperatures; a lack of victim response; thin, cracking ice.) Say "Don't go onto the ice to try to rescue someone unless you know the ice is thick enough to step on."

4. Review with students how to perform reaching assists. Ask "During an ice rescue, what would be a good position for distributing your weight so that the center of gravity is low?" (Answer: Lying down with legs spread.)

5. Have the students create and act out an ice rescue scene. The rescuer should lie prone with legs spread. He or she may either extend a long object such as a pole, oar, stick, or ladder or hold out an arm or leg. If the rescuer extends an arm or leg, he or she should take every precaution to secure his or her body to something solid.

6. Discuss getting help. Outline the procedures.

7. Discuss what to do if you are a victim:

• Yell for help.

• Try to kick and slide back onto the surface.

• Once on the surface, lie flat on the ice and pull yourself with your arms onto the bank.

shark

- If the ice breaks again, keep breaking it as you move closer to shore.
- If you can't climb out, wait for someone to come to your rescue. Keep still and calm. Stay warm by keeping your arms close to your body and legs together.

Performance Criteria

The student should

→ know something about ice safety and

→ be able to demonstrate an ice rescue scene.

Objective: To learn first aid for heat disorders

Discussion Guidelines for Instructors

1. Tell students the following trigger story:

   "You are on the beach. It's a hot day, and you're watching a volleyball game that people have been playing for a long time. Suddenly, one of the players faints on the court. You go over to see if you can help. The player is not conscious; her skin is very red, hot, and dry."

2. Ask "What should you do?" (Answers: Cool the body quickly with cool water, ice packs, or other means.)

3. Emphasize that hot, red, *dry* skin is a sign of heat stroke. This is a real emergency, so call an ambulance. Ask how many of the students know how to call an ambulance. Explain about emergency numbers in your area.

4. Discuss the following precautions regarding heat:

   - Exercising in water is one of the safest ways to remain physically fit even when temperatures soar. Still, sun and sand, high temperatures, and too much exercise may create problems even for swimmers. Discuss why it is not a good idea to exercise too strenuously during warm weather, particularly early in the summer before the body has had time to adapt to hotter temperatures.
   - Encourage the students to share anecdotes about becoming ill after too much play or too much beach on hot summer days.

- Ask "What can we do to protect ourselves?" (Answers: Use sunscreen and wear a hat, take it easy, drink fluids.)
- Ask "Why is it good to swim even on hot days?"

5. Introduce a brief discussion of evaporation and humidity at this point. Explain that it is evaporation of sweat from our skin that cools us. When the air is humid, evaporation takes place more slowly. This means that people should not overexert themselves when it's humid, as it is harder for the body to cool down. They also should wear absorbent materials that wick sweat away and light clothing that allows air to circulate around the body.

6. Discuss simple rules about what to do for people overexposed to heat:

   - Take the victim to a cool place.
   - Give him or her small amounts of liquid (if the victim is conscious).
   - Let the victim rest.
   - If the body temperature seems elevated and the skin is hot and dry, get medical help quickly.

Performance Criteria

The student should

→ be able to describe the symptoms of heat stroke;

→ know how to protect himself or herself and others from too much heat while swimming and on land; and

→ know immediate first-aid procedures for these conditions.

Objective: To learn first aid for cold disorders

Discussion Guidelines for Instructors

Frostbite and hypothermia

1. Explain that the main dangers of exposure to cold are frostbite, which is tissue damage caused by the cold, and hypothermia, which is when the body temperature becomes abnormally low.

2. Discuss frostbite prevention:

shark

- Wear thin layers of clothes to keep in the heat.
- On very cold days, cover all exposed areas of the skin, especially the hands, ears, and nose.
- Understand why swimmers should know about protection from the cold.

3. Discuss the symptoms of superficial frostbite:
   - Severely waxy, white, or grayish skin
   - Coldness and numbness in the affected area; possibly tingling, stinging, or aching feelings
   - Surface feels crusty or stiff; underlying tissue is soft when touched gently and firmly

4. Discuss symptoms of hypothermia:
   - Uncontrolled shivering
   - Bluish color
   - Shock
   - Cold to touch

5. Have students develop safety rules for protection from the cold, such as the following:
   - Never go to sleep outside when the weather is freezing.
   - Keep moving in freezing temperatures no matter how tired you are.
   - Wear protective suiting, for example, if skin diving.

6. Talk about the fact that hypothermia is likely to occur if someone ends up in cold water. To increase their ability to survive when immersed in cold water, students should follow these rules:
   - Stay calm.
   - Decide whether to swim for your boat or shore or to stay where you are. This will depend on how cold the water and air are, how strong the current and wind are and their direction, and how far you are from your boat or shore. Students should remember that it is harder to swim in cold water, and it also is difficult to tell how far away things are when you are in the water.

- If your boat is capsized and is floating, you should hold on to it. It makes it easier for rescuers to see you; it may also allow you to keep part of your body out of the cold water and to rest. If the boat is not floating, but you are near other objects that float, grab one of them.
- If there is nothing to hold on to that floats, stay in the HELP position and try to relax until help arrives. Keep your clothes on for warmth.

7. Discuss what to do for victims of frostbite or hypothermia:
   - If someone is exposed to the cold, see that he or she warms up *gradually,* preferably at room temperature, or heart failure may result.
   - Use blankets.
   - Do not put ice-cold or hot water on frostbite.
   - Keep the victim warm and get medical help at once. Observe a victim of hypothermia for 48 hours.

Performance Criteria

The student should
- → be able to describe the symptoms of frostbite and hypothermia;
- → know how to protect himself or herself and others from too much cold while swimming and on land; and
- → know immediate first-aid procedures for these conditions.

Objective: To learn the appropriate treatment for shock

Discussion Guidelines for Instructors

1. Ask "What is shock?" (Answer: Shock occurs when the body doesn't provide enough oxygenated blood to all tissues, which can lead to tissue damage.)
2. Ask "What can cause shock?" (Answers: Extreme anxiety or worry; sudden fright; an injury or medical condition causing a loss of body fluids or pooling of body fluids.)

shark

3. Ask "Have you ever seen anyone who has gone into shock? What did he or she look like?" (Answers: Pale skin; rapid pulse; rapid and shallow breathing; cold and clammy skin; nausea and vomiting.)

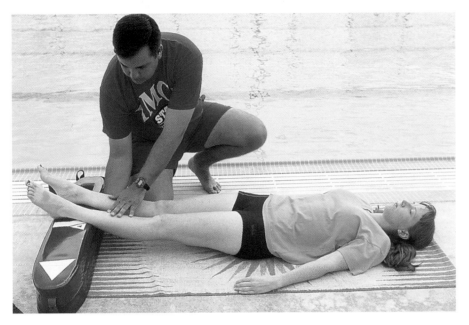

Treating a victim with shock

4. Say "To treat someone who is in shock, do the following:
   • Check the victim's airway, breathing, and circulation. If the person is not breathing, do CPR.
   • Check for and treat any serious injuries.
   • Have the victim lie down on his or her back (unless he or she is unconscious or vomiting, or has a head or spinal injury, a possible stroke or heart attack, difficulty breathing, or chest injuries). Raise the person's legs 8 to 12 inches. (Do not raise the legs higher than this, and do not lift the foot of a bed or stretcher to lift the entire body.)
   • Lay a blanket or coat on the person to conserve body heat.
   • Do not give the person anything to eat or drink."

Performance Criteria

The student should
   → participate in the discussion,
   → be able to list the symptoms of shock, and
   → know the basic treatment for shock.

Objective: To review rescue breathing procedures

Materials Needed:
a CPR manikin, pocket mask(s), alcohol wipes or rubbing alcohol and cotton swabs

Discussion Guidelines for Instructors

1. Review the steps of rescue breathing with students (see Guppy, Minnow, Fish, and Flying Fish levels).
2. Discuss the problems of doing rescue breathing on a victim who has neck or back injuries. Also discuss the possible consequences of moving a victim who has neck or back injuries.
3. Explain the necessary steps to take if the victim vomits.
4. Discuss the benefit of the modified jaw-thrust technique as an effective way to open the air passage in an unconscious, nonbreathing victim; in an unconscious victim trying to breathe; or when a head tilt or chin lift can't be used. Emphasize that this technique should be used when spinal injury is suspected.
5. Review with students the emergency procedures (see Flying Fish level).
6. Say "It's important to use barrier protection when we practice rescue breathing as well as when we actually perform it on a victim. What could we use as a barrier?" (Answer: A pocket mask, a microshield.)
7. Say "After we practice rescue breathing on the manikin, we need to disinfect it to clean off the germs. What do you think we could use to clean it?" (Answer: Rubbing alcohol.)
8. Have the students practice rescue breathing on the manikin using a pocket mask. Disinfect the manikin afterward.

shark

Instructor Note: Have one pocket mask for each student, or disinfect a single pocket mask between each use.

Performance Criteria

The student should

→ be able to demonstrate the steps of rescue breathing on a CPR manikin (as well as how to decontaminate the manikin) and

→ be able to list three special precautions—checking for neck and back injury, mouth injury, and vomiting—in preparing to perform rescue breathing on a victim.

Objective: To learn about first aid for an unconscious victim with an obstructed airway

Materials Needed:

a CPR manikin, pocket mask(s), alcohol wipes or rubbing alcohol and cotton swabs

Discussion Guidelines for Instructors

1. Say "How can you tell if you have come upon a person who is unconscious?" (Answer: If you ask the person if he or she is OK and get no response.)

2. Say "If the person doesn't respond, you should then check the person's airway. You remember how this is done. Show me." Have students demonstrate on a manikin. The students should use the head tilt/chin lift method, then place an ear over the victim's mouth and nose while keeping the airway open; look at the victim's chest, listening and feeling for breathing; then, if there is no breathing, give two slow breaths. They should use barrier protection.

3. Ask "What can you do if the air doesn't go in?" (Answer: Retilt the head and try another breath. If it is unsuccessful, suspect choking. This is also known as an obstructed airway.)

4. Say "Now, if the air is not going in, we only have a few minutes to save this person's life. We should try the following procedure."

Step One

Give up to five abdominal thrusts. Perform them like this:

- Straddle the victim's thighs.
- Put the heel of one hand against the middle of the victim's abdomen, slightly above the navel and well below the sternum's notch. The fingers of the hand should point toward the victim's head.
- Put the other hand on top of the first hand.
- Press inward and upward, using both hands, for up to five quick abdominal thrusts. Each thrust should be a separate, distinct effort to open the airway obstruction.
- Keep the heel of the hand in contact with the abdomen between abdominal thrusts.

Step Two

Perform a finger sweep (for unconscious victims only). Follow these procedures:

- Use your thumb and fingers to grasp the victim's jaw and tongue and lift upward to pull the tongue away from the back of the throat and away from a foreign object.
- With the index finger of your other hand, slide the finger down along the inside of one cheek deep into the victim's mouth and use a hooking action across to the other cheek to dislodge any foreign object.
- If a foreign object comes within reach, grab and remove it. Do not force the object deeper.

Step Three

If these steps are unsuccessful, give one rescue breath, do up to five abdominal thrusts, then do a finger sweep. Continue through these steps in a rapid sequence until the object is expelled or the EMS arrives.

5. Have students practice on a manikin. Remind them to disinfect the manikin when they are finished.

Performance Criteria

The student should

→ be able to demonstrate how to open an obstructed airway for an unconscious victim.

Summary

Shark

Summary of Performance Criteria

Component 1: Personal Safety

- Participate in the discussion of rafting and tubing safety.
- Participate in the discussion of open-water safety.
- Participate in the activity and discussion regarding swimming in rough water.
- Take own heart rate and swim within own target heart-rate range.

Component 2: Personal Growth

- Participate in the discussion of service to others, give three examples of how to serve others to build a better world, and perform one self-chosen volunteer assignment for the YMCA.
- Describe the advantages and disadvantages of being caring, honest, respectful, and responsible.

Component 3: Stroke Development

- Swim the crawl stroke for 100 yards, streamlining efforts and cutting the distance per stroke by 20 percent; and perform a front start and front flip turn.
- Swim the breaststroke for 100 yards with a pullout (a transitional movement from the wall), starts, and turns.
- Swim the inverted breaststroke for 50 yards.
- Swim the back crawl for 100 yards and perform transitions with a dolphin kick, streamlining, starts, and turns.
- Swim the overarm sidestroke for 50 yards (25 yards each on the left and right sides).
- Demonstrate the butterfly stroke for 25 yards, streamlined and using a push-off with starts and turns.
- Swim the trudgen crawl for 50 yards.
- Swim the individual medley for 200 yards: the butterfly stroke, backstroke, breaststroke, and freestyle with starts and turns.

Component 4: Water Games and Sports

- Participate in learning how to do a front walkover in the water.
- Participate in performing synchronized swimming skills that involve more than two people.
- Participate in creating synchronized swimming pattern formations with others.
- Participate as a team member and perform the team's synchronized swimming routine.
- Swim the water polo medley: head-up butterfly stroke with a rotary kick, head-up backstroke with a rotary kick, rotary kick forward with the hands in the water, and head-up freestyle (widths).
- Pass the ball, alternating the right and left hands (first in shallow water, then in deep).
- Participate in a five-minute wetball game in deep water.
- Don skin diving equipment in deep water with ease, perform a surface dive, and retrieve an object from the bottom of the pool and return it to the side of the pool.

Component 5: Rescue

- Know something about ice safety and demonstrate an ice rescue scene.
- Describe the symptoms of heat stroke, frostbite, and hypothermia; know how to take protective measures against too much heat or cold while swimming and on land; and know immediate first-aid procedures for these conditions.
- Participate in the discussion of shock, be able to list the symptoms of shock, and know the basic treatment for shock.
- Demonstrate the steps of rescue breathing on a CPR manikin (as well as how to decontaminate the manikin) and list three special precautions in preparing to perform rescue breathing on a victim.
- Demonstrate how to open an obstructed airway for an unconscious victim.

shark

Porpoise Level

The Porpoise level is the final level of the Youth and Adult Aquatic Program, and it differs from the other levels in that it can be structured as just a class or expanded to be a club.

The club format is more flexible and allows older children and teens the opportunity to develop a program that fits their interests, one that they can participate in for years.

Class Format

The class format is similar to that in the previous levels. However, you can add interest to the class and extend the number of sessions by including activities that will appeal to older students' interests and use their high-level swimming skills. Such activities might include the following:

→ taking part in courses such as YMCA Aquatic Safety Assistant or YMCA Aquatic Personal Safety and Survival;

→ taking a course in snorkeling and skin diving (information available from the YMCA SCUBA office);

→ taking a CPR course or first-aid course;

→ going on field trips to places such as the fire department (tour an ambulance and talk to the EMTs) or different water environments;

→ bringing in speakers from outside aquatic groups such as the U.S. Coast Guard Auxiliary, boating clubs, or SCUBA clubs;

→ learning to evaluate each other's strokes; and

→ learning about other YMCA programs and helping to implement character development in those programs.

Component 1: Personal Safety

Objective: To improve leg strength while treading

Materials Needed:
a diving brick (or comparable object)

Discussion Guidelines for Instructors

1. Have students start treading in a circle. Alternate kicks among scissors, double scissors, circle, and rotary.

2. Begin a trigger story about going out to the beach with friends. Pass the brick to one of the students, who must continue treading and tell the next part of the story. He or she must hold the brick and tell a story for at least 30 seconds before passing it on to the next person. Continue the story and the passing of the brick until all students have had a turn.

3. As students practice, increase the time until they can tread two minutes with the brick.

Performance Criteria

The student should

→ be able to tread water for two minutes while holding a diving brick.

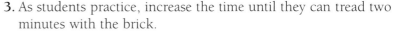 **Objective:** To learn how to enter a boat from deep water

Materials Needed:

PFDs, one for each student; a boat (canoe, rowboat, dinghy, inflatable raft)

Discussion Guidelines for Instructors

1. Ask "Where do you think it is best to enter the boat when you are in the water?" (Answer: From the stern or back of the boat.) "Why do you think so?" (Answer: Otherwise the boat might tip over.) "If that is not possible, try entering from the side. For inflatable boats, it is easier to get in from the side. Be careful not to capsize the boat. If others are in the boat, have them try to balance the weight as they help you get in."

2. Place a boat in the deep end and have students put on PFDs and practice getting into and out of the boat from the water while you spot them.

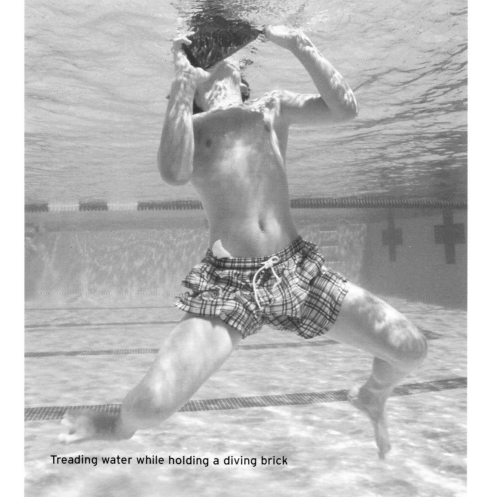

Treading water while holding a diving brick

Entering a raft from deep water

Performance Criteria

The student should

→ be able to enter and exit a boat from deep water.

Objective: To learn how to disrobe and inflate clothing in aquatic emergencies

Materials Needed:

Students should wear clean cotton long-sleeved shirts and cotton or denim pants to class over their swim suits and bring large plastic bags with their names on them to hold wet clothing.

Discussion Guidelines for Instructors

1. At the previous class meeting, tell students to wear a clean, long-sleeved cotton shirt and cotton or denim pants over their swimming suits and to bring plastic bags with their names on them to hold the wet clothing after the activity. Send home a note with students explaining what the students need to bring to class and why.

2. Ask, "If you found yourself in cold water, fully clothed and with no help around, what problems would you have?" (Answers: Sinking, staying warm to prevent hypothermia.) "What could you do to help yourself?" (Answers: Perform the resting stroke, keep my clothes on to help guard against hypothermia.)

3. Ask "How could you use your clothes to help you float?" (Answer: Inflate them with air.) "Let's see if you can find a way to do that. Get into the water and see what you can come up with." See what they can do. Here are some ways in which clothing that is being worn can be inflated with air.

Inflating a shirt or jacket: While treading water, tuck your shirt in or tie the ends together. Button all buttons except the top one. Take a deep breath, lean forward, and pull the shirt up to your face and exhale into it. Keep the front of the shirt underwater and hold the collar closed. The air will rise into the opening and then continue rising around the body to form an air pocket in your shirt. Make sure the shirt is kept tight around the neck so the air will stay trapped. Exhale several breaths into the shirt.

Inflating a shirt

Another method is to button the shirt up to the neck. Then hold the front of the shirt out with one hand, keeping it just under the water, and lean back a little. From the surface, strike the water with your free hand and drive it down below the shirttail. The air carried down from the surface will bubble into the shirt. Repeat the steps as necessary to reinflate.

Inflating layers of clothing: Roll on to your back, and, underwater, lift the front of the clothing or coat away from your body. Cup your hand and push air bubbles into the clothing or coat. The bubbles will rise to the shoulders, providing extra buoyancy.

4. Say "If you found yourself in warm water and were fully clothed, with the possibility of being able to swim to safety, you might want to take off some of your clothes. Let's see if you can figure out how to take your clothes off while treading." Let them try. "The best way to do it is slowly and calmly. The shoes would come off first. If you wanted to save them for when you reached shore, you could tie them together and hang them around your neck. Next you would take off your pants. First you would open all buttons, snaps, or zippers, then slowly slide the pants down your legs and take one leg out at a time. Finally you would take your shirt off, undoing all the buttons and then slowly removing your arms from the sleeves, one at a time."

5. Say "After we took off our clothes, we probably would be getting tired. Is there anything we could do to help us float?" (Answer: Inflate our clothing to help us float.) Ask "How else could our clothes be helpful?" (Answer: If one of the people with us is hurt or unconscious, we could use the inflated clothing to support him or her.) Then say "It's your turn again. Let's see if you can come up with a way to inflate your clothing." Let them try inflating their clothing. Here are some methods they could use.

Inflated clothing: Inflated pants can provide more support than an inflated shirt, but if both are to be used, the shirt should be inflated before the pants. The clothing must be kept wet to prevent air from escaping.

Inflating a shirt: After removing the shirt, tie the sleeves together just below the slits in the cuff. Find the shoulder opening in the sleeve and, while holding it open, submerge and exhale beneath the sleeve hole so the air rises and inflates the sleeve. Tie this sleeve shut while you locate the other sleeve and repeat the process. Slip your head between the two inflated sleeves. The rest of the shirt should be open on your chest. Take the two shirttails and tie them behind your back, which will help keep the air from escaping. In this way it supports your upper body.

Inflating pants: After removing the pants, tie a square knot in the legs as close to the bottom as possible. Next close all fastenings. The splashing method is the most preferred method of inflation. Hold the back of the waistband under while splashing air bubbles

Inflating pants

into the opening with your other hand. The air bubbles created by the splashing will be trapped in the pants. Once the pants are inflated, you will need to keep the open waist area underwater. To prevent air loss through this opening, tuck the waistband through the crotch. Now slip the feet between the two inflated legs. With the shirt supporting the upper body and the pants supporting the legs, you should have adequate support. If you are not using an inflated shirt for buoyancy, place your head and arms between the two inflated pant legs.

porpoise

6. Say "Keep in mind that you can only inflate clothing that is closely woven, such as cotton or denim. Also, if there are holes in the clothing, it is difficult to keep the clothes inflated." Remind the students that they should only remove their clothes in warm water. They should keep their clothes on in cold water to help prevent hypothermia.

Performance Criteria

The student should

→ know how to disrobe in the water and

→ know how to inflate a shirt and pants while in the water.

Component 2: Personal Growth

Objective: To understand the role of being a leader

Materials Needed: pencils and paper

Discussion Guidelines for Instructors

1. Say "Describe a person you look up to. What makes you look up to him or her—what is it that that person does?"

2. Ask "If you had a younger kid walk around with you for a couple of days, would you feel good about what that kid saw? Would you want him or her to do the same types of things you do? What types of behavior would he or she see? Do any of you have someone you think looks up to you?"

3. Ask "What types of behavior would you want someone to see?"

4. Ask "If you want to be a more caring person, what could you do? A more responsible person? A more respectful person? A more honest person?" Have them give some examples. Then hand out a piece of paper and have them write down three goals for each of the values. Collect these, and at each class return the goals to them and have them mark what progress they have made.

5. Say "Being a role model is important and has far-reaching implications and consequences. When someone looks up to you, you are leading him or her. You want to lead that person in the right direction. Once you realize that others are watching you, you can be

more conscious of doing the right things and modeling the behaviors you want them to do."

Performance Criteria

The student should

→ participate in the discussion and

→ reach the goals he or she made.

Objective: To participate in group problem solving and to practice being a leader and a follower

Discussion Guidelines for Instructors

1. Have students form a circle in chest-deep water and hold hands. They should hold hands throughout the activity.

2. Have students tangle themselves by going under or over the arms and legs of others in the circle.

3. Have students try to untangle themselves without letting go of each other's hands.

4. Then assign one of the students to give commands that tangle the group again.

5. Assign a different student to give commands that untangle the group.

6. Afterward discuss the differences in the activity when no one was given the leadership role and when someone was given the leadership role. Ask "Which was faster? How did you feel different?"

Performance Criteria

The student should

→ participate in the activity and

→ be able to accept the roles of being a leader and being a follower.

Objective: To observe the behaviors associated with caring, honesty, respect, and responsibility.

Discussion Guidelines for Instructors

1. Review what each of the four values mean and what behaviors reflecting those values look like.

2. Ask each of the students to observe others and to bring back to the group examples of people demonstrating each of the values. They also should bring back examples of people not demonstrating those behaviors. For the observation, assign students to different swim classes to assist an instructor or to walk around the lobby or gym.

3. After a period of time, meet with your students again and discuss the examples they observed. Discuss ways in which, once they see behaviors that reflect the values, they can reinforce those same behaviors.

Performance Criteria

The student should

→ be able to observe and report on examples of behavior that do and do not reflect the core values, and

→ suggest ways that he or she can reinforce behaviors that do reflect the core values.

Objective: To learn about fitness

Instructor Note: *For more information on fitness and fitness components, check the YMCA fitness resources in the Y Program Store catalog.*

Discussion Guidelines for Instructors

1. Discuss the four components of fitness: speed, strength, endurance, and flexibility. Ask students how these components are included in their swim lessons.

2. Divide the class into two groups. Assign each group one of the components and give them the task of coming up with an activity or game in the water for that component.

3. Have each group lead the other group in playing the activity or game.

4. Repeat, this time assigning groups a different component.

Performance Criteria

The student should

→ participate in the discussion,

→ participate in the group in developing an activity or game, and

→ understand the four components of fitness.

Component 3: Stroke Development

Objective: To increase the speed of strokes

Materials Needed:

a variety of swimming aids, such as kickboards, flotation belts, hand paddles, pull buoys, fins, or PFDs; a stopwatch

Discussion Guidelines for Instructors

1. Have each student pick three strokes or arm/leg actions to try.

2. Have each student choose three pieces of equipment that he or she thinks may help him or her go faster.

3. Ask students to predict which of the pieces will help them move faster; then have them swim for 25 yards with the equipment they chose.

4. Once they've finished, chart their time for each stroke or arm/leg action. Ask if their predictions were correct.

5. Discuss why each piece of equipment either helped them swim faster or slowed them down.

6. Have them try again, first with the same pieces of equipment and then with different ones. Discuss how proper stroke mechanics are important to improve speed. Relate the results to the different laws of the physics of swimming described in chapter 7 of *Teaching Swimming Fundamentals.*

7. Have students set a goal for improving the speed for each of their strokes. Have them count the number of arm cycles it takes for

porpoise

them to do a length of the pool and chart it. Also time each of their strokes for 25 yards. Then have students set an improvement goal for the end of the session. Help them determine realistic ones. Work with students to improve their efficiency and speed for each of the strokes using the drills in appendix A. Recognize students at the end of the session for working hard to meet their goals.

Performance Criteria

The student should

→ participate in the activity.

Objective: To swim a 200-yard individual medley: butterfly, backstroke, breaststroke, and front crawl with starts and turns

Discussion Guidelines for Instructors

Have students work on their 200 IM. Help them with their transitions between the different strokes.

Performance Criteria

The student should

→ be able to swim a 200-yard individual medley: butterfly, backstroke, breaststroke, and front crawl with starts and turns.

Objective: To learn the double-trudgen crawl stroke

Skill Description

The double-trudgen crawl stroke combines two scissors kicks with the front crawl stroke arms. To perform the double-trudgen crawl stroke, the student executes one scissors kick to the breathing side, then a second scissors kick to the other side. He or she uses a slower arm stroke so that each arm does a complete stroke and recovery before the other arm strokes. (This is called a *catch-up stroke*.) The student does a scissors kick with the leg on the breathing side as the body rolls. He or she then does a scissors kick with the leg on the other side as the body moves to accommodate the first kick. The student usually inhales at the start of the recovery on the breathing side, although it is acceptable to breathe on alternate sides.

Discussion Guidelines for Instructors

1. Say "Let's see you do your single-trudgen stroke."
2. Say "Now let's see if you can try to use the scissors kick on the other side as well. This is the double trudgen."
3. Ask "How does the stroke feel? Is it tiring or restful? Can you think of anytime when you would want to use this stroke?"

Performance Criteria

The student should

→ be able to perform the double-trudgen crawl stroke for 50 yards.

Porpoise Series Swim Information

These experienced swimmers can swim lengths back and forth, although for some activities you may want them to swim down and walk back. Students usually use the middle lanes of the pool. You will usually be on deck to be able to observe better. Have students stretch before beginning their series swim.

Component 4: Water Games and Sports

Objective: To develop a synchronized swimming routine with others and perform it to music in front of others

Materials Needed: music on tape or disc, a tape or CD player

Discussion Guidelines for Instructors

1. Divide the class into small groups. Have each group put together a routine using strokes, figures, and formations. Let them pick out some music to use.
2. Allow them some time during a few classes to make up and practice their routine.
3. At the end of the session or during some other special event, have the students perform their routines.

Instructor Note: *If students are interested in learning additional synchronized swimming strokes, get one of the following resources from the Y Program Store: the Coaching Creative Synchronized Swimming Effectively book (Item No. 5022) and video (Item No. 5278), and Creative Synchronized Swimming (Item No. 5277). Or they can take the YMCA Synchronized Swimming Instructor certification course or contact United States Synchronized Swimming at 317-237-5700.*

Performance Criteria

The student should

→ participate in a small group to develop a routine and perform it to music in front of others.

Objective: To learn offensive and defensive strategies in wetball

Discussion Guidelines for Instructors

1. Ask "If you are playing offense, what do you think you should be trying to do?" Help the students to come up with the following strategies:
   - Be aware of where the ball is.
   - Be aware of the location of your team's players and your opponents.
   - If you are the player controlling the ball, locate a teammate who is unguarded and closer to the other team's goal. Avoid dribbling the ball when you have the opportunity to pass the ball forward to a teammate.
   - If you are in control of the ball and are unguarded, try to dribble the ball forward to the opponent's goal.
   - If you have the ball and are guarded, pass the ball to any unguarded teammate.
   - If you don't have the ball, try to swim or to move to an open area in the offensive end of the pool. Swim away from the other team's players. Get into an area where you can receive a pass and score a goal.

2. Ask "OK, if you are playing defense, what are you trying to do?" Help the students to find the following strategies:
   - Be aware of where the ball is.
   - Be aware of where your teammates and opponents are.
   - Immediately and quickly swim or move back into your defensive end of the pool (the goal which you are protecting) and get between the goal and the offensive players.
   - Have each defensive player guard one of the offensive players remaining between that player and the goal to help prevent the offensive player from getting open for an easy shot.

3. When playing a game, talk about each of the roles and positions. Make sure each of the players gets a chance to play all the different positions.

4. Explain the following safety rules to the players:
   - Never run on the deck.
   - Always enter the water feetfirst.
   - Never punch or engage in dangerous play.
   - Take all goggles off before the balls enter the pool. (A ball hitting the face of a player wearing goggles could cause serious injury.)

- If a player needs corrective lenses, he or she may wear only safety-certified glasses.
- All players should wear proper caps with ear guards.
- Mouthpieces are recommended for all players.
- Never wear jewelry, wristbands, or watches.
- Warm-up, stretching, and cool-down periods should be a part of each practice and game.
- Trim your fingernails to prevent scratching.

Performance Criteria

The student should
→ be able to understand offensive and defensive strategies in wetball.

Objective: To play a game of wetball for 10 minutes

Materials Needed:
ball; four cones (use two cones for each goal); wetball caps with ear guards, one for each student

Discussion Guidelines for Instructors

1. Divide the class into two teams and have the students play a 10-minute wetball game in deep water.
2. Point out to students how they can improve their play in both offense and defensive roles.

Performance Criteria

The student should
→ be able to play in a game of wetball for 10 minutes.

Component 5: Rescue

Objective: To learn about hyperventilation

Discussion Guidelines for Instructors

1. Ask "What do you think hyperventilation is?" (Answer: Fast, deep breathing.)
2. Ask "How can hyperventilation occur?" (Answers: During periods of personal stress people may hyperventilate. Some people may try to hyperventilate purposely to be able to swim underwater a longer distance without taking a breath. Hyperventilating lowers the amount of carbon dioxide in the blood, and the level of carbon dioxide in the blood is what triggers the brain to initiate breathing.)
3. Ask "What are symptoms of hyperventilation?" (Answers: Dizziness, numbness, tingling in the hands or feet, shortness of breath, breathing rates higher than 40 breaths per minute.)
4. Ask "Why is it dangerous to hyperventilate before swimming?" (Answer: The oxygen level may drop to a point at which the swimmer blacks out before he or she feels the need to breathe. Drowning can result. This is why we limit the time and distance of underwater swimming and always swim with a buddy in a supervised area. To help prevent hyperventilation before swimming take two to three slow, deep breaths.)
5. Ask "What do you think you can do to help someone who is hyperventilating?" (Answers: Calm and reassure the person; encourage the person to take slow, deep breaths and hold them for a few seconds; don't have the person breathe into a paper bag.)

Performance Criteria

The student should
→ participate in the discussion and
→ understand the causes of hyperventilation and steps to remedy it.

porpoise

Objective: To carry a 10-pound object (diving brick or weight) 15 yards while swimming

Materials Needed:

10-pound diving bricks or other objects of similar weight, one for each student

Discussion Guidelines for Instructors

1. Ask students how they could carry a weight with them while they swim.

2. Give each student a 10-pound diving brick or something similar of the same weight. Ask them to try swimming different ways, keeping the top of the object out of the water.

Elementary backstroke with a diving brick

Performance Criteria

The student should

→ be able to swim 15 yards carrying a 10-pound object, keeping the top of it on the surface of the water.

Objective: To perform the approach-crawl stroke for 25 yards

Discussion Guidelines for Instructors

1. Ask "How could you swim and continuously watch an object? Let's see."

2. Say "To keep your eyes focused on an object, you should swim with your head up and minimize the movement of your head. Would it also help if you kicked harder? Why do you think so?" (Answer: With your head up, your feet drop lower in the water, and you are not as streamlined as you are when you are swimming with your face in.)

Approach crawl stroke

Performance Criteria

The student should

→ be able to perform the approach-crawl stroke for 25 yards.

porpoise

Objective: To perform a stride entry, swim the approach crawl to an object, and retrieve the object and return it to the side of the pool

Materials Needed: a kickboard or other floating object

Skill Description

The stride entry should be done only in water over seven feet deep and from a height of no more than three feet. To perform the stride entry, the student holds the arms out to the sides with the hands slightly above the shoulders. He or she leans forward, then steps out away from the edge. As the student's body enters the water, he or she forces the legs together using a scissors kick and brings the arms forward and down to slow the jump and to keep the head above water.

Discussion Guidelines for Instructors

1. Have students stand on the deck. Toss a kickboard or other floating object about 20 feet into the pool. Ask "How do you think you could get in the water quickly without taking your eyes off an object?" Let them try.

2. Have them try leaping into the water. Ask "Does your head stay above the water? How could you do this and keep your head above water? Is there something you can do with your arms that may help you keep your head above water?" Let them try a few times.

3. Once the students have gotten the idea of the stride entry, have them swim the approach crawl to the object, pick up the object, and bring it back to the starting point. They can swim the object back with whatever stroke they think they can use and get the object back.

Performance Criteria

The student should

→ be able to perform a stride entry,

→ be able to swim the approach crawl to the object, and

→ be able to retrieve the object and return it to the side of the pool.

Objective: To review the steps of rescue breathing

Materials Needed:

five cards, with a rescue breathing step on each one; five kickboards; a CPR manikin; a toy telephone

Discussion Guidelines for Instructors

1. Set up a row of kickboards on deck so that there's one kickboard per card. The cards should not be in any particular order. Put a manikin at the end of the row.

2. Assign one student to represent the EMS (emergency medical service) at the opposite end of the row from the manikin. Assign the other students to do the following:

   • Get the cards, unscramble them, and put them in the correct order.

   • Call the steps out.

   • Perform the rescue breathing steps on the manikin as they are called out.

   • Make the phone call to EMS on the toy phone.

3. After the call is made, the person designated as EMS picks up a kickboard as the step is called out and moves to the manikin (victim).

4. Discuss how, in a real emergency, a lot of things are going on. In such a situation, students would need to stay focused on their task until EMS arrives and takes over.

Performance Criteria

The student should

→ participate in the activity.

Club Format

When the Porpoise level is offered as a club, it can become a program that keeps swimmers in your program on an ongoing basis. It also can provide a source for future YMCA instructors or aquatic volunteers. It does this by giving swimmers who have successfully completed the Shark level a chance to develop their leadership skills, provide community service, and create and participate in challenging, exciting adventures. Whether participants are interested in kayaking, boating, synchronized swimming, wind surfing, water skiing, skin or scuba diving, search and rescue, or other water activities, the Porpoise Club can provide a tantalizing introduction to what may become lifelong pursuits.

Some of the activities that can be offered through the Porpoise Club already may be available in other YMCA programs. However, no other program for this age level offers the variety and scope of aquatic activities that the Porpoise Club does.

Program Format

Usually the club is formed at the beginning of a school year. It can be enlarged by adding new groups every four months or during school breaks. It starts with all members meeting together, but later the members divide into special interest groups that hold their own additional meetings.

To keep the program flexible and appealing, we recommend that participants initiate and lead the activities. They can begin by setting general value-focused "house rules" for meetings and activities (not rigid, formal rules and regulations). They then can set meeting days and times for both the group as a whole and, later, for subgroups.

Club meetings, which usually last about an hour, can be scheduled either prior to a weekly class or at a separate time. During the weekly class, participants learn new water skills or refine their strokes. You can use the activities described at the beginning of this chapter or add elements based on club members' interests.

Adult Leadership

Adult Porpoise Club leaders may be paid staff or volunteers. They should expect to serve as coaches and consultants, rather than instructors. Adult leaders should be mature, able to relate well to participants, and interested and skilled in aquatic activities. Other essential qualifications include honesty, reliability, and the ability to relate comfortably to parents and to the larger community. Leaders should be good role models and respect matters of confidentiality.

Program participants themselves may help recruit their own leaders. They may find their teachers, community leaders, and parents more than willing to take on this challenge.

Acting as a club leader differs from being an instructor. The club leader's role is to assist individual club members in reaching their potential and to help the club function effectively as a group. For the club to perform effectively, it must meet the following conditions:

→ Members possess a clear sense of the purpose and goals of the group.

→ Club members develop consistent but flexible operating procedures. A structure is needed, but not a rigid one.

→ Members share leadership. The club leader must encourage them to be aware of their duties and to take responsibility for them. When members feel responsible, they will say and do whatever is necessary to help the club move ahead. This creates a sense of belonging, a critical need of older children and teens.

→ Group members set aside sufficient time to select, plan, implement, and evaluate their activities and analyze their effectiveness as a group.

→ Group members make decisions efficiently and effectively and frequently can reach consensus.

→ The group makes good use of the skills, interests, and talents of all its members.

→ The group balances activities between meeting individual needs and group goals.

→ Members demonstrate a high degree of commitment to the group.

porpoise

→ Members have a high level of trust in each other, which encourages open communication.

→ The group is not dominated by its official leaders or by any other member or group of members.

If you are a leader, you can aid the group in reaching this level of effectiveness by helping members accept leadership roles and learn about responsibility. Give them the responsibility for planning and running activities. You are present just to oversee the program. Be a good role model, and guide and protect members when necessary. Also, since the program is under the direct supervision of the local YMCA, make sure that all club activities are in keeping with local YMCA policies.

To learn more about working with teen clubs, see the *YMCA Teen Leadership Manual* or take the Teen Leadership Director training course.

Recruitment

The core group of Porpoise Club members may be recruited from current class members in the Shark level of the Youth and Adult Aquatic Program. These members may then bring in classmates, friends, relatives, and others who have a comparable aquatic skill level.

Schedule an information night for parents and kids. This provides an opportunity for them to meet the program leadership and other participants, as well as answer questions about the program.

The club can attract members by stressing adventure, something most older children and teenagers find alluring. Participants are responsible for creating and implementing real adventures for themselves. Under the proper conditions and with appropriate leadership, they can safely enjoy activities and get a genuine sense of accomplishment and personal pride.

Club Development

In the first meeting, include a general overview of the club's purpose and goals. The meeting can be chaired by the aquatics director, an instructor, or a previously recruited adult volunteer. Whoever chairs the meeting should stress the following points about the Porpoise Club:

→ It offers those who are good swimmers and who are interested in aquatics an opportunity to develop their own program.

→ It gives participants a taste of a variety of aquatic activities so they can intelligently choose those they like best.

→ It allows participants to develop leadership skills.

→ It helps participants serve others while enjoying themselves.

→ It lets participants create real adventures of their own choosing.

→ It provides a healthy atmosphere and social opportunities.

→ It develops human potential—spirit, mind, and body.

After each participant has the opportunity to introduce and talk about himself or herself for a minute, start with a brainstorming session. Ask club members to call out any aquatic activities that come to mind, then list them. It doesn't matter if they do or don't like the suggestions; the idea is to generate a list of possibilities. (Possible activities are unlimited, but could include sailing, skin diving and snorkeling, SCUBA, competitive swimming, water polo, water skiing, and aquatic leadership and instruction.) When they have finished, display the list for everyone to see.

Give each participant a number of index cards. Ask the participants to write the name of each activity at the top of a card, one to a card. Next to the name, they should write one of the following words:

→ *Definitely*—This indicates that the person would very much like to pursue this activity.

→ *Curious*—This says that the person might want to learn more about the activity and participate in it.

→ *Maybe*—This shows that the person would watch this activity but not necessarily participate in it.

Participants should make copies of the cards for themselves, then hand in the originals. These cards should be treated as secret ballots. Participants should not be swayed by friends or neighbors, but rather give their own opinion.

From this survey, construct a list of activities in order of club members' preference. Also ask club members to sort their copies of the cards, prioritizing the activities by individual preference. Then form small common interest groups based on these preferences. Include no more than 12 people in a group. If more than one group wants to pursue the same activity, have them choose different aspects of the activity. For example, if two groups wanted to do synchronized swimming, one group could pursue the art form and the other group could try the competitive form.

At this point, club development proceeds in three phases: the initial organization phase, a sampler phase, and a subgroup and service phase.

Initial Organization Phase

This first phase takes about three weeks. During this time, club members carry out the following tasks:

→ Pinning down specific activities to pursue

→ Determining who wants to join which group

→ Choosing leaders and researchers within each group to gather information about specific activities in which the group is interested

→ Lining up speakers who are experts in the fields of special interest to make presentations

As individuals and groups take on topics to research and speakers to recruit, questions may arise. Bring these to the group for resolution.

Sampler Phase

This second phase takes about three months. During this time, club members do research, gather data, interview people, and contact community groups and organizations. The recruited speakers and presenters make their presentations, which may involve audiovisuals and field trips to observe and to try out different activities. Speakers might include the U.S. Coast Guard Auxiliary, boating club members, yacht club members, lifeguards, professional athletes, or experts from the YMCA.

Subgroup and Service Phase

This final phase also takes about three months. In this period, the club divides into smaller special interest groups that meet twice monthly (or more often if members want to). The club then meets as a whole once a month to plan joint activities, social events, outreach programs, and volunteer efforts, as well as to take care of business matters.

During this phase each club member should be able to get a good feel for at least three or four activities. Some members may choose to pursue only one or two in depth.

Service projects also are added during this phase. Possibilities are endless, but here are some common ones:

→ Helping swim instructors with classes at lower Youth and Adult Aquatic Program levels

→ Working in the pool with special population children

→ Greeting families on the first day of a session to direct them to the pool and classes, hand out swim information, and answer basic questions about the program and facility

→ Helping with swim registration

→ Running fundraisers for World Service and the club such as breakfasts, pasta dinners, bingo games, or ice cream socials

→ Cleaning up the area around the outdoor pool just before summer opening

→ Holding a swim meet with a YMCA in another country by faxing event results to each other

→ Attending water shows with groups of senior adults or small children

→ Creating a slide show or videotape, if equipment is available, and going on lecture tours of schools, community organizations, and local business groups

Activities such as these may act as a springboard to participation in a Leader's Club or other volunteer opportunities.

By this phase, the main club elements should be in place. A sample schedule might look like this:

→ Weekly 45-minute water class

→ Every other week (or more) subgroup meetings

→ Monthly club meeting

→ Volunteer projects

porpoise

Social Activities

Some Porpoise Club members may wish to choose colors, emblems, club sweat bands, or other ways to identify themselves. All will want to make social events and activities an intrinsic part of the club. Members should decide on their own activities and should be responsible for planning, implementation, and follow-up. Social activities should be once a month or so throughout the school year for the entire group. At the monthly meetings the club can vote on and designate committees and individuals to carry out different aspects of the activities. In this way subgroups can stay involved with each other.

Some possible activities include these:

→ Peer-group skills performance in areas such as competitive diving, skin diving, synchronized swimming, and rescue

→ Family nights, where club members perform or families and members free swim

→ Outings to see water shows or to windsurf or boat

Social activities also can be used as recruitment activities for new members and adult leaders.

Recognition

Many successful clubs use a point system to recognize members for their level of involvement. The aim of the system is not to foster competition but rather to provide standards by which a club member can measure involvement. One system awards one or more points for each of the following actions:

→ Attending club meetings

→ Participating in community service projects or volunteer hours

→ Participating in fundraising events

→ Participating in training events

→ Participating in multi-club events

→ Writing an article for the club newsletter

→ Serving on a committee

→ Assuming an official leadership position

→ Meeting deadlines for turning in fees or forms

→ Paying dues on time

→ Serving as a "big brother" or "big sister" to a new member

→ Recruiting new members

Once you designate the number of points per activity, you then can determine a maximum number of possible points and decide the range of points needed for each level of recognition. Here is one example:

→ 0–20 points = not recognized

→ 21–40 points = a certificate

→ 41–60 points = a T-shirt or pin

→ 61–80 points = a plaque or trophy

Traditionally recognition is presented at the end of the year, but it can be done on a quarterly or monthly basis as well.

Summary

Porpoise

Summary of Performance Criteria

Component 1: Personal Safety

- Tread water for two minutes while holding a diving brick.
- Enter and exit a boat from deep water.
- Learn about inflating clothes and disrobing in the water.

Component 2: Personal Growth

- Participate in discussion about the role of being a leader and reaching personal goals.
- Participate in the leader/follower activity and accept the role of being a leader or a follower.
- Observe and report on examples of behavior that does and doesn't reflect the core values, and suggest ways to personally model and reinforce behaviors that do reflect the core values.
- Participate in discussion about the components of fitness, participate in a group in developing an activity or game, and understand the four components of fitness.

Component 3: Stroke Development

- Participate in the activity of finding ways to increase the speed of strokes.
- Swim a 200-yard individual medley: butterfly, backstroke, breaststroke, and front crawl with starts and turns.
- Perform the double-trudgen crawl stroke for 50 yards.

Component 4: Water Games and Sports

- Participate in a small group to develop a synchronized swimming routine and perform it to music in front of others.
- Understand offensive and defensive strategies in wetball.
- Play in a game of wetball for 10 minutes.

Component 5: Rescue

- Participate in the discussion of hyperventilation and understand its causes and steps to remedy it.
- Swim 15 yards carrying a 10-pound object, keeping the top of it on the surface of the water.
- Swim with eyes up and forward throughout the length of the swim.
- Perform a stride entry, swim the approach crawl to an object, and retrieve the object and return it to the side of the pool.
- Participate in an activity reviewing the steps of rescue breathing.

Drills for Improving Strokes and Building Fitness

To improve their strokes, students need to change one or more of the parts of their strokes, such as the arm stroke, leg kick, breathing, or coordination and timing patterns.

Changes in these parts can lead to increased speed, improved endurance, or enhanced stroke efficiency.

These variables can be measured by

- → observation,
- → timing with a stopwatch or pace clock over a 25-, 50-, or 100-yard distance for speed,
- → counting the number of lengths swum continuously without stopping (for endurance), or
- → counting the number of strokes performed per distance (for resting strokes) or the number of stroke cycles divided by the speed (for competitive strokes) for efficiency.

Changes in speed, endurance, and efficiency don't just happen automatically if students swim more laps. Students need guidance from you or another observer who knows what to look for in their strokes. (See chapter 7 of *Teaching Swimming Fundamentals* for stroke observation sheets for each of the strokes.) They also need to perform the appropriate stroke drills to improve those parts of their stroke that are not efficient. Such drills typically modify one or more aspects of a stroke in order to get the swimmer to emphasize a particular part of the stroke pattern. When used regularly, drills can substantially improve students' strokes.

After students have had the opportunity to explore the strokes in the beginning levels and have developed the basic concepts of the strokes, you can offer them a variety of drills to refine their strokes based on their particular problems. These drills can be used across either the width or the length of the pool. Many drills are designed so the students correct themselves by overcompensating for the improper technique they are using. Some of the drills include the use of IFDs such as kickboards, pull buoys, or arm paddles.

This appendix includes drills and suggested activities for series swims and the following strokes: the front crawl stroke, back crawl stroke, breaststroke, butterfly stroke, sidestroke, and elementary backstroke. These are just a few of the many possible drills and activities. Look at books and videos on swimming to find additional ones, or make them up on your own.

Series Swims

To build swimmers' endurance and add variety to series swims, try these variations for upper levels:

→ Swimming continuously

→ Resting one minute between lengths or laps at first, then reducing the resting period as endurance grows

→ Swimming one length fast and the next length slow or combinations of fast and slow lengths (1 fast, 2 slow; 2 fast, 1 slow)

Front Crawl Drills

The following drills help students improve their arm stroke, kick, breathing, and combinations of these elements.

Arm Stroke

These drills are performed with a kick, unless otherwise noted.

→ Human stroke: This is a "long pull" version of the dog paddle in which the arm action alternates. Emphasize either the **S** pull or "sweep out in the catch, sweep in for the midpull, and accelerate the sweep out for the finish." Perform arm recovery underwater, with the hands and arms streamlined to minimize drag. Ideally, keep the face in the water, using rotary breathing, but to begin, the face can stay out of the water.

→ Human stroke sculling drill: Keeping the arms entirely in the water, with palms facing downward and fingers pointing down, scull both arms symmetrically in a "figure 8" or "waxing the car" action. This will make you move yourself forward without pulling backward.

→ One-arm crawl: Swim the crawl recovering the arm out of the water, but use only one arm per length. Fully extend the remaining arm ahead of the body. Emphasize the **S** pull and the "sweep out, sweep in, accelerated sweep out" pattern with one arm at a time.

→ One-arm crawl holding board: Same as the one-arm crawl except the arm that is not pulling holds on to a kickboard. This helps if you have trouble keeping the non-pulling arm at the side. Be careful to maintain trunk roll as a natural part of the pull.

→ Fist swim: Alternate swimming lengths with hands in fists and hands open.

→ Closed fist: This drill keeps you from feeling the water on your hand, forcing you to focus on the "feel" of the entire arm. Closing the fist cuts the hand off from the sensations of the water.

  Closing the fist can be combined with most of the other arm stroke drills. Emphasize the "sweep out, sweep in, sweep out" of the **S** pull and the bent-arm pull and the "power" of the hand.

→ Human stroke with a high elbow recovery: This is similar to the human stroke drill, except that you recover with the elbow and upper arm rising above the surface while the hand and wrist stay in the water.

→ Pull buoy swim: Place a foam pull buoy between your thighs and swim the crawl stroke (or any of the other preceding drills). The pull buoy provides additional buoyancy that can minimize kick action while emphasizing arm action. It's especially good for swimmers who can't float or who have relatively weak flutter kicks that cause their bodies to incline.

→ Hand paddle swim: This is swimming wearing hand paddles. The paddles add significant surface area, and thus drag-lift forces, to the hands. It's much like wearing leg weights to run, with the weights producing an overload. Use paddles of an appropriate size for short periods of time, as hand paddle use can cause shoulder injuries.

  The hand paddles should be slightly bigger than your hand. Swim the crawl stroke or any of the drills for distances between 25 and 200 yards. If the hand paddle pulls away from your hand at any time during the pull, it may indicate a point where you are creating drag forces that are impeding your forward progress. You can use additional stroke drills to correct the drag detected using the paddles.

→ Fins: Fins add propulsive force to your feet. This gives you more time to work on improving your arm stroke and speeds you up significantly.

→ No splash: Try to have your hand enter the water without making a splash.

→ Throw away: Pretend you have a weight in your hand and that, after you complete your pull, you are throwing the weight out of the water.

→ Shoulder roll, breathe both sides: Each time the arm comes out on each side, breathe. Turn your head to each side and look at your elbow. This emphasizes the feeling of slicing through the water and body "balance" while in the 45° position.

→ Hand touch: Extend both arms forward with locked elbows. Start stroking, but keep one arm extended until the other arm has stroked and touched the hand of the extended arm. Then the extended arm strokes and the stroking arm extends forward. The stroke hesitates, as you are stroking with one arm.

   Watch the hand on the extended arm as you stroke (you can see 90 percent of it). Stroke with an **S** pull. Emphasize the pull and extending the arm straight to touch the other hand.

   • Rub ears off: Lift your arms and elbows so your shoulders graze your ears. This emphasizes the shoulder roll and high elbows and allows you to see the extension of your arm straight forward, like sighting down a rifle barrel. Look at the arm and hand placement.

   • Right and left arm breathers: Extend the left arm with a locked elbow and stroke with the right arm. Breathe on every stroke of the right arm. Then reverse, with the right arm extended and the left arm stroking. This is a good drill for timing the breathing with the arm stroke. It also helps in learning alternate breathing, in which you breathe every three strokes. Alternate breathing sometimes helps smooth out strokes that are choppy.

   • Chicken wing swim: Swim short distances with the thumbs tucked into the arm pits so the upper body is propelled by the "wings" created by the forearms and upper arms bent at the elbows. The hand must enter the water first. Fingertips should enter the water in a "knifing" fashion, like a knife stabbing soft butter. The hand does not "slap" the water. Keep the arm in a **V** shape. The feeling of having your elbows bent severely is the same feeling you want to have during arm recovery.

   This drill is a good one for correcting a persistent windmill-type stroke, with the hand over the elbow. If this is a problem, swim close to the wall. You will either bend the elbow or hit the hand on the wall.

→ Thumb touch: As you stroke, touch your thumbs to your thighs before starting your overarm recovery.

→ Fingertip drag: Drag your fingertips when your arm recovers. This insures a good elbow bend.

→ Chicken drag: Combine the fingertip drag and the chicken wing actions.

→ Variations on arm propulsion: Use pull buoys or fins so you can pay more attention to arm recovery. Keep your arms bent (flexed) at the elbows as much as you and your stroke style permit.

→ Toaster: Do this to better understand the arm stroke. Pretend you are putting a piece of bread in one hand. Place it into the toaster, spread the butter, and then lift the elbow as it pops out of the toaster. Do it again.

→ Catch-up/overlap stroke: This drill is like the one-arm crawl except that the arm actions alternate. Keep the non-pulling arm fully extended ahead while the other arm completes its power and recovery phases and catches up to the second arm in the front glide position. Then the second arm pulls and recovers while the first arm remains extended.

   Emphasize the kick and proper arm technique. Hold a small wooden stick in front to ensure good entry and extension. Switch the stick from one hand to the other as the arms rotate.

→ Efficiency: Try to decrease the number of strokes you need per length or width or the number of stroke cycles divided by the speed.

Kick

These drills all use the flutter kick.

→ Front flutter kick, arms extended forward, head up: Swimming like this increases leg resistance, so you have to use more power to propel yourself. (This also points out Newton's law of action and reaction.) When your head is up, your hips and legs drop, making it harder to move forward.

→ Front flutter kick, arms extended forward, head down: Swim with your head down, ears between your arms. This points out the difference between swimming with your head up or down. (This again points out Newton's law of action and reaction and the importance of streamlining and alignment.)

→ Front flutter kick with "rubber feet": Pretend that your foot is cut off above the ankle and replaced with a rubber foot. This emphasizes that the kick comes from the hips, thighs, and lower back and that feet should be relaxed.

→ Front flutter kick, heels out of water only: As you kick, think about only the heel coming out of the water, not the toes.

→ Front flutter kick on side: With one arm extended, flutter kick on your side.

→ Front flutter kick, six-kick drill: Have one arm extended and one arm back to the side. Give six kicks each stroke to turn your body a quarter turn (about 45°) in order to produce a "slicing" effect through the water. It gives you a feel for how the shoulders should be rolled. You can try switching arm positions halfway across.

→ 25 kick, 25 swim, 25 kick: With a kickboard, flutter kick 25 yards. Leave the board by the side of the pool, turn, and swim 50 yards of a full crawl stroke. Return to the side where you left the kickboard, pick up the kickboard, and flutter kick back to the starting point. This can also be done using a pull buoy and/or hand paddles during the swim.

→ Front flutter kick with fins: The added force may help improve kick efficiency, ankle flexibility, and coordination.

→ Kick variations: Try some of the following:

a. Kick with your head down, using a kickboard, breathing every six kicks.

b. Kick with your head down (no kickboard), arms extended and wrists crossed and locked.

c. Kick alternating sides; do 12 kicks on one side with your bottom arm out, then pull and change sides.

d. Kick with your hands behind your neck and your chin on the surface.

e. Kick with your arms by your sides. Alternate the side on which you breathe every six kicks.

f. Kick underwater.

Breathing

→ Shipping/spitting water: If you have a great deal of difficulty getting a breath while stroking, practice shipping and spitting water. Shipping is taking water into your mouth without swallowing it or choking. Essentially you breathe "over" the water, keeping it under the tongue and breathing gently. Spitting is taking pool water into the mouth and spitting it out again without choking or swallowing it.

→ Single-stroke cycle swim: Perform only one complete stroke cycle with rotary breathing, then stop and start over. Emphasize exhaling prior to breathing.

→ Bobbing/human stroke drill in shallow water: Submerge, push off the bottom, and exhale as you do the human stroke to the surface. Get a quick breath at the surface and submerge again. Be sure to get a breath of air each time you come up above surface, but only a quick one.

→ Kicking and breathing: Using a kickboard while face down, flutter kick with your face submerged. Breathe to the side by rotating your head, not lifting it. Simulate stroking by moving the breathing-side arm through the water prior to taking the breath. Keep half your face in the water.

→ Human stroke with breathing: Do the human stroke and use side rotary breathing, exhaling underwater.

→ One-arm swim with kickboard: Forcefully exhale during each arm pull toward the breathing side. Attempt to have only your mouth break the surface of the water for the inhalation.

→ Alternate side breathing (for intermediate and advanced swimmers): Swim one width or length breathing on the right side and the next one on the left. It will help you focus on the feel and timing of breathing on both sides.

Progressive Drills

Use one or two (or more, depending on the students' level) of these drills for each width or length to help improve their strokes. Using different drills helps them keep focused. Assign drills to students based on their needs. For example:

→ One width/length each of the chicken wing, chicken drag, finger drag, and normal swimming

→ One width/length each of a kick only, pull only right arm, pull only left arm, and normal swimming

→ One width/length each of a pull only right arm, pull only left arm, arms stretched out front and kick, and normal swimming

→ One width/length each of a kick, pull only right arm, pull only left arm, and normal swimming

Back Crawl Drills

These drills work on the arm stroke, kick, body position, and combinations of these.

Arm Stroke

→ Back finning: On your back, flutter kick and vigorously "fin" with your arms by extending them from the elbow.

→ Back sculling: On your back, move through the water by sculling (making figure 8 movements) with your hands at your side near your hips. Then try sculling with your hands extended over your head.

→ One-arm back crawl: Swim the back crawl with one arm while holding the other arm at your side. As your pulling arm begins to pull, the opposite shoulder should "pop" out of the water from the normal roll of your body. Your body should be tilted or rolled a quarter roll. The head remains in a fixed or steady position. Emphasize good hand entry, an elbow bend, and a strong kick. Alternate the arm used for each width or length. This develops the

shoulder roll, a high shoulder position on the recovery, and a streamlined position.

→ Right arm/left arm drills: Same as the one-arm back crawl, except arms alternate each stroke. It develops the shoulder roll and allows you to concentrate on arm movement.

→ Catch up/overlap back crawl: Keep one arm extended straight ahead of the body while the other arm completes its power and recovery phases and catches up to the second arm. Then the second arm pulls while the first arm remains extended.

→ Hand paddle back crawl: This is swimming wearing hand paddles. The paddles add significant surface area, and thus drag-lift forces, to the hands. It's much like wearing leg weights to run, with the weights producing an overload. Use paddles of an appropriate size for short periods of time, as hand paddle use can cause shoulder injuries.

The hand paddles should be slightly bigger than your hand. Swim the back crawl stroke or any of the drills for distances between 25 and 200 yards. If the hand paddle pulls away from your hand at any time during the pull, it may indicate a point where you are creating drag forces that are impeding your forward progress. You can use additional stroke drills to correct the drag detected using the paddles.

→ Pull buoy: Swim while holding a pull buoy between your legs. This allows you to concentrate on your arm stroke.

→ Kickboard: Swim while holding a kickboard between your thighs and crossing your ankles. This will increase your resistance, making you have to use stronger arm movements.

→ Arms-only swim: Swim using your arms only, not your legs.

→ Shoulder roll: Swim, concentrating on making sure the shoulder leads the overarm recovery.

→ Pinky first: Swim, concentrating on making sure the pinky finger enters the water first.

→ Double arm: Swim using a flutter or dolphin kick. Bend the elbows and work on shoulder flexibility.

→ Half arm: Start your stroke cycle with your thumb up, then stop your arm at the midpoint and return it to the side. Alternate arms.

→ Backstroke shoulder roll: Roll the shoulder and elbow during six kicks on one side, then roll to the other side and do six more.

→ Slide-push drill, no kick: Use both arms simultaneously on just the push phase of the stroke. The movement should be similar to the arm movement in the elementary backstroke, except the arms do not come back any farther than the chest.

→ Double-arm recovery: Move both arms up and over on the vertical recovery. Notice the hand entry position.

→ Rub ears off: As your arms come up and over in the overwater recovery, the shoulders and upper arms brush (rub) against your ears. This helps you develop the stretch of your arm coming back entering the water.

Kick

These are all done with a flutter kick.

→ Kicking with a kickboard: Try one or more of the following body positions while kicking with a kickboard:

  a. Hold the kickboard across the chest.

  b. Hold the kickboard with arms overhead, squeezing your ears with your arms.

  c. Hold the kickboard under the head like a pillow.

→ Kick variations: Try some of the following:

  a. Kick with your arms to your sides, toes to the surface.

  b. Kick with your hands on your thighs and look at the splash of your feet.

  c. Kick wearing fins for any of the kicking or arm drills (develops streamlining, strengthens the legs, and develops a feel for the kick).

→ Kicking while one-arm swimming: Swim with one arm (see one-arm back crawl), but emphasize kicking extra.

→ Side flutter kick: Flutter kick either with a kickboard or lying on one side. If you find yourself moving one way or another, your kick is not symmetrical. Try both sides.

→ Back flutter kick, arms at side: Imagine you have rubber feet as you kick. This helps with body position and ankle looseness.

→ Back flutter kick, one arm back, one arm at side: Swimming like this helps you develop a feel for your body and arm position and for streamlining your body as you move through the water. You can also try this with both arms back.

→ Back flutter kick, arms stretched, hands clasped: Watch as your instructor demonstrates this position on the deck. This stretches the body. If he or she then lowers the hands to the head, you can see the body muscles relax. This causes the hips to drop to a sitting position and deepens the kick.

  Try swimming with arms stretched and hands clasped with palms toward each other. Elbows should be locked and the body stretched. This position is very important, as it does three things:

  a. It holds your head in a comfortable position, where you won't get water over your head. The water usually hits your forehead at approximately a 45° angle.

  b. It arches your back, lifting your tummy and legs.

  c. It keeps your toes pointed so you can make the water "boil" at the surface.

→ Six-kick drill, one arm back, one arm at side: Extend one arm and keep one arm at the side. Kick six times, then pull and switch arms. Develop a cyclic rhythm and timing.

Body Position

→ Superman: Clasp your arms overhead and kick, trying to keep your hips at the surface. This helps streamline the body.

→ Body roll: With your arms at your sides, roll to the left side and kick 12 times. Stroke, then roll to the right and kick 12 times. Continue alternating to the end of the width or length. Then try it again, kicking 6 times on each side.

→ Quarter drill: Place a quarter on your forehead and swim the length of the pool without letting the quarter fall off.

Progressive Drills

Use one or two (or more, depending on the students' level) of these drills for each width or length to help improve their strokes. Using different drills helps them keep focused. Assign drills to students based on their needs. For example:

- → One width/length each of one left arm, one right arm, arms clasped overhead and kick, and a normal stroke
- → One width/length normal stroke, arms only, and legs only
- → One width/length side flutter left, side flutter right, normal stroke, and normal stroke

Breaststroke Drills

The following drills cover arm stroke, kick, breathing, coordination, and combinations of them.

Arm Stroke

- → Fins: Wearing fins, do the dolphin kick and use the breaststroke arm stroke.
- → Pulling drill: Pull three times with the right arm, three with the left arm, then three alternating arms.
- → Arm position: Place a water log, inner tube, or mat around your chest, under your armpits. Pull only with your head up. The water log or other flotation device prevents your pull from moving behind the shoulders. It also strengthens your arms.
- → Arm pull: Start with small wrist sculls and build gradually to a full-sized arm pull. Alternate pulling with a straight arm and a bent arm.
- → Arms extended, "roll" wrists: This develops the timing and thrust of your kick. Pull to your elbow, then pull to your chin. When you pull, reach up and over, then pull down strongly.
- → Arm pull-downs: Extend both arms and pull straight down and back, perpendicular to your shoulders. Then retract the arms up and extend them straight forward again. This develops power in your pull and helps the timing of your breathing if you breathe late.
- → "No kick" pulls: Swim wearing paddles for the hands and/or a small tube, pull buoy, or kickboard between the thighs. Do not

kick. Be aware of the push, or "press," against the water. This develops your feel for the pull, helps streamline it, and improves the lift of your elbows.

- → Arm stroke—breaststroke: Have students lie on the deck with chest over the side. Have them try the arm pull in the water. The side of the pool will limit their arm pull. This will help sensitize students to the idea that the pull is a short pull.
- → Bronco busting kickboard riding: Have swimmers sit on a kickboard or water log. Have them use the breaststroke arm motion to move. Legs should not be used. Reinforce with swimmers that they should see their hands at all times.

Instructor Note: *The student's head should not move up or down and the forehead should be dropped slightly. The student should develop a power pull that will "pull for air," so that he or she lifts the shoulders on the pull just enough to get a breath of air. On the glide, the water should hit the student's forehead; on the pull, the water should hit just under the chin.*

- → One-arm breaststroke pull: Swim with one arm, either with a pull buoy between the legs or using a dolphin or normal breaststroke kick.
- → Pull-out drill: Swim using two underwater pulls.
- → Arm variations: Try some of the following:
  - a. Breaststroke pull keeping the head up, with or without a pull buoy between the legs.
  - b. Breaststroke using a catch-up arm stroke.
  - c. Breaststroke with three kicks and one pull. Breathe at the right time throughout the drill.

Kick

- → Push kick: Do the breaststroke kick holding on to the wall. Your instructor will stand behind you and use his or her hands on the soles of your feet. You should push off the instructor's hands, which will provide resistance for an effective kick and develop your feel for pushing water with the feet.
- → Chin kick: Perform the breaststroke kick while keeping the chin at the surface of the water.

→ Finger hit: Hold your hands clasped in the small of your back so your heels hit your fingertips on the kick recovery. Take a breath with every kick at the proper time. Your heels should touch your fingertips to emphasize flexing the foot up and pushing the water back with the soles of your feet.

→ Treading: Tread water using the breaststroke kick. Keep your hands out of the water or on your head. Bob up for air using the breaststroke kick for a minute, rest, then bob up again. This conditions your legs and develops their thrust. It also gives you a feel for pushing water with the feet.

→ Breaststroke kick on kickboard: Try one or more of the following:

a. Kick with your face in the water. Lift your chin to breathe a short time after the kick is completed. This promotes streamlining the body and general conditioning.

b. Kick with the head up looking straight ahead, which gives you more power, better body position, and general conditioning.

c. Kick with the head down and arms extended. Breathe at the same point in the stroke that you would if you were swimming.

d. Hold the board at a right angle to the bottom of the pool to create drag, which you must overcome.

→ Breaststroke kick: To help swimmers learn the feel of the kick and the dorsiflexion of the foot, have swimmers lie on top of a kickboard at the edge of the pool. Swimmers will move clockwise around the pool wall. They will hold onto the gutter with one hand and with their foot against the wall. All toes should be against the wall. They should push with their foot against the wall. Then have them try the other side. Remind students this is a push, not a kick. Then have students move away from the wall and pretend that they are swimming in a very narrow pool. They should try to use both imaginary walls to push themselves forward.

→ Rotary (eggbeater) kick: Do the rotary kick using a kickboard.

→ Breaststroke kick, arms extended: Try one or more of the following:

a. Extend the arms with wrists crossed and keep the chin at the surface.

b. Extend the arms with wrists crossed. Keep face in the water and streamline the body.

c. Keep head up. This drops your hips, which forces you to kick harder and promotes general conditioning and leg power.

d. Extend the arms and keep the hands up (develops more power in the kick).

→ Breaststroke kick, arms behind back: Clasp your hands and rest on hips.

→ Explode kick: Extend the arms forward (hand over hand, wrists and elbows in), lift your head, and breathe. Your hands may drop or press downward while you breathe, then return to the surface. Drop your head and kick with an "explosive thrust," driving your streamlined body forward. Emphasize the "whip" of the legs coming back and the "squeeze" of the legs and feet as they come together. This drill develops an awareness of power and streamlining in your stroke, strengthens the stroke, and gives you a better feel for it.

→ Explode, kick, glide: Kick explosively, then glide for a count of four with arms extended forward (hand over hand, wrists and elbows in). Hold the shoulders tight against the jaw. This helps develop a feel for the glide and body streamlining.

Breathing

→ Build up glide: Start with a long glide, then reduce the length of the glide with each stroke.

→ Reducing breaths: Have the students breathe and kick half the length of the pool, getting a breath, initially, every fourth kick, then every third, every second, and, finally, each kick.

Coordination

→ Stroke rhythm: Pull, kick, and glide, grabbing your thumb and holding it for a count of 1, 2, 3, 4. After doing this for one width or length, then try doing it for a count of 1, 2, 3; for a count of 1, 2; and finally, for a count of 1. This helps develop the thrust of the stroke for exploding into the glide, and holding the glide helps develop the rhythm of the stroke.

Try to stay streamlined during the glide. Bring the legs together and keep the arms fully extended. The elbows should be in and the shoulders tight into the jaws.

→ Bowl-of-frosting arm pull: This technique helps students achieve a proper arm pull. Say "Imagine you have a big bowl of chocolate frosting in front of you. Lean forward and place your hands in the bowl, up to your elbows. Scrape the chocolate off the sides of the bowl, lick your hands, and stretch out. Remember to 'lick and kick' for proper stroke coordination."

Progressive Drills

Use one or two (or more, depending on the students' level) of these drills for each width or length to help improve their strokes. Using different drills helps them keep focused. Assign drills to students based on their needs. For example:

→ One width/length each of the kick only, pull with dolphin kick, and normal stroke

→ One width/length each of right arm only, left arm only, and normal stroke

→ One width/length each of the kick only, pull with dolphin kick, catch-up arm stroke, and normal stroke

Butterfly Drills

The drills in this section address arm stroke, kick, coordination, and combinations of those elements.

Arm Stroke

→ One-arm swim: Swim using only one arm, with the other arm extended. Alternate the arm used for the pull, and don't breathe with the stroke. This helps develop the timing of the arms and legs. Also try a double one-arm swim, in which you take two right arm strokes with the left arm extended, then two left arm strokes with the right hand extended.

→ One-arm swim with kickboard: Same as the one-arm swim except the arm that is not pulling holds on to a kickboard.

→ Closed fist: Alternate between swimming one width or length with hands open and one with hands in fists.

→ Fins or hand paddles: Swim the butterfly wearing fins or hand paddles.

→ Build up: Pull three times with the right arm, then three times with the left, and finish with a complete stroke. Use the normal kick.

→ Standing butterfly drill: Perform this bending over in shallow

water. Alternate using the right and left arm to do the butterfly arm stroke. Isolate each arm and correct the entry of the hand and arm. In correct entry, the thumbs should drop in first, almost lining up with the eyeballs. Hands should then press out, squeeze in, then press out again (breathe at this time). Then the arms move out over the water to the side and around. Thumbs drop in again to complete recovery.

→ Walking butterfly drill: Perform this bending over in shallow water. Then try swimming a few strokes, and stop. This lengthens your stroke and gives you the feeling of moving.

→ Arms-only swim: Swim using only the arms. For the legs, hold a pull buoy between the legs, or an innertube (with little air) or rubber band around ankles for resistance, or drag the legs. This gives you more time to concentrate on arm movements.

→ Butterfly catch-up drill: Swim the butterfly using a catch-up arm stroke.

→ Arm variations: Try some of the following:

   a. Butterfly kick with an underwater pull.

   b. Off the wall, do several underwater butterfly pullouts in a row.

   c. Butterfly swim as usual, but pause at the end of each stroke (helps develop an explosive finish).

Kick

→ Kick stretched out: Watch the instructor demonstrate the correct butterfly (dolphin) kick, which is similar to the flutter kick except both legs are together. Then try the kick with your hands stretched out in front. Emphasize that the waving motion of the kick starts from the shoulders and goes through the hips, legs, and feet.

Instructor Note: Students can wear flotation belts when you teach this kick.

→ Butterfly kick on side: Do six kicks on one side, then pull with the lead arm and do six kicks on the other side.

→ Kick on surface: Kick on the surface with your head down and arms extended. This emphasizes swimming the butterfly with the head down. It gives you a feel for streamlining, alignment, and performing the butterfly. Also try kicking on the surface with the head up and arms extended to experience the difference (it's more difficult).

→ Right-leg butterfly kick: Extend the arms and kick with the right leg only. This improves your feel for the kick and isolates the action of the right leg. It may show that one leg is weaker than the other. Do the same with the left leg.

→ Kick-kick-stop: Try this first with a kickboard, then without one. Extend your arms and kick on the beat that the instructor gives you.

Instructor Note: *Set a cadence that's slightly fast so the swimmer doesn't rest on "stop." Repeat it a few times before the swimmer starts so he or she can get the rhythm. This drill should start the development of a two-beat kick and good kick timing. (See also the kick-pull-kick-stop drill under Coordination.)*

→ Arms behind the back: Do any of the kick drills that are to be done with extended arms with the arms behind the back instead. Keep kicking while breathing. Put rubber bands on the ankles and above the knees. This develops more body movement in the kick.

→ Fins: Try doing any of the previous drills with swim fins.

→ Kicking game: Swim through a plastic hoop doing the butterfly kick.

Instructor Note: *Exercise care when you use underwater drills, as students will not be able to see where they are going as easily as they can on the surface.*

→ Kick the width of the pool underwater: Try one or more of the following:

a. Kick underwater with hands at sides (develops feel for propulsion and leg and body movements).

b. Kick underwater with arms extended forward (develops feel for leg and body movements while arms are extended).

→ Kick using a kickboard: Try one or more of the following:

a. Hold the kickboard to the chest, push away from the wall, and undulate on your back.

b. Kick with the head up.

c. Kick with the head up and elbows locked straight (conditions, gives a feel for body undulation, emphasizes the rhythm of the kick, improves power on second kick).

d. Kick with the head down and face in water.

e. Kick with the head down and breathe every two kicks as when swimming.

f. Put both hands about a third of the way up the kickboard and allow the head to raise up for a breath on one kick and lower for the other.

→ Kick variations: Try some of the following:

a. Kick while holding on to the pool gutter with one hand and pressing the other hand against the wall a foot or two lower.

b. Dolphin kick on the back.

c. Dolphin kick on the back with the hands extended over the head.

d. Kick underwater with arms extended and a streamlined body.

e. Dolphin kick on the side and alternate sides.

f. Dolphin kick on the side, alternating between a small and a large kick.

g. Butterfly kick with arms extended and the face in the water.

h. Butterfly kick with the arms trailing behind the back and the face in the water (develops a continuous kick and the feel of starting the kick from the head).

i. Butterfly kick with the arms trailing behind the back and the face in the water.

j. Lift the chin to breathe every fourth kick, and continue the kick while breathing.

k. Butterfly kick with the arms at the sides. On the first kick, have the chin touching the chest; raise it on the second kick.

Coordination

→ Push off: Push off the bottom, take one stroke of the butterfly, then return to the push-off position.

→ Kick-pull-kick-stop drill: Start in a layout position. Do one kick, then start a keyhole pull. As the hands start to press past the tummy, the second kick takes place. The legs "wham" down as the hands finish the press. The hands and arms then retract close to the body and the hands extend out, similar to the breaststroke recovery (this is the stop portion). Start over again. This drill develops the double kick with one-arm pull.

After you perfect this drill, go short distances with the arms coming out of the water. Emphasize the double kick.

→ Breathing: Stand bent over in shallow water. Lift the chin to breathe as the arms press back at the hips. Use alternating left and right arm stroking to practice matching the breathing position to the stroke. Then work on breathing with the mouth just out of the water, rather than lifting the chin up. Develop a strong press out to breathe.

→ One-arm pull: Swim the butterfly using one arm to pull and one arm extended, with side breathing. This helps develop the timing for breathing. Alternate the arm used for the pull.

→ Kick-pull (for air)-kick: The "stop" portion of this drill has been dropped, as there is not a true stop in this drill. Work on getting the mouth just out of the water—"breasting over the water"—rather than lifting the head back. Breasting can be done with a slight tilting of the head to the side for easier shoulder movement.

→ Coordination variations: Try some of the following:

  a. Practice doing the flying porpoise to help get the rhythm again.

  b. Practice doing the stroke slowly and emphasize the rhythm of the stroke.

  c. Practice breathing every other stroke.

  d. Practice breathing every two strokes.

  e. Butterfly kick with an underwater pull.

  f. Off the wall, do several underwater butterfly pullouts in a row.

  g. Swim the butterfly as usual, but pause at the end of the stroke (this helps develop an explosive finish).

  h. Swim the butterfly with the hands touching in front to lengthen and streamline the stroke.

Progressive Drills

Use one or two (or more, depending on the students' level) of these drills for each width or length to help improve their strokes. Using different drills helps them keep focused. Assign drills to students based on their needs. For example:

→ One width/length each of the kick, pull with right arm, pull with left arm, and normal stroke

→ One width/length each of the normal stroke, arms only, legs only, and normal stroke

→ One width/length each of the normal stroke with fins, arms only, legs only, and normal stroke

→ One width/length each of the dolphin kick (with or without fins), dolphin kick on the right side, dolphin kick on the left side, dolphin kick on the back, and dolphin kick on the front

→ One width/length using two right arm strokes only, with the left arm extended, then two left arm strokes only, with the right arm extended

Sidestroke Drills

The drills in this section address arm stroke, kick, and coordination.

Arm Stroke

→ Sculling/treading water: Practice the flutter back scull and treading water using a scissors kick, designating which foot is to go forward.

→ Pull buoy: Watch the instructor perform the arm stroke, with one ear in the water and face out of the water, the lower arm stroking no higher than the chest, the extended arm pulling halfway and the top arm the rest of the way, hands passing each other, and a stretch and glide at the end of the stroke. Then place a pull buoy between your legs or a flotation belt around your waist and practice the stroke.

→ Side-to-side: Stand in chest-deep water and lean forward with one shoulder in the water and arms in the glide position. Practice the arm stroke, alternating which shoulder is in the water to gain practice on both sides. First practice one arm at a time, then try both together.

→ One-arm swim: Pull with one arm, leaving the other arm in the air.

→ Apple tree: Move your arms as if you were picking an apple from a tree, putting it in a basket, then reaching for another.

Kick

→ Kicking at the side: Hold on to the edge of the pool at the gutter and practice the sidestroke kick on each side. Make sure you have the correct body position, and place your top hand on the wall where it will stabilize you the best.

→ Kicking with kickboard: Lay one arm over the kickboard for support and put the other hand on the hip with the elbow in the air. Watch your elbow to make sure it stays pointed up.

→ Group kicking: Everyone in class lies on the same side, four to five feet apart. As a group, you all recover your legs, then stop; extend your legs toward the pool wall, then stop; execute a thrust, then stop; and recover the legs, pause, set the feet, pause, extend the legs, pause, set the feet, and thrust. After you've mastered the parts of the kick, you then try performing the recovery-extension-thrust in one continuous motion. This drill also can be performed on land, with the legs extended over the edge of the pool, or as an individual drill in which you are supported by a buddy or a kickboard.

Coordination

→ Arm-leg coordination: With or without a flotation device, practice coordinating each arm with the leg action. Then try the entire stroke, first with a flotation device, if desired, then without one.

→ Rhythm: As you swim, slow down and repeat to yourself "pull, kick, glide, 2, 3."

→ Kicking with a kickboard: Support your bottom arm (hand) with a flotation device. Practice coordinating the top arm and kick. Then try practicing with just the bottom arm and the kick. Finally, try the full stroke without any flotation device.

→ Kicking with the arm assisting: Sidestroke kick with your top arm holding on to the top leg and working at the same time the leg moves. Push on the leg during the kick. This emphasizes timing of the top arm and the leg kick. Do it on both sides. (Optional breathing: Exhale with the face in the water during the glide. Inhale as the bottom arm begins the pull.)

→ Music: Swim to music of a slow or medium tempo using the full stroke. You also can swim to instructions from your instructor.

Elementary Backstroke Drills

The drills in this section address arm stroke, kick, and coordination.

Arm Stroke

→ Land exercise: Stand on the pool deck and slide your hands up your sides to your armpits. Then extend your arms with the palms facing your feet to a point just above shoulder height. Press the palms of your hands toward your feet in a sweeping motion, then slide the hands up the side again.

→ Arm movements: Think of the sequence of arm movements as either "chicken, airplane, and soldier" or "little **T**, big **T**, **I**."

Kick

→ Inverted breaststroke kick: Using a kickboard, do inverted breaststroke kicks the length of the pool while holding the kickboard to the stomach. Your feet should drop directly below your knees. The feet should be lifted toward the shins (and turned out) during the power phase. The knees should not break the surface of the water.

→ Kick with flotation device: Use a water log or barbell, then concentrate on kicking with your knees at the water's surface.

Coordination

→ Rhythm: As you swim, slow down and repeat to yourself "pull, kick, glide, 2, 3."

→ Count the kicks: Practice kicking in the water using a kickboard. Count the number of kicks per length you take, then try ways to reduce the number of kicks.

YMCA Wetball Rules of Play

The following are the rules of play for wetball as determined by the YMCA of the USA.

Lead-up Activities/Basic Skills (conducted in shallow water)

Dribbling

Moving through the water with the ball under control is one of the basic skills required in wetball.

- → Have the children wade through the water from one side of the pool to the other, dribbling or patting the ball and maintaining control.
- → Speed up the activity by having three or four at a time race each other, wading across the pool while dribbling the ball.
- → Introduce a relay doing the same thing in teams of four.
- → For those who can swim, have them repeat the activity swimming rather than wading.

Passing

While two-handed catching is permitted in wetball, one-handed passing is required, and this skill requires some practice.

- → Arrange the children in pairs about five meters apart. Have one of the pairs throw with the favored hand to the other, who may catch it with two hands but must return it with one.
- → Gradually spread the pairs, but at all times encourage accuracy of passing rather than distance.
- → Vary the throws to the right and left of the partners to practice movement by the receiver to catch the ball.
- → Arrange relay teams, seven or eight meters apart. The ball is passed to the opposite team member, who catches it and returns it. As soon as a player has caught and passed the ball, he or she goes to the back of the team line.

In the early stages of learning the skills, accuracy may be sacrificed as the children try to throw the ball more quickly. Emphasize that accurate passes are more likely to result in their team winning.

Equipment and Rules

The Pool
The pool area should not be greater than 25 yards in length and no greater than 15 yards wide, with two-meter, four-meter, and center-line markings on the side.

    The depth of water should be selected to suit the players' swimming ability. The shallow end of a pool is recommended for younger children.

The Ball
The recommended ball is a youth water polo ball or a small playground ball. During Level Three play, a youth water polo ball is best.

Goals
Two goals five feet wide by two-and-a-half-feet high made of PVC.

Caps
Water polo caps are recommended not only for team identification, but also because the protective gear will help protect players from any injury that may be caused by the ball. Each team should have a different color cap for identification purposes.

Teams
Seven players and six reserves constitute a team. Five to seven players are allowed on the field. Reserves may be substituted at the end of a quarter or after a goal. If there are more than 26 children, allow for substitutes more frequently.

    A goalkeeper should be designated and has the responsibility of protecting the goal. Goalkeepers are not permitted to go over the halfway and center lines.

The Game

The game should consist of four quarters of five minutes' duration.

→ To start the game, players line up along the goal line. At a signal from the referee, one player from each team wades or swims toward the center to the referee. The player that gets to the ball first throws the ball backward to a teammate, which will put the ball in play.

→ A goal is scored when the ball passes completely over the goal line in the goal area.

→ When a goal has been scored, the players return to their own halves and a member of the team that did not score the goal passes the ball back to a teammate to put the ball back into play.

→ Players are allowed to swim or wade to get into position and are allowed to move while holding the ball.

→ Players may catch the ball with two hands and may throw it with two hands during Level One play. During Level Two, players can catch the ball with two hands, but may throw with only one hand. During Level Three play, players must catch and throw with only one hand. The goalie may use two hands to catch or throw the ball in all levels.

→ The ball can be dribbled by pushing it along in front of the player. The ball can be stolen from a player who is dribbling the ball, provided that the player is not contacted.

→ If the ball goes out of bounds and is last touched by a defender or goalkeeper, a corner throw shall be taken by an attacker from the two-meter line near the side of the pool.

→ No player may tackle another player, whether in possession of the ball or not. (Tackling means a player is not allowed to pull another player back, dunk, grab or hold, or pull under.) A free throw is awarded.

→ No player may swim on or over an opponent's back.

→ No player may take the ball under water.

→ An infringement of the rules results in a free throw, signaled by a whistle blow from the referee. A flag the color of the cap of the player who gained the free throw is raised by the referee. It is to be taken from the spot where the foul occurred outside the two-meter line. They must release the ball within five seconds (by tossing it to themselves, but they cannot score unless another player has touched the ball).

→ No player is allowed to enter the opponent's two-meter area unless the player has the ball or the ball is in front of the player.

→ Any foul by a defending player in the four-meter area that stops a shot on goal shall result in a penalty shot if the offensive player is facing the goal and his advantage is compromised by the defenders who are behind him or side by side. The penalty shot may be taken by any opposition player from the four-meter line; there shall be no interference by any opponent.

The goalkeeper must stay behind the goal line until the referee blows the whistle, and can then attempt to stop the penalty shot. When the whistle has blown, the penalty shot must be taken immediately and without faking.

→ The penalty for tackling a player should be exclusion from the game until the next goal is scored, or 20 seconds, whichever comes first.

→ The penalty for abusive language or misconduct is exclusion for the remainder of the game with no substitute.

→ The penalty for aggression is exclusion from the game for the remainder of the match with no substitute. Aggression is defined as deliberately striking or attempting to strike another player with the intent of injury or harm.

→ Coaches should implement all rules with discretion and judgment, encouraging a free-flowing and continuous game. At the same time, unsportsmanlike behavior or deliberate body contact should be discouraged.

→ Regularly rotate player positions to give players the opportunity to experience a variety of positions.

→ One team should wear white caps and the other blue, except the goalkeepers, who must wear red caps. If possible, the caps should be numbered from 1 to 13, with the goalkeeper wearing cap No. 1.

The Referee

→ The referee is in charge of the game. He or she moves up and down along the side of the pool, always watching, always alert. He or she starts and stops the play, makes neutral throws (fair to both teams), signals when a goal is scored, and calls penalties.

→ To make it easy to show the players what his or her decision is, the referee carries a stick with a flag or pennant at each end—one dark blue and the other white—to match the colors worn by the two teams.

→ When the referee blows his or her whistle to stop play, he or she raises one flag or the other to indicate which team is being penalized, which team is to get the free throw, and so on.

For more information on playing wetball and the rules of play for different levels, call the Associate Director for Aquatics at the YMCA of the USA (800-872-9622 ext. 142). The *United States Water Polo Level One Coaching Manual* is available through the Y Program Store (item 5271). A certification course is offered for YMCA Wetball (Water Polo) Instructor/Coach.

Introduction to Water Polo

❶ *Positioning*

The basic setup for a polo team is six players and one goalie in the pool at a time.

❷ *Start of Play*

The beginning of each quarter begins with a sprint to the half. Each team lines up on the wall or two-meter line to start. When the referee blows the whistle, the two players closest to the referee sprint toward the ball, which is dropped at halfway. The player next to the sprinter also sprints to back them up. The sprinter that reaches the ball first throws the ball back to his or her players to start the play.

1* 2 3 G 4 5 6

* *Sprinter*

❸ *Fouls*

Fouls can be ordinary or major. Ordinary fouls are best understood as minor fouls. Minor fouls are called throughout the game for infringements such as reaching over a player's back if the offensive player isn't holding the ball. Most major fouls occur when a player holds, sinks, or pulls back an opposing player not in control of the ball.

❹ *Free throw*

When a player is fouled by a defender (a player on the team defending their goal), he or she receives a free throw. This is a pass that the defender may not block or interfere with in any manner. The player receiving a free throw has three seconds to put the ball in play, either by passing to a teammate, dribbling the ball, or popping it in the air to himself or herself. The ball must be touched by another player after a free throw is awarded prior to a shot being taken. If it is not, the ball will be turned over to the opposing team.

⑤ *Shot clock*

The clock that displays the time of possession, in which a team must take a shot (also called a possession clock). Teams have 35 seconds to shoot the ball during each possession. If they do not, the ball will be turned over to the opposing team.

⑥ *Dribble*

The method a player uses to swim with the ball.

⑦ *Ejection*

A major foul that requires a player to go to the penalty area for 20 seconds (also called a kickout). This results in a 6 on 5 play. The player may return to the game only when the referee or desk waves him or her back in. The player may not push off the wall or deck to return to the game.

⑧ *Penalty Shot*

A shot awarded to the offense when a defender commits a major foul within four meters of his or her own goal. Any offensive player currently in the pool (no goalies) may take a free shot at the goal when the referee blows his or her whistle. He or she may take it no closer than four meters, and he or she may not fake or delay. The defending goalie may not move to block the shot until the referee blows his or her whistle.

⑨ *Red*

The period of time immediately prior to the expiration of the shot clock or game clock. Some teams yell "red" when either of these clocks indicates 10 seconds or less.

⑩ *Press*

A type of defense in which everyone is covered tightly, player-to-player.

⑪ *Zone Defense*

A type of defense in which players are assigned an area to defend. Defensive players must assume responsibility for covering any offensive players entering their area.

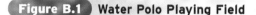
Figure B.1 Water Polo Playing Field

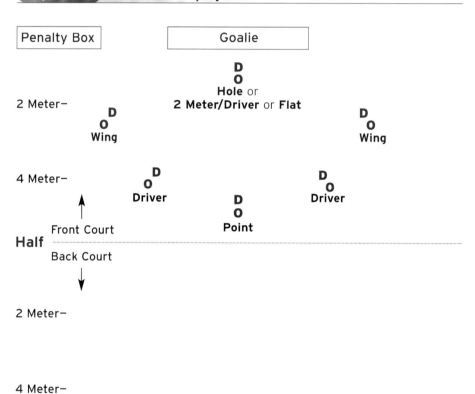

YMCA Swim Lessons Level Logos

Shown on this and the next page are the logos for each of the levels in the YMCA Swim Lessons program. They can be used on information sheets, handouts, and flyers, even on t-shirts.

Parent/Child and Preschool Program

Kipper

Inia

Shrimp

eel

perch

Pike

Ray

Starfish

Youth and Adult Program

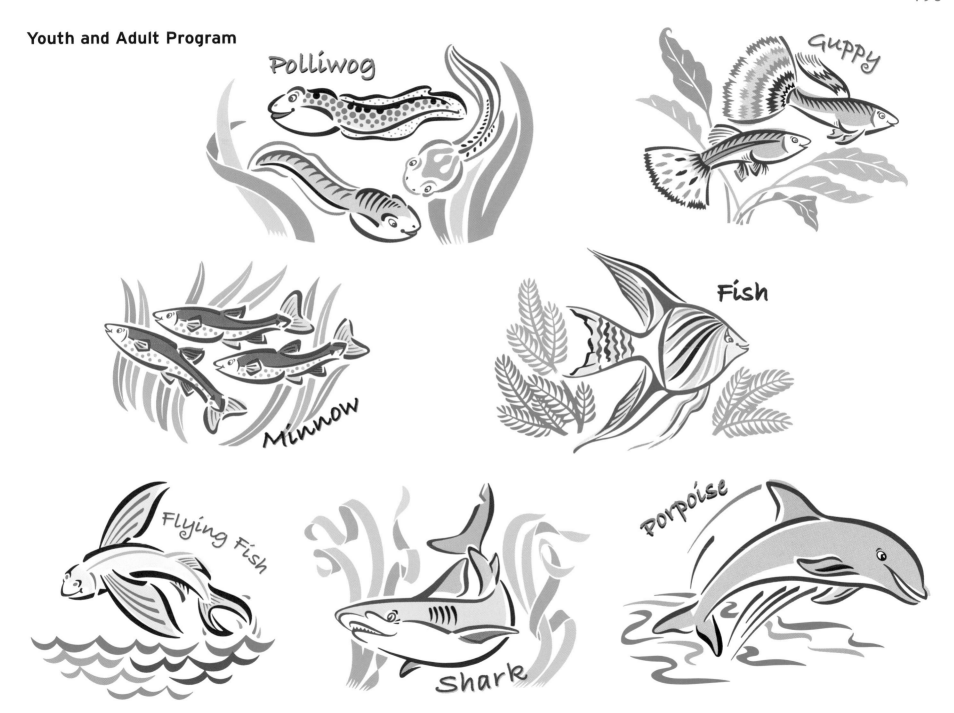

Polliwog

Guppy

Minnow

Fish

Flying Fish

Shark

Porpoise

Resource Organizations

United States Canoe Association, Inc.
606 Ross Street
Middletown, OH 45044-5062
513-422-3739

U.S. Coast Guard
2100 Second Street S.W.
Washington, DC 20593-0001
202-267-1060
Fax: 202-267-4423

U.S. Diving Inc.
Pan American Plaza
201 South Capitol Avenue, Suite 430
Indianapolis, IN 46225
317-237-5252
Fax: 317-237-5257

U.S. Synchronized Swimming
Pan American Plaza
201 South Capitol Avenue, Suite 510
Indianapolis, IN 46225
317-237-5700
Fax: 317-237-5705

U.S. Water Polo
1685 West Uintah
Colorado Springs, CO 80904-2969
719-634-0699
Fax: 719-634-0866
USWP@uswp.org

YMCA Scuba Program
5825 Live Oak Parkway, Suite 2A
Norcross, GA 30093
770-662-5172
Fax: 770-242-9059

Additional Resources for Your Aquatics Program

For details about these additional items, current prices, and a complete listing of available accessories, contact the Y Program Store, P.O. Box 5076, Champaign, IL 61825-5076, phone (800) 747-0089. To save time, order by fax: (217) 351-1549. Please call if you are interested in receiving a free catalog.

YMCA Swim Lessons manuals

5412   YMCA Swim Lessons Administrator's Manual (Approx 416 pp)

5418   Teaching Swimming Fundamentals (208 pp)

5420   The Parent/Child and Preschool Aquatic Program Manual (Approx 208 pp)

YMCA Swim Lessons training videos

5434   Teaching Swimming Fundamentals Video

5435   The Youth and Adult Aquatic Program Video

5436   The Parent/Child and Preschool Aquatic Program Video

Aquatics

5285   Principles of YMCA Aquatics (144 pp)

5243   Everybody Swims, Everybody Wins (11-minute video)

5322   Water Fun and Fitness (176 pp)

5296   Aquatic Games (144 pp)

5229   YMCA Pool Operations Manual (Second Edition, 160 pp)

Aquatic Safety

5328   YMCA Splash (150 pp)

5428   Aquatic Safety Training Video (9-minute video)

Lifeguarding

5334   On the Guard II (Third Edition, 272 pp)

5342   Instructor Manual for On the Guard II (Third Edition, 568-page notebook and 93-minute video)
          *Note: *This manual may only be purchased by certified YMCA lifeguard instructors with a sanction number.*

Competitive Swimming and Diving

5302   Principles of YMCA Competitive Swimming and Diving (152 pp)

5287   Rookie Coaches Swimming Guide (80 pp)

5290   Coaching Swimming Successfully (200 pp)

5423   Swimming Drills for Every Stroke (208 pp)

5258   Swimming Into the 21st Century (272 pp)

Water Polo

5271   United States Water Polo Level One Coaching Manual (78 pp)

Index

Illustrations have italicized page numbers

A

accent high-elbow recovery 131
accident prevention 114
accordion pattern 153, *154*
adventure, and risk taking 123-124
airways, obstruction of 90, 160
alcohol, cautions 65
alternate ballet leg 128
approach-crawl stroke 171, *171, 172*
Aquatic Safety courses 140
aquatics programs, common elements 3-4
arm actions
    for back crawl stroke 182-183
    for breaststroke 184
    for butterfly stroke 186
    for elementary backstroke 189
    for front crawl stroke 72-73, 179-180
    for sidestroke 188
    for treading water 37
    for underwater swimming 126
arm recovery, with back paddle 23
assistance, asking for 31

B

back alternating overarm stroke 75, *75*
back alternating paddle stroke *47,* 47-48
back crawl stroke
    crawl combined with 131
    drills for 182-184
    endurance and improvement 125
    flip turn 138-139
    skill refinement 102, 147-148
back float *15, 36, 38*
    learning 14, 15-16
    without IFD 36
back paddle stroke
    with flotation belt *23*
    learning 23
    with PFD *68*
back somersault, in water *49,* 49-50
backstroke
    with diving brick *171*
    skill refinement 102, 125

synchronized swimming variations 106
    variations 131
back symmetrical paddle stroke 48, *48*
back symmetrical stroke 76, *76*
backyard pool safety 119-120
ballet leg 128
ball handling *28, 89*
    blocking a ball 134-135, *135*
    endurance 135
    improvement of 88-89
    learning 28
    shooting the ball 134
    skill refinement 107-108, 155
    while paddling 58-60
    while treading water 120
beach precautions 44, 143
better world, building 144-145
big buddy projects 145
bilateral breathing 124
boating
    introduction to 5
    and lifejackets 40
    safety 4, *65,* 65-66, 96-97
    traffic laws 96
boats
    capsize procedures 68, *69,* 121-122
    entering from deep water *163,* 163-164
    getting in after falling overboard *97,* 97-98
    getting in and out of swamped boat 98, *98*
    getting in and out with assistance 18-19, *19*
    getting in and out without assistance 40-41, *41*
    moving around in 41
bobbing *39,* 39-40
body composition 123
body control 146
body heat preservation 39
body position, drills for back crawl stroke 183
bone density, and floating 14
breaststroke
    butterfly combined with 131
    drills for 184-186
    endurance and improvement 124
    front rudimentary 74
    sidestroke combined with 131
    skill refinement 101-102, 146-147

synchronized swimming variations 106
    variations 131
breaststroke roll 132
breathing
    bilateral 124
    for breaststroke 185
    for front alternating paddle stroke 44-45
    for front crawl stroke 72-73, 181-182
    rotary 72-73, 101
    rudiments 44-45
    and somersaults 49
    while floating 15
bubbles, blowing 13, 39-40
buddy system
    at beach 44
    for skin diving 93, 156
    for underwater swimming 70, 127
buoyancy 14
butterfly stroke
    breaststroke combined with 131
    drills for 186-188
    learning 103
    skill refinement 126, 148-149

C

canoes. *See* boats
canoe sculling *50,* 50-51
capsized boat procedures 68, *69,* 121-22
cardiorespiratory endurance 123
caring
    demonstrating 42-43, 70-71, 100
    describing 21
    and leadership roles 166
    observing behaviors of 167
catch-up stroke 168
caution, learning about 43-44
chain formation 151-152, *153*
character development 4. *See also* personal growth
circle kick 76-77, *77*
class expectations 12
closed-end classes 3
clothing
    floating in 120
    inflating for emergencies *164,* 164-166, *165*
    swimming with 69, *69,* 95, *95*

cold disorder first aid 157-158
colds 93
combination strokes 131
comfort in water 12
competitive swimming 5
cooperation, learning through games 100
coordination
    drills for breaststroke 185-186
    drills for butterfly stroke 187-188
    drills for elementary backstroke 189
    drills for sidestroke 189
core values 145. *See also* caring; honesty; respect;
        responsibility
corkscrew 132
CPR manikins *62,* 115-116, 140, 159
cramps, treating 99, *99*
crawl stroke *73*
    back crawl combined with 131
    with bilateral breathing and open turns 124
    front flip turn 138
    learning 72-73
    with rotary breathing *101*
    skill refinement 101, 145-146
currents, swimming in 93-94

D

danger, recognizing 29-30, 42, 115
depth
    for diving 35, 44, 55, 65, 133
    for jumping 56, 87
directional swimming 108
diver's flags 93
diving
    beginning skills 52-55
    from boats 65
    distance between divers 82
    feetfirst surface dive 110-112
    forward fall-in pike 86
    front dive 106-107, 133-134
    front standing dive with jump 86-87
    headfirst surface dive 55, 110
    kneeling dive 55-56
    long shallow dive 84-86, 146
    resources 196
    safe depth for 35, 44, 55, 65, 133

safety 35, 65, 146
springboard diving skills 5
squat dive 83
standing dives 83-88
stride dive 81-82, 82-83
targets for 87
diving boards
    adjustments for jumping 88
    proper use of 57, 65
dolphin kick
    with fins 113
    for speed in start 148, 149
    underwater 126
dolphin maneuver 77, 78
double-trudgen crawl stroke 168
dribbling 28. See also ball handling
    learning 28
    while paddling 58-60, 59, 190
drills
    about 178-179
    for back crawl stroke 182-184
    for breaststroke 184-186
    for butterfly stroke 186-188
    for elementary backstroke 189
    for front crawl stroke 179-181
    series swims 179
    for sidestroke 188-189

E
ear discomfort 27
ears, pressure on 53, 93
ear squeeze 93, 137
eel sculling 104
elementary backstroke
    drills for 189
    learning 76, 76
emergency care 6
emotional development 21
endurance
    for back crawl stroke 125
    for backstroke 125
    for ball handling 135
    for breaststroke 124
    cardiorespiratory 123
    developing 155
    and fitness 167
    improving 178
    muscular 123
    for sidestroke 125
    skill refinement 145-147, 147-149

for treading water 120-121
for wetball 136, 155
equipment
    mask and fin care 113, 127
    mask construction 113
    snorkel care 138
    for wetball 191
eye squeeze 93

F
fat, and floating 14
feetfirst sculling 104
feetfirst surface dive 110-112, 111
finning 25
    learning 25
    for treading water 37
fins
    deep water activities 155-156
    introduction to 112-113
    in underwater swimming 126-127
first aid
    basics 116
    for cold disorders 157-158
    for heat disorders 157
    for obstructed airway 90, 160
fish level
    about 92
    logo 195
    objectives summary 8 table 1.1
    performance criteria summary 117
    personal growth 99-100
    personal safety 93-99
    rescue 114-116
    stroke development 101-103
    swim information 103
fitness
    concepts of 122-123
    learning about 167
flat sculling 25
flexibility 123, 167
flip turns
    for back crawl 138-139
    skill refinement 146
floating
    back float 14, 15-16, 36
    and body fat 14
    and bone density 14
    and breathing 15
    in clothing 120
    duration 94, 120

and muscle mass 14
flotation belts
    for confidence 13
    at guppy level 48
    at polliwog level 24
    and somersaults 49
    in stroke development 5
flotation devices. See instructional flotation devices
    (IFDs); personal flotation devices (PFDs)
flu 93
flutter kick 113, 126
flying fish level
    about 118-119
    logo 195
    objectives summary 8 table 1.1
    performance criteria summary 141
    personal growth 123-124
    personal safety 119-123
    rescue 139-140
    stroke development 124-126
    swim information 126
    water games and sports 126-139
flying porpoise 53, 54
formations 151-154
forward fall-in pike 86
front alternating arm stroke 72-73
front alternating paddle stroke 44-45, 45
front crawl stroke
    drills for 179-181
    exercises 131
    stroke variations 130-131
    synchronized swimming variations 105-106
front dive
    off one-meter board with three-step approach 133-134
    in tuck and pike positions 106-107
front flip turn 138
front float 15, 36
    learning 14-15
    without IFD 36
front paddle stroke
    with flotation belt 22
    learning 22-23
    with PFD 68
front rudimentary breaststroke 74
front somersault, in water 49, 49
front standing dive with jump 86-87
front symmetrical paddle stroke 45-46, 46
front walkover 151, 152
frostbite 157-158

fun
    through games 21
    with wetball 109-110

G
games. See also water games and sports
    ball dribbling 28
    ball push pass 29
    Heads, Shoulders, Knees, and Toes 21
    treasure hunt 27-28
goalie skills 134-135
goal setting 20, 70, 124
goal-setting form 71 fig. 4.1
goal shooting. See under ball handling
goggles, masks compared to 93
group efforts. See teamwork
guppy level
    about 34-35
    logo 195
    objectives summary 7 table 1.1
    performance criteria summary 63
    personal growth 42-44
    personal safety 35-41
    rescue 60-62
    stroke development 44-48
    swim information 48
    water games and sports 49-60

H
hand pitch 26
Hawaiian stroke 106, 131
head congestion 93
headfirst surface dive 55, 55, 110, 111
head position, changing 132
health, personal 122
healthy lifestyle habits 121
heart rate
    monitoring 72
    range chart by ages 144 fig. 7.1
    target range 144
heat disorder first aid 157
Heimlich maneuver 90, 90
help
    summoning 30
    using telephone for emergencies 31
HELP (heat escape lessening posture) 39, 96
honesty
    demonstrating 42-43, 70-71, 100
    describing 21
    and leadership roles 166
    observing behaviors of 167

huddle position 96, *96*
hyperventilation
    learning about 70, 170
    while bobbing 40
hypothermia 65, 66, 157-158

I
ice rescues 156-157
individual medley 150, 168
inland waterways, cautions 44
instructional flotation devices (IFDs) *16*
    about 4
    at fish level 103
    in stroke development 5
    use of 12-14
instructors
    as role models 4
    spotting at ladders 57
    wearing PFDs as behavior model 68
inverted breaststroke 147, *147*

J
jumping
    from one-meter board 56-57, *57*
    from one-meter board, with arm swing *87,* 87-88
    into pool away from side 19-20
    into pool with PFDs 17-18

K
kick. *See* leg actions
kickboard drills 26
kickboards 13, 16
kip maneuver *129,* 129-130, *130*
kneeling dive 55-56, *56*

L
ladders, proper use of 57
lakes, cautions 44
leadership roles 166
leg actions
    for back crawl stroke 183
    for breaststroke 184-185
    for butterfly stroke 186-187
    for elementary backstroke 189
    for front crawl stroke 72-73, 181
    for sidestroke 189
    for treading water 37, 67
    for underwater swimming 126
leg cramps, treating 99, *99*
leg strength improvement 162-163

lifejackets 16-17. *See also* personal flotation
    devices (PFDs)
lifesaving sidestroke 125
lifesaving skills 172
lifestyle habits 121
logos, YMCA swim lesson levels 194-195
long shallow dive 84-86, *85,* 146

M
marine life 143
masks
    deep water activities 155-156
    goggles compared to 93
    introduction to 112
    in underwater swimming 126-127
mask squeeze 93, 137
minnow level
    about 64-65
    logo 195
    objectives summary 7 table 1.1
    performance criteria summary 91
    personal growth 70-72
    personal safety 65-70
    rescue 89-90
    stroke development 72-76
    swim information 76
    water games and sports 76-89
murky water 126
muscle mass, and floating 14
muscular endurance 123
music 105-106, 131

N
National Safe Boating Council 17
nutrition, discussing 121

O
obstructed airways 90, 160
open turns 101-102, 124
open-water safety 143
out-of-water recovery 132
overarm recovery 72-73, *73*
overarm sidestroke 148, *149*
Over-the-Waves breaststroke 131
oyster maneuver 79, *79*

P
paddle rescue 139-140
passing a ball *59,* 190. *See also* ball handling
patience, learning about 43-44

peer grouping 3
personal flotation devices (PFDs) *16, 18*
    in boats 18, 65
    correct use of 38
    jumping into pool with 17-18
    learning about 16-17
    learning to swim longer with 68
    swimming with clothing and 95, *95*
personal ground rules 123
personal growth
    about 4
    at fish level 99-100
    at flying fish level 123-124
    at guppy level 42-44
    at minnow level 70-72
    objectives summary 7-9 table 1.1
    at polliwog level 20-22
    at porpoise level 166-167
    at shark level 144-145
personal health 122
personal safety
    about 4
    at fish level 93-99
    at flying fish level 119-123
    at guppy level 35-41
    at minnow level 65-70
    objectives summary 7-9 table 1.1
    at polliwog level 11-20
    at porpoise level 162-166
    at shark level 143-144
pets, and home pools 119
physical fitness
    concepts of 122-123
    learning about 167
pike position
    forward fall-in 86
    front dive 106-107
plank position *105*
plank synchronized swimming figure 104-105
polliwog level
    about 10-11
    logo 195
    objectives summary 7 table 1.1
    performance criteria summary 33
    personal growth 20-22
    personal safety 11-20
    rescue 29-32
    stroke development 22-24
    swim information 24
    water games and sports 25-29

ponds, cautions 44
pool
    introduction to 12-14
    jumping in away from side 19-20
    rules of 11, 119
    safe diving depth 35, 44, 55, 65, 133
    use of 4
porpoise level
    class format 162
    logo 195
    objectives summary 9 table 1.1
    performance criteria summary 177
    personal growth 166-167
    personal safety 162-166
    rescue 170-172
    stroke development 167-168
    water games and sports 169-170
porpoise level club
    adult leadership 173-174
    club development 174
    organization 175
    program format 173
    recognition 176
    recruitment 174
    social activities 176
positive values, reinforcement of 100
pressure
    equalizing 53
    on outer ear 93
Principles of YMCA Aquatics 35, 65
program levels
    components of 4-6
    objectives summary 7-9 table 1.1
    structure 6
progressive drills
    for back crawl stroke 184
    for breaststroke 186
    for butterfly stroke 188
    for front crawl stroke 182
prone float. *See* front float
pulse
    measuring 72
    and target heart-rate range 144
push pass game 29, *29*

Q
quarries, cautions 44

R

rafting safety 143
reaching assists *31, 60*
  emphasis on 140
  learning 31-32, 60-61
  practice at 89-90
  skill refinement 139-140
recovery to a stand 15
referee, for wetball 192
relaxation exercises 20
rescue
  about 6
  at fish level 114-116
  at flying fish level 139-140
  at guppy level 60-62
  at minnow level 89-90
  objectives summary 7-9 table 1.1
  at polliwog level 29-32
  at porpoise level 170-172
  at shark level 156-160
rescue breathing 62, *62*
  review of 159-160, 172
  skill refinement 115-116, 140
resources
  organizations 196
  publications 197
respect
  demonstrating 42-43, 70-71, 100
  describing 21
  and leadership roles 166
  observing behaviors of 167
responsibility
  demonstrating 42-43, 70-71, 100
  describing 21
  discussion of 145
  with having a pool 119
  and leadership roles 166
  observing behaviors of 167
resting stroke 66, *66*
revolving crawl 131
risk taking 123-124
river rapids 143
rivers, cautions 44
role models, instructors as 4
rolls 132
rotary breathing 72-73, *73*, 101
rotary kick *109, 136*
  learning 109
  while treading 135-136
rough-water swimming 143-144

routines
  combining skills into 132
  developing 155
  performance of 169
rowboats. *See* boats
rudimentary rhythmic breathing 44-45
rudimentary sidestroke, with scissors kick 74-75, *75*

S

safety. *See also* personal safety
  awareness of 42
  in backyard pool 119-120
  for boating 4, 65-66, 96-97
  for diving 35, 65, 146
  learning through games 100
  in open water 143
  for rafting 143
  for skin diving 93
  with sun 20, 98-99
  for tubing 143
  in waterparks 120
safety equipment 43
safety swim, learning 38
sailboat maneuver *127,* 127-128
sculling
  learning 25-26
  skill refinement 104
  for treading water 37
self-discipline 70
self-esteem 4
series swims 3, 179
service to others 144-145
shallow-water blackout 70
shark level
  about 142
  logo 195
  objectives summary 9 table 1.1
  performance criteria summary 161
  personal growth 144-145
  personal safety 143-144
  rescue 156-160
  stroke development 145-151
  swim information 151
  water games and sports 151-156
shock, treatment for 158-159, *159*
side alternating paddle stroke *46,* 46-47
side paddle stroke
  with flotation belt *24*
  learning 24

sidestroke
  breaststroke combined with 131
  drills for 188-189
  endurance and improvement 125
  rudimentary, with scissors kick 74-75, *75*
  skill refinement 102
  synchronized swimming variations 106
  variations 131
single ballet leg 128, *128*
sinus squeeze 93
skin diving safety 93
slippery decks 44
snorkel
  deep water activities 155-156
  learning to use 137-138
social development 21
somersaults
  learning 49-50
  in synchronized swimming 106
  variations 131
speed
  and dolphin kick 148, 149
  and fitness 167
  increasing 178
  of stroke 167-168
sports. *See* water games and sports
squat dive 83, *84*
standing dives 83-88
star pattern 154, *154*
starting blocks, cautions 35, 65
starts
  and open turns 101-102
  skill refinement 145-147, 147-149
static stretching 48
stationary sculling 25
straight-arm recovery 131
streams, cautions 44
strength, and fitness 167
stretching 48, 103
stride dive
  from high-stride position *82,* 82-83, *83*
  from low-stride position *81,* 81-82
stride entry 172
stroke development
  about 5
  enhancing efficiency 178
  at fish level 101-103
  at flying fish level 124-126
  at guppy level 44-48
  at minnow level 72-76

objectives summary 7-9 table 1.1
  at polliwog level 22-24
  at porpoise level 167-168
  at shark level 145-151
  standard progression 22
strokes:
  approach-crawl 171, 172
  back alternating overarm 75
  back alternating paddle 47-48
  back crawl 102, 125, 131, 138-139, 147-148
  back paddle 23
  backstroke 102, 106, 125, 131
  back symmetrical 76
  back symmetrical paddle 48
  breaststroke 74, 101-102, 106, 124, 131, 146-147
  butterfly 103, 126, 131, 148-149
  catch-up 168
  crawl 72-73, 101, 124, 131, 138, 145-146
  double-trudgen crawl 168
  elementary backstroke 76, 189
  front alternating arm 72-73
  front alternating paddle 44-45
  front crawl 105-106, 130-131
  front rudimentary breaststroke 74
  front symmetrical paddle 45-46
  Hawaiian 106, 131
  inverted breaststroke 147
  lifesaving sidestroke 125
  overarm sidestroke 148
  Over-the-Waves breaststroke 131
  resting 66
  rudimentary sidestroke 74-75
  side alternating paddle 46-47
  side paddle 24
  sidestroke 74-75, 102, 106, 125, 131
  symmetrical paddle 74
  trudgen crawl 149-150
stroke speed 167-168
sun safety 20, 98-99
supine float. *See* back float
surface, swimming up to *51,* 51-52
surface glide *52*
  to bottom *52,* 52-53
  and recovery 52
survival skills 4
swimming
  with clothing 69, *69*
  with clothing and PFD 95, *95*
  with 10-pound weight 171
  up to surface *51,* 51-52

symmetrical paddle stroke 74
synchronized swimming
    about 5
    beginning skills 81
    performance of routine 169
    plank figure 104-105
    resources 196
    stroke variations 105-106

T
tandem formation 153, *153*
target heart-rate range 144
teachable moments 21
teaching guidelines 12
teamwork
    discussing 144-145
    group problem solving 166
    learning 99-100
telephones, for emergency assistance 31
throwing a ball. *See under* ball handling
throwing assists *61*
    distance and accuracy improvement 140
    emphasis on 140
    learning 32, 60-61
    practice of 89-90, 114
treading water *37*
    with breaststroke kick *94*
    with diving brick *163*
    endurance 120-121
    learning 37
    leg strength improvement 162-163
    with rotary kick 135-136
    with scissors kick *67, 95*
    skill improvement 94-95
    variations on 67
treasure hunt game 27-28
trudgen crawl stroke 149-150, *150*
tubing safety 143
tub position *26*, 26-27
tuck position, front dive 106-107
turns
    flip turn 138-139
    open turns 101-102, 124
    skill refinement 145-147, 147-149

U
underwater basics
    going down pole *27*
    learning 27-28

underwater swimming
    about 5
    learning 126-127
    with mask and fins *126*
United States Canoe Association, Inc. 196
United States Coast Guard (USCG) 16, 17, 196
U.S. Diving, Inc. 196
U.S. Synchronized Swimming 196
U.S. Water Polo 196

V
victims, recognizing danger 29-30
volunteering 144, 145

W
water depth
    for diving 35, 44, 65, 133
    and jumper's body size 56
    for jumping from one-meter diving board 56, 87
    for kneeling dive 55
water games and sports
    about 5-6
    at fish level 104-113
    at flying fish level 126-139
    at guppy level 49-60
    at minnow level 76-89
    objectives summary 7-9 table 1.1
    at polliwog level 25-29
    at porpoise level 169-170
    at shark level 151-156
water logs 16
watermanship 155
waterpark safety 120
water polo
    introduction to 192-193
    lead-up skills 58-60, 88-89, 107-108
    resources 196
waterwheel maneuver *80*, 80-81
weather awareness 42
weighted swimming 171
wetball *110*
    about 5
    endurance improvement in deep water 136
    equipment for 191
    five-minute game in deep water 155
    learning 89
    offensive and defensive strategies 169-170
    playing for fun 109-110
    referee 192

rules of 191-192
    ten-minute game in deep water 170

Y
YMCA Cool Pool Rules 11, 20
YMCA courses 162
YMCA Scuba Program 196
Youth and Adult Aquatic Program, changes in 3

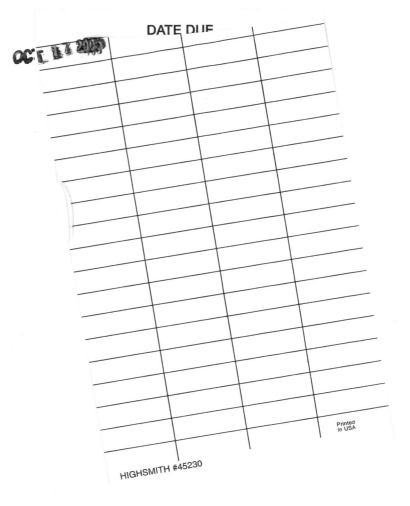